More Than L.I.P. Service

A Lifetime Investing Plan

More Than L.I.P. Service

A Lifetime Investing Plan

by

Alvin H. Danenberg, C.F.P.

PennWell Publishing Company
Tulsa, Oklahoma

Disclaimer

All of the information in this book has been taken from sources believed to be reliable, but the accuracy cannot be guaranteed. There is no guarantee that the investing plan described herein will be profitable or will equal past results. Also, individual results will vary based on which mutual funds or other securities are used and when investments are made. The Lifetime Investing Plan is designed to be used for long-term investing (minimum of five years). Contact a financial advisor to determine if this program fits individual goals.

© Copyright 1997 by
PennWell Publishing Company
1421 South Sheridan/P.O. Box 1260
Tulsa, Oklahoma 74101

Library of Congress Cataloging - in - Publication Data

Danenberg, Alvin H.
  More than L.I.P. service : a lifetime investment plan / by Alvin
H. Danenberg.
    p. cm.
  Includes index
  ISBN 0-87814-655-5
  1. Finance, Personal. 2. Investments. 3. Mutual funds. 4. Asset
allocation. I. Title.
HG179.D328 1997
332.6--DC21

Printed in the United States of America

1 2 3 4 5 01 00 99 98 97

ACKNOWLEDGMENTS

This book has come together with the assistance of several unselfish individuals who took time from their daily schedules to give me excellent professional criticism and helpful advice.

I want to thank William C. Prewitt, M.S., C.F.P., and Kyra Morris, C.F.P. (both fee-only Certified Financial Planners) and Ira Krakow (editor of the Internet newsgroup called *Persfin Digest*—an outstanding resource for financial planning advice through the Internet). These individuals critiqued the entire book. Their input has been invaluable and immeasurable.

I also want to thank Arnold L. Cornez, J.D., an expert on offshore asset protection. He helped me with the new tax laws and how they affect offshore asset protection trusts.

Another thanks goes to Jacob Needleman for extending permission to me to include his *Money and the Meaning of Life* as a foreword.

Last, but not least, I want to thank Sue, my wife, and president of the Alvin H. Danenberg Fan Club. She made English out of my gibberish and spent many grueling hours reading, rereading, and re-rereading before I got it straight.

Again, thanks to the great people and their great efforts.

CONTENTS

Money and the Meaning of Life

by Jacob Needleman

Jacob Needleman is a professor of philosophy at San Francisco State University and the author of many books, including *The New Religions*, *A Sense of the Cosmos*, *Lost Christianity*, *The Heart of Philosophy*, *The Way of the Physician*, *Sorcerers,* and *Money and the Meaning of Life*. His work on *Money and the Meaning of Life* has received national attention from NBC News, CNN, and Bill Moyers' "A World of Ideas."

Usually, our concerns about money are reduced to getting or managing it, but it is almost impossible to find serious and useful thought about the relationship between the quest for money and the quest for meaning. What is the role of money in the pursuit of spiritual development, the transformation of the self spoken of by the great teachers and philosophers of all epochs and cultures?

Surely, it has become necessary to address this question. In no other culture or civilization of which we know has money been such a pervasive and decisive influence. In the world in which we now live, the device called money enters into everything human beings do, into every aspect and pocket of life. Therefore any serious search for self-knowledge and moral self-development requires that we take money more, not less, seriously than we are accustomed to taking it. It is necessary to study money with the aim of understanding that aspect of ourselves engaged with money. Therefore, it is necessary to include the truth about our relationship to money within the sphere of our moral and spiritual self-inquiry. This process is not easy, as money in certain respects acts on our minds in the way that questions about sex affected earlier generations—as a decisive force that few of us can face squarely without hypocrisy. Yet, face it we must.

The task of studying our relationship with money requires that we set aside our moralizing about it and requires that we free ourselves from imaginary pictures of how we behave with money. It means seeing an immense aspect of ourselves with a new and freer turn of mind. From this more impartial perspective, money

becomes a key to understanding the deeper structures of human nature, a means of studying the very ancient and perennial idea of the individual's two fundamental natures—the "angel" and the "demon"; the spirit and the world; time and eternity.

The human being is, or is meant to be, a synthesis of these two warring aspects within ourselves. To bring them together is the "peace that passeth understanding." Only when these two aspects of our nature are in relationship does our life have great meaning, but before we can bring them together, we must first clearly see them in their separateness and opposition. This introspection takes great sincerity, for it is always painful to verify the statement of St. Paul that "the good that I would do, that I do not." In this context, money is the great key to studying the worldly aspect of human nature. In contemporary culture it is an irreplaceable means for seeing ourselves as we are and for taking our real measure.

Seen from this point-of-view, money becomes—not so much sacred in itself but—embraced in the sacred question of who we are and what we are meant to be in this life and in this civilization.

Money is an integral part of life. But, money is only one small part of the total you. Don't believe even for a second, that it is any more important than anything else. (See Table X.1: Life. It illustrates what I describe next.

Table X.1: Life

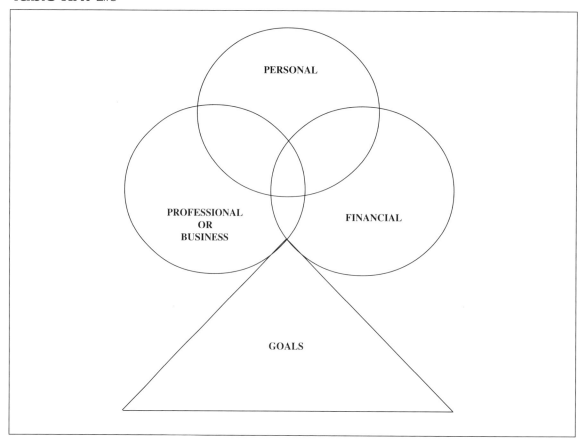

I envision life as three spheres interacting and balancing on a triangle. There are the personal sphere, the professional or business sphere, and the financial sphere.

The personal sphere is where everything you do personally and with your family occurs. It holds the emotions, the hopes, the faith, and the realities of your life. The professional or business sphere is where you conduct your business. Whatever you do for a living is within this influential sector. The financial sphere is the money side of it all. Your investments and your planning are one small part of this category.

These spheres don't work alone; they function together. Sometimes it is difficult to determine into which sphere a particular activity belongs. Everything that occurs in any one sphere affects something in the other two spheres.

The fulcrum on which all of this balances is a triangle that encompasses all of a person's goals. The spheres are the realities and the goals are the motivators. Altogether, that's life.

You are in for a surprise. You are going to learn a simple yet powerful investing program—one that you can start immediately and one that you can use for a lifetime. This book is not about how to make money; it is about how to invest the money that you do make. This plan will work for those with $1,000 to invest as well as for those with $100,000 to invest.

You may have purchased this book for a variety of reasons. Maybe you are recently divorced and feel financially disadvantaged. *More Than LIP Service* will level the playing field! Maybe you want a new investment approach. *Well, here it is!* Maybe you want to get a handle on your financial life. *Now you can!* Or, maybe you're just curious. *I can satisfy that too!*

The reason I have written this book is to share the knowledge I have learned over many years. Personally I have had many investment *downs* before enjoying investment *ups*. It all started when I graduated from dental school.

After my graduation in 1974, I was approached by many financial experts who befriended me. I followed their advice only to find out that they placed their own best interests above mine and their other clients.

Over time, these experts successfully persuaded me to invest in some very poor deals—a special "whole life insurance policy" designed to make me a millionaire, several "hot stock tips" with exceptional growth potential, the futures market for real leverage, real estate as an inflation hedge, and tax shelters to reduce my taxes.

This is what happened to me. Perhaps you can relate. The whole life insurance deal turned out to be a scheme which would have resulted in my owing a bank over $60,000 if I had continued with it. The hot stock tips only cost me 80% of all my investment. My initial $5,000 investment in the futures market eventually netted me a $15,000 loss. My real estate condominiums have gone down in value ever since purchasing them. (Anybody want some great condos?) Finally, the tax shelters which were recommended by my tax attorney finally cost me $160,000 in IRS penalties, back taxes, and interest after being ruled fraudulent.

This is a good place for me to interject and clarify an important point. I do not want you to assume that financial professionals such as insurance agents, stock brokers, real estate agents, and tax specialists are to be avoided. On the contrary! Most of us need advice from these individuals, and many of us need some of the products they sell. I have related my story to emphasize how a few poor advisers have affected me. From this you should deduce that you need to watch out for your own best interests.

Following my painful experiences, I vowed to educate myself to prevent this from ever happening to me again. I studied and eventually became a Certified Financial

Planner. I began writing financial articles and giving seminars. Eventually I wrote my first book.

In my first book, *VAP: Value-driven Asset-allocation Plan*, I described a detailed method of investing in no-load mutual funds, integrating technical and fundamental data. Then, in my second book, *21 1/2 Easy Steps to Financial Security*, I took the reader through the process of understanding the various parts of a financial plan. I made the parts easy-to-follow and easy-to-assemble. My emphasis for the investing part of that book continued to be in no-load mutual funds.

For this, my third book, I recognized a need to present a plan for the motivated individual who wants to be an investor but does not want to spend hours studying the market—for an individual who simply "wants it to happen." Again, the investment vehicle is no-load mutual funds but with a twist. This plan is as close to being a *cookbook approach* as is possible.

With this plan, basically you will dollar-cost-average every month into a select group of no-load mutual funds. Then, once a year, you will do a little housekeeping to spruce up your portfolio. That's it!

The average compounded return rate of a portfolio invested following my plan from Jan. 1, 1985 through June 30, 1996 was 16.8% a year. The details are in chapter 13. However, I will use 14% throughout this book as the average annual compounded return for you to target as your investment return goal. Although there is no guarantee that you will be able to accomplish this, there is precedence to respect this as a very real possibility.

I have found that most people want to accumulate wealth, but they just don't know how. Reading this book will show you how and the book goes even further than that. Once you reach that level of wealth you have set as your goal, I will show you how to maintain that lifestyle for the rest of your life.

Most potential investors are intimidated by all the confusing information that is thrown at them daily. To add to this confusion, the financial industry tries to make the concept of investing much more difficult than it has to be. This book cuts through the confusion and eliminates the difficulty.

Let me emphasize a critical concept—the sooner you begin, the more time you will have for your money to make more money. This phenomenon is known as compounding. Some knowledgeable scholars have actually called compounding "the eighth wonder of the world." It's a mathematical process that can turn pennies into fortunes.

OK! If wealth accumulation is your goal, what are your options?

- You could do a great deal of research and develop your own method.
- You could shoot wild darts and invest in every hot tip that comes your way.
- You could let someone else invest for you and take your money gladly.
- You could sit back, relax, read this book, and then take action! (I like this choice.)

I am going to give you some "LIP." Let my Lifetime Investing Plan (LIP) become your Lifetime Investing Plan. You will have a direct shot at making your money work for you and you will not be plagued by making frequent market-timing decisions. You will invest regularly, clean house once a year, and let the system perform!

This book is going to help make your dreams come true! As I have already hinted, you are going to discover a plan that takes the mystery out of investing and sets up a framework to build your investments for the rest of your life—simply and mechanically. Maybe you won't make the same mistakes as I did, or maybe you already have, and you are ready to get back on track. Whatever your perspective, I have some important answers for you that can be found in this book.

To make your experience with *More Than LIP Service* meaningful, you will need to purchase a financial calculator. This is a calculator that does "time value of money" calculations. Several brands are available. Purchase one and read the general instruction booklet to understand the overall operation of the calculator. I use the HP10B for my examples throughout this book. I also present my own interpretation of how to understand "time value of money" calculations.

The core of my philosophy is an investment program that can be used from birth to death. It is a concept of using aggressive vehicles in a conservative structure. Much more about that later—for now, you need to know that my plan is simple. The letters of the word simple spell out the philosophy:

S:	Set your goal
I:	Implement your plan
M:	Monitor for success
P:	Provide for yourself and your family
L:	Live without financial fear
E:	Enjoy the harvest of your efforts

Along the way, you might want to share this book with your closest friends and relatives—giving them the same opportunity to learn how easy it can be to invest for the future. One of the greatest gifts you can give to yourself or anyone else is the knowledge of how to take control of the financial future. It is important to start as soon as possible and to stay committed to this plan.

The layout of this book is different from most books on investing:
- First of all, as you can see, this book is in an 8 1/2" X 11" format with a lay-flat spine. This allows you to use the book as a workbook.
- The text pages have wide margins to give you a place to make notes. Don't just read this book, write all through it—it's your workbook.
- Finally, as a purchaser of this book, you can receive free, the most recent issue of the quarterly publication, *Danenberg's Lifetime Investing Plan*. Four times a year, this four-page newsletter can help you choose the funds for your Lifetime Investing Plan. It will provide you with the names, phone numbers,

and additional pertinent information about the two recommended no-load mutual funds over the last three- and five-year periods for each of the asset categories discussed in chapter 8. It will also summarize the current stage of the U.S. Business Cycle and the Relative Value Ratio, both of which are also described in chapter 8. (I told you I was going to make this simple for you!) To receive your free issue, return the postcard that is attached to this book. If the postcard is missing, send your written request to: Danenburg's LIP, 17 Arabian Dr., Charleston, SC 29407.

Don't hesitate to reread any portions of the book that may seem somewhat complicated. You are building a foundation of financial knowledge for yourself, brick by brick. Be sure the bricks are firmly in place and the cement is dry before adding the next layer.

The first two chapters will help you organize your financial life by *crunching* your personal financial data into a financial statement and cash flow statement. You will know exactly where you stand financially. Chapters 3–5 emphasize the importance of inflation, compounding, and dollar-cost-averaging as they relate to the future value of money. Investing in taxable versus tax-deferred vehicles is also compared. Chapter 6 covers money traps which can get in the way of your financial progress, and Chapter 7 addresses financial goal planning. Chapters 8 and 9 introduce the stock market, mutual funds, and risk.

Chapter 10 gets very personal and, among other things, asks you to look deeply into yourself to understand how much of a risk you are willing to take. Chapters 11 and 12 explain the business of investing in no-load mutual funds, and chapter 13 puts the entire plan together for you. Chapters 14–16 explain how tables can be prepared to assist you in staying on track with your investment program up to and throughout your retirement years. Various retirement options are suggested. Chapter 17 is a bonus chapter that discusses asset protection.

Appendix I includes blank forms. You can copy these forms and personalize them for your permanent records. Appendix II includes a typical issue of the quarterly newsletter, *Danenberg's Lifetime Investing Plan* and a description of how to use the information. Appendix III includes an alphabetical listing of almost all no-load mutual funds, grouped within LIP's asset categories. Appendix IV helps you understand the prospectus, the statement of additional, and the current reports. Finally, LIP Gloss is a glossary that highlights the terms used throughout the book.

The bottom line is that investing for a lifetime is not complicated and can be accomplished by anyone who is motivated and has the time to make it happen. The most important step is to get out of the mind-set within which you have been working, and to get started on your journey of making things happen for you. Visualize the following metaphor:

Your entire life has been spent sitting in a rectangular box. The box is three feet wide and four feet long. The sides of the box are two-and-a-half feet high. For whatever reason, you have functioned within this box. All of the things you felt you needed to do during your life you were able to do inside this box. Suddenly you look up, and you see that there is no lid on this box. You realize that there never was a lid on the box. You stand up, and you can see beyond the confines of the box. You can actually step over the side of the box and leave it. For the first time you are outside the box, and the whole world lies in front of you.

By leaving your previous confines, you can explore many new and exciting ideas that will challenge you and make you grow. By changing your mind-set, you will see new opportunities.

Throughout this book I will use examples of real life situations. I will introduce you to various fictitious individuals who will gladly share situations from their storybook lives to help you see the comparisons in your own life. Treat them kindly; they are a product of my imagination.

The following preview of my Lifetime Investing Plan is meant to whet your appetite. Chapters 1 through 12 will build the foundation before the details of this plan are fully explained in chapter 13.

Preview of LIP
(Lifetime Investing Plan)

1. Select the best performing and riskiest no-load mutual funds over the last three- and five-year periods from each of five distinct asset categories.
2. Establish an account with a discount broker.
3. Dollar-cost-average equally into each fund on a regular basis, ideally monthly.
4. Once a year, determine if your current funds continue to satisfy Rule #1. If not, make the necessary changes.
5. Equalize the dollar amounts in each fund at the end of the first 12 months of investing.
6. Continue to dollar-cost-average monthly for the next 12 months.
7. Once every 12 months, repeat the process starting with Rule #4.
8. As your need for income develops, liquidate a specific percentage of your portfolio equally across all asset categories, and move needed cash into a money market account.

It is time to get out of your rectangular box. It is time for you to accept a new challenge and let go of old paradigms. It is time to consider a new way of investing for a lifetime.

Create Your Personal Financial Statement

Some Background First

Most of us pursue excellence in our business or professional lives. We take continuing education courses to sharpen our working skills, and we read our trade journals to broaden our awareness. We do what we feel is necessary in order to be the best we can be in our chosen field of employment. We know exactly who we are and what we have to offer. We deliver excellence to our customers.

There is one area, however, that we often neglect. This is an area of our lives where we frequently accept *average* as the rule. This is one area where we pay others to tell us what to do, and we nod in compliance without question. This is the area of investing for our future. In this area we often accept financial mediocrity. Why is this so? There are probably many reasons for our complacency:

- First, we don't have any formal training in financial planning. Our basic education comes from commissioned salespeople who sometimes have a biased perspective when selling us a financial product. We are their prey because we have discretionary dollars to buy what they have to sell. There is at times a conflict of interest on the part of these salespeople. On one hand they are telling us what we need to buy to meet our needs, yet on the other hand they are making a commission only if we purchase what they have to sell. The conflict is that they may not advise us of the items we really need if they do not have those products to sell. Only a few of these salespeople take the time to help us understand where we are financially before they try to sell us something. How can we know where we are going if we don't know where we are starting?

- Another reason deals with impulse buying. When we are sold individual financial products (such as life insurance, annuities, mutual funds, etc.), we are only buying isolated items. (It's like walking past a clothing store, seeing some things that catch our eye, and buying them on the spur of the moment. However, when we get home, the clothes and accessories we bought don't match our wardrobe.) How do our various financial purchases fit together? Do they provide us with a total formula to reach our goal? Do we even have a goal? (More about goals in chapter 7.)

- Still another reason is that the field of financial planning and investing seems confusing. There are so many different experts telling us what to do and why. It is hard to decipher what is right for us. Facts and statistics that are presented are conflicting, and we usually feel inadequate to make the right decisions.

The Here and Now

Before you can plan where you want to go financially, you need to know where you are now. This is a must before you ever buy any financial product. If the product does not help you reach your goal, then you don't need it no matter how great an opportunity it is touted to be. Here's an analogy:

> Mike was a frugal shopper. He always looked for bargains. While shopping one afternoon, he came across the sale of sales. For the price of one, he could purchase five bags of dog food—a well known, high-quality brand. He couldn't pass up the deal. When he got home, his wife was confused and angry. You see, they didn't own a dog!

Of course this is silly, but it emphasizes my point because it is so ridiculous. No matter what the product is, no matter how great the deal, it only makes sense if, and only if, it complements your financial program.

First, you need to get a handle on where you are financially. Assume you were playing one of the popular board games such as Monopoly®. You would be given a specific amount of play money at the beginning, and you would know exactly where you were financially before you rolled the first dice. With this bankroll, you could buy and negotiate your way around the board. Your objective would be to increase your bankroll and only to purchase what was necessary to control the board. You always would know where you were financially. You would add up the dollars and all the real estate you had accumulated around the board and then subtract any money you owed.

To know where you are financially in the real world, you need to do the same thing—only there is more data required to give you the answer. Data collection is time consuming, but it is necessary.

> For example, Mike needs to get a loan for his professional practice. He goes to the bank to request a loan, but the loan officer demands to see specific information first. He tells Mike to record all of his income, all of his debts, and all of his assets. From this information, the loaning institution can decide if Mike's money needs are a risk that the bank wants to assume. In other words, the bank wants to know where Mike is financially; it wants Mike's personal financial statement.

Personal Financial Statement

Your personal financial statement defines your net worth. It is the value of everything you own minus everything you owe. The detail comes from the various categories that you must address to make the bottom line accurate. The major categories are assets and liabilities. There are three subcategories under assets: cash & cash equivalents, invested assets, and use assets. There are two subcategories under liabilities: short-term liabilities (12 months or less) and long-term liabilities (more than 12 months).

As with all of the forms in this book, you can create your personal financial statement by hand from the blank, ready-to-use forms in Appendix I.

Collecting the data means that you will need to set aside the time to diligently go through various financial papers, personal items, and business files. Some people will take less than an hour to complete their personal financial statements. Others may take several days to gather all of the necessary numbers. But, gather them you must. This is the starting point in the ongoing process of investing for a lifetime.

Most of the individual elements in the Personal Financial Statement are self explanatory. For definitions, go to the LIP Gloss (Lifetime Investing Plan Glossary).

After you have completed your personal financial statement, you will know where you stand financially. You should update this statement at least once every year to help you track your financial growth. File your statements in a safe place. You may want to purchase a 3-ring binder with dividers. Label each divider for each type of form you will generate from this book. Retaining these forms over time will document your overall financial growth. A current statement will also help you with various financial transactions such as obtaining a bank loan or purchasing real estate.

Updating your statement every year will be easier than the initial data gathering process. First, you will know where to go for the numbers; second, you will have organized the process so that it will not be so cumbersome the next time around.

Gathering Data

First, go to the sources that are easily available. Look at your checkbook, bank statements, and cash-on-hand to obtain the proper figures. Call your insurance company if you have a cash value life insurance policy to determine your cash value balance.

Then, check your brokerage house statements to determine the market value of various securities you own. Any stock certificates that you personally hold also must be valued. If your personally held certificates are listed on the major stock exchanges, all you might need to do is check their current selling prices in the financial pages of your newspaper. If they are not listed, the easiest and most accurate way to determine their value is to take the certificates to your broker, transfer them into your account, and let the broker research their value.

Your retirement accounts including qualified retirement plans, non-qualified retirement plans, IRAs, etc. need to be summarized. If the information is not on your monthly statements, contact the fiduciaries of the plans, and inquire about their market value.

A more difficult task will be to place an accurate value on such assets as collectibles and real estate. You may have to contact various appraisers to obtain realistic numbers. When valuing automobiles, boats, household items, etc., be sure to use the market value—not what you paid for them nor what it would cost to replace them.

For assets that are difficult to value, it is always better to underestimate their worth than to overestimate it. Remember, your net worth is where you are financially at any time. This is not only information for your private use, it is also information that can be used for obtaining a loan. An honest mistake will result in an inaccurate net worth. If you should overestimate the value of an asset on purpose to obtain a loan, your net worth would appear to be higher than it actually is. This is fraud and carries all of the legal consequences!

When valuing your business, you will also need the assistance of an accountant and/or an appraiser. Once you understand how they go about determining the value of your business, it will be easier for you to make the calculations in the future. Do not include the

value of goodwill. Often this is a highly debatable figure on which you cannot depend when you sell your business. Be realistic.

When you get to the liabilities, all of them should be pay-off balances. Do not include the additional interest charges that will accrue in the future. Use the actual pay-off balance as if you were to pay off the debt today. To obtain these pay-off balances, call the lending institution which holds the loan or mortgage.

Table 1.1 is an example of Mike and Jodi's joint financial statement. For your own personal financial statement and for that of your spouse, there are reasons to own assets individually in your name and individually in your spouse's name. Various means of owning assets are described under "Titling of Property" in LIP Gloss. However, in this example, all of the assets are clumped together to give a total picture.

Table 1.1: Mike and Jodi's Personal Financial Statement is their financial status as of the date of the statement. As you can see, numbers have been gathered and added to the form. Subtotals have been determined and added to the summary section at the end of the statement. All liabilities were subtracted from all assets to arrive at a net worth for Mike and Jodi.

Now go to Appendix I, make a copy of the blank form *Personal Financial Statement*, and begin your process of investing for a lifetime. But, this is just the beginning. You next need to know where your dollars are coming from and where they are going.

Table 1.1: Mike and Jodi's Personal Financial Statement

Table 1.1: Mike and Jodi's Personal Financial Statement
Year:1996

ASSETS   **NOTES**

I. Cash/Cash Equivalents
    A. Checking account   4,000
    B. Savings account   10,000
    C. Money market fund   7,000
    D. Life insurance cash value   3,000
    E. Cash on hand   1,000
          Total Cash/Cash Equivalents   25,000

II. Invested Assets
    A. Portfolio Assets
        1. Common Stocks/Listed   15,000
        2. Retirement Benefits/IRA 24,600
    B. Active Assets
        1. Dental practice net value 300,000
          Total Invested Assets   339,600

III. Use Assets
    A. Personal residence   165,000
    B. Automobiles   30,000
    C. Jewelry   5,000
    D. Computers   5,000
    E. Miscellaneous household contents 20,000
          Total Use Assets   225,000

LIABILITIES

I. Short-Term Liabilities (pay-off balances where applicable)
    A. Credit card debt   8,000
          Total Short-Term Liabilities   8,000

II. Long-Term Liabilities (pay-off balances where applicable)
    A. Loans for automobiles   15,000
    B. Loans for other personal assets 12,000
    C. Mortgage on personal residence 115,000

          Total Long-Term Liabilities   142,000

SUMMARY

ASSETS (fair market value)
    Total Cash/Cash Equivalents   25,000
    Total Invested Assets   339,600
    Total Use Assets   225,000
          Total Assets   589,600

LIABILITIES (pay-off balances)
    Short-Term   8,000
    Long-Term   142,000
          Total Liabilities   150,000

NET WORTH (Total Assets - Total Liabilities)   **439,600**

Create Your Cash Flow Statement

Cash Flow

Cash flow is like a water spigot. Turn it on full force, and water gushes through. Close it off a little, and the stream slows down. But, if it is turned on full force for too long, the source may dwindle, and the flow may slow to a trickle. If there were no water left in the system, nothing could come out of this spigot. The well, so to speak, would run dry.

You are in control of the cash that flows through your financial spigot. You have the power to open or close the tap—to channel its flow in various directions or to various expense categories. Imprudent use of your resources could cause your financial well to run dry.

When you want to buy something, you can either pay cash, write a check, charge it, or receive a bill directly from the source where you purchased the item. Eventually, money will pass from your resources to the individual or organization from which you made the purchase.

If you want to be methodical, you could keep track of your money. Keeping track lets you know how much was available and where it was directed. You could identify what was spent on specific items and services as well as what was kept in savings. At any given moment, you would know your cash flow—the *coming in* and *going out* of your hard-earned dollars.

What I am getting to is a structured method that enables you to identify exactly where your money is being spent. Once the facts are known, you could redirect the money that is overspent in certain areas to other sectors that are in need of more attention. With your Cash Flow Statement, you will be able to project your future expenditures and assure yourself that enough money will be available for your investment programs.

Don't skip this exercise of developing your own cash flow statement. If you jump into investing without knowledge of where the resources are to fund your investment goal, you could wind up with no investment. A cash flow statement will not only show you what you have spent and where it went, it will more importantly assist you with finding the extra necessary dollars to fund your investment program. It's like *cut* and *paste* in computer jargon. You'll *cut* from a frivolous category and *paste* into the investing category.

Gathering Data

To create your cash flow statement, you need to gather data. As in chapter 1, data collection takes time and thoroughness on your part. To prepare your cash flow statement for the previous 12 months, you would have to recreate the past. You would need to gather information on all income (i.e., earned income, unearned income, capital gains, annuities, and retirement plan distributions), and all expenses to make the statement meaningful and accurate. If all of your transfers of money were carried out by writing checks, then assembling all of your checks for the past 12 months and organizing them into categories would be relatively easy. If all of this information were already on a computer spreadsheet, then the task ahead would be simple.

However, if you just don't have the time, or you don't have the desire to collect past information, then you could create your cash flow statement by starting today and working forward.

After several months of keeping track of all of your income and expenses, you will get a perspective of your spending lifestyle. As you develop specific financial goals and methods to reach these goals, you will be able to go back to your cash flow statement to determine where the dollars could come from to fund your investment vehicles.

Cash Flow Statement

It's time to get down to the basics and start your cash flow statement. The major categories are cash inflows and cash outflows. Cash outflows can be subdivided into three distinct headings: savings and investments, fixed cash outflows, and variable cash outflows.

Fixed cash outflows are expenses over which you have no (or little) control. Rent, utilities, telephone, and mortgage payments (to name a few) are costs of living that you must meet to maintain your lifestyle. They are not easily adjusted, but they can be changed with some effort.

Variable cash outflows, on the other hand, are at your discretion most of the time. They are much easier to change. You can spend less on entertainment, vacations, dining out, and the like if you need to save money for some other expenditure. Also, adjusting these variable expenses would not alter significantly your standard of living.

A cash flow statement always balances. Total cash inflow will always equal total cash outflow since whatever is not spent remains either in your checking account, in your savings account, or in your pocket.

The individual items under the various headings of a cash flow statement are self explanatory. You can set up your statement either monthly, quarterly, or annually. My recommendation is to do it monthly so it conforms to your monthly payments for debts, your monthly bank and investment statements, and other monthly financial matters. Monthly data also gives you valuable information to view and compare seasonal changes.

Table 2.1 shows an example of Mike and Jodi's joint cash flow statement. They once again have gathered all of the data to fill in the standard form in Appendix I. For ease of explanation, it is summarized as annual inflows and outflows. As you can see, the totals of the subcategories of expenses (savings & investment, fixed, and variable) must add up to equal the total of all income. If it doesn't, you have missed something. Remember, miscellaneous cash that is spent is an expense. Don't forget what you have spent it on. If you do, estimate its category as best as you can. Also, remember money at home or in a checking account has to be included as *savings* at that moment in time.

Now go to Appendix I, make a copy of the blank cash flow statement, and begin your own accounting.

One objective of keeping this statement current is to determine the resources available to make investments. Look first at the outflow categories. Additional discretionary income to put into investments can sometimes be found by consolidating high-interest debt and refinancing it over a longer period of time at a lower interest rate to reduce current outflows. If done properly, this may not increase the total interest you will have to pay over the long-term, and it can provide the extra necessary cash for investing. Even if more interest is paid over a longer period of time, freeing up money now could be beneficial to fund your other investment goals. As I mentioned earlier, another source is to curtail impulsive and excessive spending from various variable expense categories and to redirect those dollars to the investment category.

Methods of increasing inflows might be more difficult. You could consider taking on a part-time job. Possibly your spouse may consider employment of some type. You could be entrepreneurial and creative, and begin an in-home business. You might be able to earn a raise at work by demonstrating your worth to your employer. You might be able to improve your own business by being more efficient and thereby more profitable.

Increasing your income is possible but more involved than changing your expenditures. If raising income levels can be accomplished, it usually takes a longer time to happen and then to impact your situation, than do those changes in the expense categories that I have already suggested.

Credit Card Debt

I can't leave this area without emphasizing the damage that excessive credit card debt does to your financial situation and your mental health. No one is immune. This is an insidious disease that can overwhelm the most logical minds and strongest bodies. It's a malignancy that can devour your best intentions and invade your sense of balance. It can stop you dead in your tracks.

Table 2.1: Mike and Jodi's Cash Flow Statement

YEAR:1996

INFLOW:

Gross salaries 96,000

Dividend income 750

Interest income 350

TOTAL CASH INFLOW: 97,100

OUTFLOW:

SAVINGS & INVESTMENT: 5,000

Fixed Outflow:

Auto insurance 5,000

Debt payments 4,000

Income taxes 29,000

Life insurance premiums 11,470

Mortgage payments* 15,000

Personal property taxes 750

Telephone 600

Utilities 1,800

TOTAL FIXED OUTFLOW: 67,620

Variable Outflows:

Attorney/Accountant fees 1,500

Auto: gas, repairs 2,960

Clothing and personal items 4,000

Entertainment and vacations 4,000

Food 6,700

Gifts/contributions 500

Home repairs/Maintenance 1,320

Household furnishings 2,000

Medical/Dental care 1,500

TOTAL VARIABLE OUTFLOW: 24,480

TOTAL CASH OUTFLOW: 97,100

*includes principal, interest, taxes and insurance

The Benefits of Credit Cards. Credit cards are an excellent way to purchase goods and services. Credit cards allow the user easily to make a transaction and to have recourse if something goes wrong with the purchase.

There is ease and convenience associated with these cards of plastic. Carrying one allows you to leave your checkbook and large amounts of cash at home. Using one also permits you to make purchases over the telephone.

There is also recourse with these cards because of important leverage. Here is an example of recourse: Assume you charged your purchase and then later felt that you required a refund. Also, assume that the merchant refused to give you a refund. You could complain to the credit card company and have the charge credited back to your account. The credit card company would then investigate your complaint and if reasonable would require the merchant to make the refund.

If you made the original purchase by cash or check instead, you could have a difficult time negotiating a refund if later you felt entitled to one.

The Disease of Credit Card Debt. Life is great using credit cards as long as you pay off your credit card statement each month. The potential for disaster occurs when you begin to carry a balance.

Once you get into the habit of carrying a balance and paying only the minimum required each month, you also begin to accumulate consumer debt. The debt you are paying off gets more expensive than you think. You see, in addition to paying the charged amount and interest, you must also pay taxes on the earned income you use to pay this credit card debt (i.e., federal income tax, state income tax, Social Security tax, Medicare tax). Here's an example of the extra cost:

Assume you must pay 31% federal income tax and 7% state income tax along with the required 6.2% employee Social Security tax and 1.45% Medicare tax on all earned income. For every $1 you pay in credit card charges and interest, you must earn about $1.84 so that there is enough money to also pay the various taxes due! So, if you must pay $700 in credit card charges and interest, you will really have to earn approximately $1,288 ($700 x $1.84 = $1,288) to pay the debt and the necessary taxes! ($588 goes to the previously mentioned taxes, and $700 pays the debt.)

Here's a scenario where the convenience of credit cards transformed into a menacing disease:

Meet Justin Tyme. Justin is a lot like you and me. He earns a good income and has good credit. He has been using his credit card to purchase those things he believes he needs. Most of these are spur-of-the-moment purchases. He feels good when he buys something for himself. Just recently, his credit card statement showed a balance of $2,900.

Wow! That was more than he remembered charging. But, after checking over his statement, he realized that all those charges were his. Since he didn't have the extra cash to pay off the whole balance, he decided to pay the minimum amount due and

let the remainder carry forward to next month. Big mistake! It became too easy for him to just pay the minimum due and let the balance ride.

Justin Tyme's credit card spending habit did not change even though he started carrying a balance. Since his cash flow could not keep up with his expenses, his credit card debt began to grow.

Plastic became easier for Justin to use. More and more credit card companies started sending him pre-approved credit cards. With them, he was able to accumulate more and more debt which added to his already overburdened deficit. He also earned higher credit limits with many lending institutions—just another element that encouraged him to charge more.

At some future point, Justin began to have difficulties in making the minimum monthly payments on all those credit cards. Stress was building. The disease became a malignancy. He began to panic. How could he ever pay off his debt and emerge whole from this debilitated condition?

Treatment. Justin needs to evaluate what he really needs, and stop spending spontaneously. Justin should begin a repayment plan, allocating an exact amount of money which he can afford each month to reduce this debt. He should pay off the highest interest rate debt first. If possible, Justin could investigate consolidating his debt into one loan at a lower interest rate than he was paying for his credit cards. One way he could do this would be to apply for a personal loan from his bank. He would take his personal financial statement to the loan officer, discuss the purpose of the loan, and negotiate a payment plan that could work.

By paying the same amount each month to reduce the outstanding debt, Justin will be able to accurately calculate when he will be debt free. He will be treated, but he will not be cured. A cure will come to Justin Tyme only after he understands that the proper use of credit cards is never to allow a balance to be carried from month to month. (An excellent paperback book on getting out of debt and staying out is The *Cheapskate Monthly Money Makeover* by Mary Hunt. It is available in most bookstores or directly from *Cheapskate Monthly* at (310) 630-8845.

For Justin as well as everyone else, controlling credit card debt improves cash flow. Improving cash flow means finding the extra dollars to fund your investment program.

OK! Chapter 1 has enabled you to know where you are financially; this chapter has shown you where you can find the dollars to make your lifetime investing program viable. Both statements are like snapshots of your financial situation at a specific moment. Yet, both need to be put into motion since your financial life is dynamic, not stagnant.

The groundwork is being laid, and sources of available dollars are becoming evident. Let's move on to making money *with money* by first understanding what happens to the mighty dollar over time.

Inflation and Other ...ions

Over time, the mighty dollar is affected by many factors. Some of these are the *ions* of infla**tion**... reces**sion**... disinfla**tion**... depres**sion**... defla**tion**. These five economic terms can become confusing and misleading if they are not defined properly. You should know their meaning and how they affect your financial life.

Inflation is a rise in the prices of goods and services when spending increases relative to the supply of goods and services. Basically, this means that too much money is chasing too few goods and services. But, there are many causes of the inflationary problem. The result over time is a reduction in the purchasing power of the dollar. I have much more to say about inflation later in this chapter.

Recession is an actual downturn in economic activity which generally begins when the Federal Reserve tightens the money supply. A recession is the contraction phase of a normal business cycle.

Disinflation is a slowdown in the rate at which prices are rising. During this time, borrowing capacity can increase because interest rates decline relative to personal income. Disinflation is the end result of a recession.

Depression is a long-term debt liquidation process which occurs when cash flow is insufficient to handle debt payments. Debt liquidation can occur either in an orderly process (slow growth) or a disorderly process (deflation).

Deflation is the actual decline in the prices of goods and services. During deflation, borrowing capacity is reduced because personal income drops further and faster than interest rates. Deflation is financially painful.

What is Real Money?

In the 5th century BC, Aristotle described the properties of money. For over 5,000 years, gold was considered real money—the medium of exchange and the store of value. Although gold is not used as money today, it is still considered by many as the ultimate money of last resort.

The following six factors identify why gold is the money of last resort and the only true store of value. The first five factors are attributed to Aristotle's perception; the last, to modern day economic conditions:

1. It is durable: Gold, more than any other solid element, is chemically inert. It cannot rot, crumble, evaporate, rust, or break.
2. It is divisible: One ounce of gold can be divided exactly into smaller pieces. Real estate, for example, cannot; diamonds cannot.

3. It is convenient: Gold can be carried physically from place to place. Real estate, again as an example, cannot.
4. It is consistent: Twenty-four carat gold is pure gold. The quality of 24 carat gold does not vary from country to country or from time to time.
5. It has intrinsic value: Gold has many useful industrial purposes. Of all the metals, it is the most malleable, most ductile, and the least reactive. It is an excellent conductor of heat and electricity and the most reflective of light. In jewelry, its utility is unsurpassed.
6. It cannot be created by governments: Probably more important than anything else, there is a finite amount of gold on this earth. Fiat paper money can be printed without concern, but gold cannot be debased in its pure state.

What is Fiat Money?

Fiat money has no value itself. It only has the value people are willing to accept. It is money that is created by the government without the backing of gold or any other commodity. It is considered the legal tender of the land.

The U.S. Government controls the supply of fiat money through its central bank, The Federal Reserve (Fed). The Fed has defined money in three different ways—M1, M2, and M3.

M1 includes all currency, traveler's checks, and checkable deposits.

M2 includes M1 plus passbook savings deposits, small denomination CDs, money market funds, money market deposit accounts, overnight repurchase agreements issued by commercial banks, and overnight Eurodollars.

M3 includes M2 plus large denomination CDs and term repurchase agreements.

M2 is the most important of these three measures of money supply and is watched closely by the Federal Reserve. M2's growth or contraction appear to move in the same direction and at the same rate as the Gross Domestic Product. To regulate economic growth, the Fed tries to regulate M2's growth. This is done by adjusting short term interest rates.

If M2 grows too quickly, then inflation becomes a threat. If M2 contracts too much, then recession becomes a threat. The Fed attempts to create steady, controlled growth of M2. This is a delicate process at best.

Inflation

Inflation! What a powerful word; what a powerful tax. That's right. Inflation is powerful, and it is a tax (of sorts). It takes the purchasing power of the U.S. dollar and whittles it down year after year. This is not much different than the actual taxes you and I pay on our income every year.

Let me call on Mike and Jodi for an example. Their income last year was about $97,000. After they paid $29,000 in federal, state, and withholding taxes, their spendable income (purchasing power) from their $97,000 income was approximately $68,000 (income – taxes = spendable income).

With inflation, an additional reduction in purchasing power occurs over time. Let's go back to the $68,000 in spendable income. If Mike and Jodi hold onto this $68,000 for one year, its purchasing power will be decreased by the annual rate of inflation. (Everyone's personal inflation rate is different because of the types of purchases an individual will make. Using the Consumer Price Index as reported by the U.S. Department of Labor as the annual rate of inflation provides a standard that is generally accepted. For my examples, I'll use an inflation rate of 4%. However, your personal inflation rate may be higher or lower depending on what you are purchasing.)

It's not that the $68,000 changes in appearance or that the face value changes to $65,280 at the end of 12 months (reflecting the dilution in purchasing power as a result of an inflation rate of 4%). What happens is that the actual paper dollars that Mike and Jodi spend look the same, but the items that their money purchases cost more each year. The annual cost of products and services increases at the rate of inflation, and therefore the value of the dollar decreases accordingly.

This dilution of the dollar every year is akin to an invisible, non-legislated tax. Income taxes reduce Mike and Jodi's $97,000 in gross earnings to $68,000 in spendable income. A 4% inflation rate further reduces this $68,000 one year later to $65,280 worth of purchasing power.

So, not only are we giving the government our money in the form of taxes, we are also allowing the government to reduce the quantity of goods or services that we can purchase through the inflationary erosion of the dollar.

What's the Big Deal?

Why do I make such a big deal about inflation? For one thing, no one else seems to bother with it. The current thinking today is that inflation is low; it has been brought under control by the Federal Reserve Board; and it just isn't worth worrying about. I totally disagree.

Inflation has been with us since the beginning of paper (fiat) money, and it will stay with us. Some economists blame it on too much money in circulation without enough growth to soak up the extra dollars. Some economists blame it on too few goods being chased by too many dollars. Some economists blame it on the Middle East. You probably have your own ideas. It doesn't matter what the real causes are. It is still out there, and we are affected by it over time.

Like almost everything else in the marketplace, inflation is cyclical. Yet, it has a steady rise over the years. Look at Table 3.1 of the Consumer Price Index.

This index is reported monthly by the U.S. Department of Labor and is considered a relatively good reflection of the inflationary rate in the United States. There are arguments about how this index overstates inflation, but there are other arguments that it doesn't include some of the inflationary pressures each of us experiences every

Table 3.1: Consumer Price Index, December Ending Values

| | U.S. Department of Labor | |
| | Bureau of Labor Statistics | |
Year	**Consumer Price Index**	**Year-Over-Year Inflation Rate**
1970	39.8	
1971	41.1	3.3%
1972	42.5	3.4%
1973	46.2	8.7%
1974	51.9	12.3%
1975	55.5	6.9%
1976	58.2	4.9%
1977	62.1	6.7%
1978	67.7	9.0%
1979	76.7	13.3%
1980	86.3	12.5%
1981	94.0	8.9%
1982	97.6	3.8%
1983	101.3	3.8%
1984	105.3	4.0%
1985	109.3	3.8%
1986	110.5	1.1%
1987	115.4	4.4%
1988	120.5	4.4%
1989	126.1	4.7%
1990	133.8	6.1%
1991	137.9	3.1%
1992	141.9	2.9%
1993	145.8	2.8%
1994	150.1	3.0%
1995	153.5	2.3%

day. Whatever the real answers are, the CPI is as good as any index to show the trend, and the trend is what really matters.

Based on year end data from 1970 through 1995, the CPI has risen an average of 5.6% (more exactly 5.55%) compounded yearly. Is that very much?

Consider what happened to the purchasing power of $1 over the 25 years covered in the table from 1970 to 1995. What you could buy with $1 at the end of 1970 would cost $3.86 by the end of 1995. That's a 286% increase in the price of goods and services. Put another way, the U.S. $1 in 1970 would be worth only $0.24 in purchasing power in 1995.

Do you think this dilution of the U.S. dollar is something to be concerned about? I do! Remember, 5.6% is the average annual inflation rate over the 25-year period I just described. It was as high as 10.1% annualized for the five-year period from the end of 1976 to the end of 1981. In contrast, it was as low as 2.8% annualized from the end of 1990 to the end of 1995. At 10.1% or even 2.8%, inflation takes away our spending power.

An example of how the mighty dollar succumbs to the ravages of inflation is shown in Table 3.2: Effects of Inflation. The table shows what $10,000 will purchase 10 years, 15 years, 20 years, and 25 years from now at various inflation rates of 4%, 5%, and 6%. As you can see, if you do not offset the inflation factor, then you are on a sinking ship.

Table 3.2: Effects of Inflation

$10,000...
and the dilution effects of various inflation rates

Inflation	10 years	15 years	20 years	25 years
4%	$6,648	$5,421	$4,420	$3,604
5%	$5,987	$4,633	$3,585	$2,774
6%	$5,386	$3,953	$2,901	$2,129

Indicators of Impending Inflation

If you believe it is important to understand that inflation poses a future threat to economic markets, then there are three indicators which are easy to follow that could help you determine if inflation is beginning to accelerate. A fourth indicator tells you what the inflation rate actually has been up to the present. All four of these indicators can be found in the *Market Laboratory Section* of *Barron's Financial Newspaper*. [*Barron's* is a weekly financial newspaper which is published by Dow Jones & Co., Inc. every Saturday. It is available in many bookstores or by subscription at (800) 328-6800.]

1. Gold is usually the first indicator to begin its rise whenever the earliest hint of future inflation develops. Since gold has been the true store-of-value throughout modern history, it is no surprise to see the price of gold rise along with inflation fears.

2. The Commodity Research Board (CRB) Index usually begins its upward trend shortly after a gold rise has already started. This index of commodity prices is an important base for rising prices in manufactured goods. As raw materials rise in price, inflationary pricing eventually is passed on to other sectors.

3. Factory Operating Rate is a measure of how overworked our factories are. As factories become busier and busier, inflationary pressures mount because of supply/demand realities. Historically, when the Factory Operating Rate (sometimes called the Factory Utilization Rate) rises above 85%, economists begin to look for inflationary pressures building in the economy.

4. Only after price increases reach the consumer level will the Consumer Price Index (CPI) scream of inflation. The CPI basically tells you the way it is.

What's the Answer for the Individual Investor?

What can we do? Well, we can fight back by investing astutely. We must invest our money with a definite purpose. We can offset the dilution effect of inflation by earning at least the current rate of inflation and also earning enough above the inflation rate to pay the taxes that will be due from our investments' unearned income. Note that this basic requirement of investing only allows us to break even with inflation. It only lets us tread water. We still are going nowhere.

Here is a formula you can use to determine the break even point with inflation. It takes into consideration the inflation rate, your tax bracket, and the taxable return you require on your investment:

X = I ÷ (1-a)

X = the required taxable return percent on the investment to break even with inflation

I = Inflation rate percent

a = combined marginal tax rate in decimal form for federal and state income taxes. (The marginal tax rate is the income tax you must pay, expressed in decimals, on the next dollar you receive in income.)

For example, assume Mike and Jodi are in the 28% federal tax bracket and 7% state tax bracket for a total tax bracket of 35%. To balance out the dilution effect of 4% inflation, they must earn 6.1538% from their taxable investments. [4% ÷ (1 - 0.35) = 6.1538%]. This represents 4% to offset inflation and an additional 2.1538% to offset the taxes due. Here is how the numbers work out:

One thousand dollars plus a 4% inflation rate means that Mike and Jodi must have $1,040 on hand one year later to offset the loss of purchasing power for that year. Investing $1,000 at 6.1538% will yield $61.54 in investment interest. After paying 35% in taxes on the unearned income ($61.54 times 35% = $21.54), $1,040 is left.

This is only the beginning of astute investing. To really succeed in investing, our investments must significantly exceed this level if we hope to produce a wealth accumulation plan that can reach our goals. It becomes very important that all of your projections of future expenses and investments take inflation into consideration. To plan for the future but to ignore inflation will render an otherwise well designed plan insufficient to meet your cash flow needs. The following scenario elaborates how planning without inflation could be disastrous.

Suppose inflation averaged 4% for the next 25 years, and Mike and Jodi believed that $97,000 could maintain their standard of living today. From that $97,000 they would pay all expenses and taxes. They arranged their finances in such a way that their retirement plans were designed to provide them with $97,000 a year beginning 25 years from now. Unfortunately, they would be in trouble. The reason: $97,000 in 25 years would only purchase $34,958 worth of goods in today's dollars. The fact is that inflation at 4% reduced the purchasing power of the $97,000. Mike and Jodi didn't see it happening, but it did. Inflation is a subtle destroyer of money.

In the previous example, Mike and Jodi planned for their future, but they miscalculated badly because they failed to take inflation into their computations.

Don't get jostled. The plan I will be discussing in detail in chapter 13 will more than offset the ravages of inflation. But, there are more building blocks of information to absorb before you can fully appreciate my plan. Chapter 4 puts together two more bricks of the foundation—compounding and dollar-cost-averaging.

The Power of Compounding and Dollar-Cost-Averaging

You have seen how inflation can beat down the purchasing power of the dollar. In contrast, money working properly can make additional money which more than offsets inflation's toll. Compounding is the process of money begetting money, and dollar-cost-averaging is a way of feeding this money machine. These processes come together to form a wealth accumulation spiral of massive potential.

Compounding

This is the point where investing gets exciting. Watching an investment grow by its own strength can be mind boggling as the numbers get bigger and bigger. The self-perpetuating power comes from compounding. In my seminars, I use an allegory that punctuates my point about compounding. Here it is for you to ponder:

In 1492, Christopher Columbus decided he was going to save for retirement. He had one penny ($0.01), and he knew he could earn 6% every year on his money which he placed in his *left* pocket. He put the penny in his *left* pocket, and every year he earned 6% on that penny. He placed the interest ($0.01 x 6% = $0.0006) into his *right* pocket for safe keeping. He never added anything to his original penny in his *left* pocket. Yet, the interest accumulated year after year in his *right* pocket.

In this story, Chris was a very healthy guy. He ate good, nutritional food and exercised daily; so, he lived until today, 1997—505 years later. Now, he thought it was a good time to retire. So, he took his one penny from his left pocket and added it to all of the simple interest he accumulated in his *right* pocket. Do you know how much Mr. Columbus had?

Well, the interest in his *right* pocket added up to only $0.30 (504 years x $0.0006 = $0.30). Along with his original penny from his *left* pocket, he had $0.31 on which to retire. Not good planning!

Since I am obviously making this story up as I go, let me change it slightly. Let's assume Chris was much more astute about investing because he heard me speak about compounding. Instead of putting the interest in his *right* pocket, he now put it into his *left* pocket with the original penny—the principal. Over the years he would earn the same 6% interest on the original penny and the interest that accumulated in his *left* pocket every year. This is called compounding.

As the story goes, at the end of year #1, he had $0.0106 in his *left* pocket (the original penny plus the 6% interest). At the end of year #2, he had $0.011236 ($0.0106 plus 6% interest). At the end of year #3, he had $0.01191 ($0.011236 plus 6% interest). This compounding continued for 504 years. How much did good ole' Chris finally accumulate for retirement?

The answer is somewhat more to Chris's liking. At the end of 504 years of compounding the original penny at 6% interest, Chris had $56,774,862,807 (56 billion, 774 million, 862 thousand, 807 dollars!) That's a lot of pocket change!

That's the beauty and power of compounding. It's amazing, just as this little story suggests. The numbers you will use will be different of course, but time will make the growth potential appear to be almost miraculous.

Table 4.1: Compounding Table shows how $1,000 compounds annually at 14% over the course of 30 years. Here is an important differentiation to make. You must understand the difference between compounded annual interest rate and average annual interest rate.

Compounded annual interest rate is what made Christopher Columbus so wealthy in the story above. It is the rate at which interest is earned that is added back to principal plus interest that was earned earlier. If $1,000 is earning 14% compounded annually, it is earning that rate of return every year on principal and reinvested interest.

Average annual interest rate is not the same rate year after year because it is determined differently and can be confusing. It is the average return on the initial principal during a specific period of time.

As the table demonstrates, $1,000 is the initial principal and is earning 14% compounded annually. At the end of five years, it has earned a total of $925 in interest. The percentage of return for this five-year period is 92.5% [($925 ÷ $1,000) x 100 = 92.5%]. To obtain the average annual return, divide 92.5% by five years, and the answer is 18.5%. The average annual return of 18.5% is different for different time periods. It is always higher than the compounded annual return which is consistent throughout.

Here's the problem. An unsuspecting investor could be sold an investment product that is yielding 18.5% average annual interest over a five-year period. The investor could mistakenly believe that the average annual interest rate is a compounded interest rate. It is not! Always know if you are being quoted an annual compounded interest rate or an average annual interest rate.

Compounding is the growth effect on the initial investment when all interest is added back to principal. When you continue to feed the compounding process with new money, then even more exciting things unfold.

Table 4.1: Compounding Table

When comparing investment results,
always compare *compounded annual interest* - not *average annual interest*

14% compounded at the end of each year

End of year	Beginning balance	14% compounded annual interest	End of year total	Average annual interest rate
1	$1,000	$140	$1,140	14.0%
2	$1,140	$160	$1,300	15.0%
3	$1,300	$182	$1,482	16.1%
4	$1,482	$207	$1,689	17.2%
5	$1,689	$236	$1,925	18.5%
6	$1,925	$270	$2,195	19.9%
7	$2,195	$307	$2,502	21.5%
8	$2,502	$351	$2,853	23.2%
9	$2,853	$399	$3,252	25.0%
10	$3,252	$455	$3,707	27.1%
15	$6,261	$877	$7,138	40.9%
20	$12,056	$1,688	$13,743	63.7%
30	$44,693	$6,257	$50,950	166.5%

Dollar-Cost-Averaging

Dollar-cost-averaging is a disciplined form of regular investing. By dollar-cost-averaging, you invest the same amount of money at specific intervals (i.e., monthly) into a financial vehicle such as a no-load mutual fund. Most importantly, dollar-cost-averaging helps the investor develop a discipline to stay committed to a goal.

Dollar-cost-averaging is as simple as it gets. It enhances the power of compounding. You decide how much money you will invest every month. Your minimum limit is dictated by the minimum deposit allowed by your investment vehicles and also by the amount you must invest to reach your goal. The maximum limit is determined by your available investable cash and your plan's contribution limit if this is a tax-deferred retirement account.

The secret here is to determine what that monthly amount will be and then to invest that same amount every month. No excuses will be acceptable. Pay yourself first!

You must consider this monthly commitment as important as your monthly mortgage payment or your monthly utility bill. You couldn't let them slide, and you shouldn't let your predetermined monthly allotment to your investment plan slide.

Here is an example of how the whole process of dollar-cost-averaging could work for Mike and Jodi. Although taxes would have to be paid on all distributions if this were not a tax-deferred account, taxes are not considered in this example.

Mike and Jodi want to invest $200 at the beginning of every month into one of the best no-load mutual funds that has been averaging a compounded annual return of 14% over the past 10 years. If their funds continue to average 14% compounded a year, in just five years they will have invested $12,000, but their investment will have grown to $17,440. They continue to invest the same $200 monthly for another five years. After 10 years of regular monthly investing, they will have invested a total of $24,000. However, compounding at 14% has allowed their investment to grow to $52,418. If they continue their program for another five years, they will have invested a total of $36,000 after 15 years. But, their investment will now be worth $122,571.

Look at what compounding will do for a regular investment program such as dollar-cost-averaging! (See Table 4.2: Compounding Table with Dollar-Cost-Averaging.) During the growth of Mike and Jodi's portfolio, they will be purchasing shares of the fund at various prices. When prices are high, they will be buying fewer shares. When prices are low, they will be buying more shares. These prices will average out over the months of their investing program, but there will be times when the market in general will not seem to be such a great place to invest. With dollar-cost-averaging, Mike and Jodi must continue to invest in bad times as well as good times, so should you!

Stages of Wealth Accumulation

Wealth accumulation is a process. It is deliberate and methodical. There is no quick gimmick; it just takes time.

The process occurs in stages. Assuming you have a plan that requires you to invest the same dollar amount at regular intervals (dollar-cost-averaging), and the money that is generated is reinvested back into the total (compounding), the stages of wealth accumulation are the same for everyone. The only difference is the amount of money actually involved. There are three stages. The first stage I call the Building Stage; the second, the Momentum Stage; and the last, the Self-Propelled Stage.

Building Stage

Throughout the Building Stage you are fueling your investment vehicle with equal dollar purchases on a regular basis. Your investment vehicle could be one of the many excellent no-load, growth-type mutual funds. (More about specific investment vehicles in chapter 8.)

Let's revisit Mike and Jodi. They have a long-term plan to invest $200 every month for a total of $2,400 a year. The dominant feature at this stage is that the total

24

Table 4.2: Compounding Table with Dollar-Cost-Averaging

14% average annual compounded interest rate;
$200 invested at the beginning of each month;
interest earned at the end of each month

End of year	Total invested	Total annual interest	End of year total
1	$2,400	$190	$2,590
2	$4,800	$577	$5,567
3	$7,200	$1,021	$8,988
4	$9,600	$1,533	$12,921
5	$12,000	$2,119	$17,440
6	$14,400	$2,795	$22,635
7	$16,800	$3,570	$28,605
8	$19,200	$4,462	$35,467
9	$21,600	$5,487	$43,354
10	$24,000	$6,664	$52,418
15	$36,000	$15,780	$122,571
20	$48,000	$34,062	$263,269
30	$72,000	$144,267	$1,111,411

return their entire portfolio earns annually is less than the amount of money they place into their investment vehicle annually. In this example, their total return from dividends, interest, and capital gains is less than $2,400 annually.

During this first stage of wealth accumulation, your infusion of money makes a big impact on the success of your plan. You are building the base. Discipline is critical at this stage. If you do not create the base, growth will occur much slower, and you may not reach your long-term goal.

The overall rate of return which your portfolio earns determines how long this stage (as well as the following stages) will last. The Building Stage could last from four to nine years if you were earning between 8% and 20% compounded a year. It is primarily a function of the total rate of return. The higher the rate, the shorter the stage; the lower the rate, the longer the stage. (See Table 4.3: Stages of Wealth Accumulation and Table 4.4: Annual Return for Given Year. The *clear* rectangle at the base of the graph represents the Building Stage.) It ends with the beginning of stage two, the Momentum Stage.

Momentum Stage

The Momentum Stage begins when your total annual contributions to your investment plan equal the total return of your portfolio annually.

Going back to the original example, this means that Mike and Jodi's total return from their portfolio is now $2,400 annually and rising.

This second stage of wealth accumulation begins to display signs of power. Your portfolio is now earning more than you contribute. Discipline is still important while your investment vehicle is picking up speed. Because of the momentum, this stage may last another two to five years before the last stage, the Self-Propelled Stage, begins. (In Table 4.3, this is the lightly shaded rectangle above the Building Stage.)

Self-Propelled Stage

The Self-Propelled Stage begins when your portfolio begins to earn twice as much as you invest annually.

Again from the original example, Mike and Jodi's total portfolio is now producing at least $4,800 annually while they are still only investing $2,400 each year.

This is the beginning of exponential growth. This is the point when your wealth accumulation seems to take on miraculous power—the power of compounding. Albert Einstein has referred to compounding as the *eighth wonder of the world*, and he certainly knew something about numbers! This stage is exciting, but it only comes after patience and commitment to your original long-term plan. (In Table 4.3, this is the dark shaded area above the Momentum Stage.)

From this point on, your portfolio will seem to grow by itself. Your continued contributions are important, but they will have much less impact than they did during the Building and Momentum Stages. It will take two to four more years before your total portfolio return is equal to three times your annual contribution. In another one to three years your portfolio return will equal four times your annual contribution. Then in less than two more years it will equal five times your annual contribution, and in approximately one more year it will equal six times your annual contribution. Even if you did not contribute another dollar to your plan during this stage, compounding would still propel your portfolio forward.

If the commitment to a financial goal can be initiated early in life, success will be yours. Time means everything. In this example, after six to fourteen years of sticking to a rigid investing schedule, the Self-Propelled Stage will take hold, and your wealth accumulation process will take on exponential growth.

No matter what your financial goal, every investment plan using dollar-cost-averaging will experience a Building Stage, a Momentum Stage, and a Self-Propelled Stage. The secret is to have a long-term plan and to begin that plan early. Start *now*! Experience the process!

Let me interject a word about taxes. Everything you earn you cannot keep. (Yes, Virginia, there is no Santa Claus!) Income taxes must be paid on all interest, dividends, and capital gains unless they are in a tax-deferred account. Interest and dividends are taxed at your tax bracket just as are your wages and salaries (earned income). However, capital gains are taxed at the capital gains rate. For 1996, the maximum ordinary income tax rate is 39.6%; the maximum capital gains tax rate is 28%.

Table 4.3: Stages of Wealth Accumulation

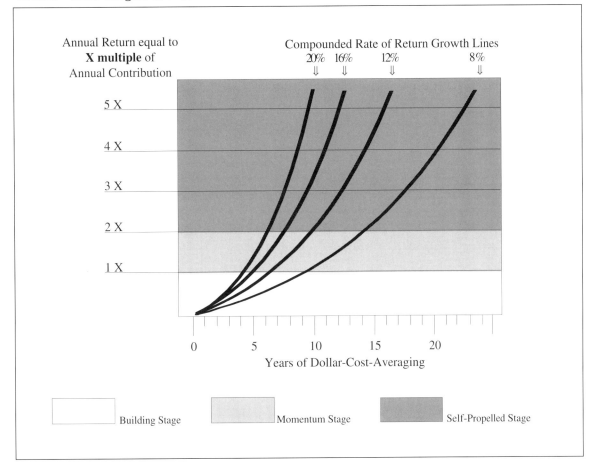

Description of Graph:
Stages of Wealth Accumulation

This graph illustrates the exponential growth of an investment compounding at 8%, 12%, 16%, and 20%. The years of dollar-cost-averaging are on the *x-axis*, and the total annual dollar returns from interest, dividends, and capital gains are on the *y-axis*. The *y-axis* is scaled for returns equal to: 1X (the annual contribution); 2X (two times the annual contribution); 3X (three times the annual contribution), etc. As you can see, the growth line of your portfolio begins to become more vertical as the years of compounding increase. The *slower* growth in the early years begins to pick up momentum until it seems to *explode* in the later years. The higher total returns take less time for the stages to unfold; the lower total returns take more time for the same stages to develop.

Table 4.4: Annual Return for Given Year

*(Multiplier Factor **TIMES** annual contribution)*
Annual contribution made at beginning of year.

		8%	10%	12%	14%	16%	18%	20%
					Annual Compounded Rate of Return			
Year of Dollar Cost Averaging	1	.0800	.1000	.1200	.1400	.1600	.1800	.2000
	2	.1664	.2100	.2544	.2996	.3456	.3924	.4400
	3	.2597	.3310	.4049	.4815	.5609	.6430	.7280
	4	.3605	.4641	.5735	.6890	.8106	.9388	1.074
	5	.4693	.6105	.7623	.9254	1.100	1.288	1.488
	6	.5869	.7716	.9738	1.195	1.436	1.700	1.986
	7	.7138	.9487	1.211	1.502	1.826	2.185	2.583
	8	.8509	1.144	1.476	1.853	2.278	2.759	3.300
	9	.9990	1.358	1.773	2.252	2.803	3.435	4.160
	10	1.159	1.594	2.106	2.707	3.411	4.234	5.192
	11	1.332	1.853	2.479	3.226	4.117	5.176	6.430
	12	1.518	2.138	2.896	3.818	4.936	6.288	7.916
	13	1.720	2.452	3.363	4.492	5.886	7.599	9.699
	14	1.937	2.798	3.887	5.261	6.988	9.147	11.84
	15	2.172	3.177	4.474	6.138	8.266	10.97	14.41
	16	2.426	3.595	5.130	7.137	9.748	13.13	17.49
	17	2.700	4.054	5.866	8.276	11.47	15.67	21.19
	18	2.996	4.560	6.690	9.575	13.46	18.67	25.62
	19	3.316	5.116	7.613	11.06	15.78	22.21	30.95
	20	3.661	5.728	8.646	12.74	18.46	26.39	37.34
	21	4.034	6.400	9.804	14.67	21.57	31.32	45.01
	22	4.437	7.140	11.10	16.86	25.19	37.14	54.21
	23	4.871	7.954	12.55	19.36	29.38	44.01	65.25
	24	5.341	8.850	14.18	22.21	34.24	52.11	78.50
	25	5.848	9.835	16.00	25.46	39.87	61.67	94.40

Description of Table:
Annual Return for Given Year

This table will tell you what your total annual return from your portfolio will be at any given year during your wealth accumulation process using dollar-cost-averaging. It identifies the multiplier to be used with your annual contribution for various annual compounded rates-of-return. This is based on equal investments made at the beginning of each year.

For example: If you invested $2,000 at the beginning of the year, and you received an average compounded rate of return of 8% at the end of each year, your total annual return at the end of year #7 (for example) would be $2,000 x .7138 = $1,428. (The multiplier is found by looking down the column "8%" and across the row "7".) If you were able to obtain a higher annual return of 14%, then your total return at the end of year #7 would be $2,000 x 1.502 = $3,004. (In this scenario, the multiplier is at the intersection of column "14%" and row "7".)

You can continue this exercise to see just how powerful the process of compounding would be for your investment program as the years increase.

There is another method to enhance the power of compounding—not paying taxes on the investment interest, dividends, and capital gains. I'm not suggesting you engage in an illegal act. I'm suggesting you use a plan that allows for tax-deferral legally. Take a peek at chapter 5 to see what I mean.

CHAPTER 5

Taxable Investing and Tax-Deferred Investing

I'm not getting into the specific investment choices yet, but I want to support further the benefits of compounding by demonstrating its power.

When you invest, your portfolio grows because of (1) reinvestment of current income, dividend, or capital gains, and/or (2) capital appreciation over time. What you actually realize in profits is taxed by the government. Money that comes out of your investments to pay these taxes leaves less money to be reinvested for compounding to proceed. If there were a way not to have to pay taxes currently, but to postpone these taxes to a much later date, then all of the money would remain in the investment to provide the maximum benefit from compounding. When taxes are paid at a later date, they would come out of a much larger investment portfolio.

One way to defer taxes is to invest in stocks or mutual funds that produce maximum growth of capital through appreciation rather than income, dividends, or realization of capital gains. In other words, you would not realize any capital gains until you sold the stock or mutual fund. The net realized gains would then be taxed as long-term capital gains after the sale. Depending on the tax laws at the time of sale, there may be lower tax rates on long-term capital gains than on ordinary income.

Another possibility for tax-deferral exists by investing in retirement programs approved by the IRS. Individual retirement arrangements (i.e., IRA, SEP-IRA, and SIMPLE), qualified retirement plans (i.e., defined contribution plans, defined benefit plan), and variable annuities allow for tax-deferral of their investment returns as long as certain rules are followed.

One disadvantage of tax-deferred retirement plans is that cash withdrawals after retirement that are subject to taxes are taxed as ordinary income even if some or all of the returns were long-term capital gains. If the long-term capital gains tax is significantly less than the tax on ordinary income when you withdraw these funds, than you will be paying a higher tax rate than you would have if the investment were not in a tax-deferred retirement program.

Another disadvantage is that there is a 10% penalty on any withdrawals before age 59 1/2 unless they are part of a series of substantially equal payments as described in chapter 15.

One way to completely avoid federal income tax is to invest after-tax dollars in tax-exempt municipal bonds. The proceeds from these bonds support state or local governmental needs or special projects. If the bond is a debt obligation from your own

state, it may also be exempt from state income tax. One disadvantage of municipal bonds is that their overall total return is lower than that from the equity markets. One major advantage is that they have a very low risk level when rated "AAA" or "AA."

Tax-Deferred Programs

Here are some definitions of various tax-deferred programs. They all allow for tax-deductible contributions with the exception of some IRAs and all variable annuities. (You may or may not be able to take a tax-deduction for your IRA contribution. This will depend on whether you or your spouse are also contributing to an employer-sponsored qualified plan. If you or your spouse are contributing to a qualified plan, then your adjusted gross income will dictate how much, if any, of your IRA contribution is tax-deductible. None of your contributions to a variable annuity are tax-deductible. Discuss these possibilities with your accountant or tax advisor.)

IRA

The Individual Retirement Account is an individual savings arrangement. It is not considered a qualified plan, but it is a tax-deferred vehicle. It can be used by anyone who has earned income. (Qualified plans are retirement plans that are approved by the IRS. They are for the exclusive benefit of employees or their beneficiaries; must be communicated to the participants in a written document; and cannot discriminate in favor of officers, stockholders, or highly paid employees. These plans also must comply with minimum eligibility, vesting, and funding requirements.)

Profit Sharing Plan

This is one of the most common qualified retirement plans. Contributions are made as a percentage of salary. The same percentage must be used for all employees.

SEP

The Simplified Employee Pension works like a Profit Sharing Plan when it comes to contributions. These contributions are made by the employer to each of the employee's IRAs. It is the easiest and least expensive defined contribution plan to establish.

401(k) Plan

This is a very popular plan with employees since they can determine how much of their own pay is to be contributed to the plan on their behalf. Sometimes there is a *matching employer contribution*.

SIMPLE

The Savings Incentive Match Plan for Employers is a new plan that began in 1997. It is a way for employers and self-employed individuals to put money into a retirement plan if no other qualified plan is in existence.

Age-Weighted Profit Sharing Plan

This qualified plan offers the benefits of a Profit Sharing Plan but permits a larger portion of the contributions to be allocated to the accounts of older employees.

Money Purchase Pension Plan

Annual contributions by the employer as specified in the plan are mandatory. As a tradeoff, a higher percentage of salary is allowed as a contribution.

Target Benefit Plan

This plan functions like the Age Weighted Profit Sharing Plan, but the annual contributions are mandatory.

Defined Benefit Plan

This plan requires mandatory contributions that are higher for older employees. The main advantage of this plan is that the annual contributions are not limited to a specific percentage of salary or to a specific dollar amount. The actual benefit at retirement is determined (or defined) based on the employee's salary now.

Variable Annuity

After you have exhausted the options of using IRAs and qualified retirement plans, variable annuities make good sense for long-term investors.

Unlike qualified retirement plans, variable annuities don't have maximum limits on how much you can invest and don't require you to invest for anyone else. They also do not require you to begin withdrawing money after age 70 1/2. Although the money you invest is *not* tax-deductible, it grows tax-deferred.

Variable annuities are basically mutual funds wrapped inside an insurance product. The life insurance component may insure that your beneficiary will receive at least the amount of all your contributions even if the equity value in the annuity falls below the total of all your contributions. Payout options range from withdrawals at your discretion to guaranteed lifetime annuities for you and your spouse.

Be sure to find one that has excellent funds in which to invest and also has low fees. Contact Independent Advantage Financial and Insurance Services at (800) 829-2887 to help you choose the best program for your needs. One program I like was announced by Jack White & Co. called *Value Advantage Plus Variable Annuity*. This is a no-load, low-expense variable annuity. Its total cost for mortality and expenses is only 0.45% in contrast to 1.24% which is the norm for this industry according to Morningstar. For more information and a prospectus, contact Jack White & Co. at (800) 622-3699.

Levels of Contributions for Tax-deductible Plans

If you are self-employed or an employer considering a plan for yourself and your employees, how would you choose the best plan? To start, the selection of a retirement plan should be based on how much the owner can contribute from earned income.

Up to $2,000

If you can only contribute $2,000 a year to a retirement plan, then all you need is a regular IRA. There is no need to spend the extra money or time to adopt a qualified plan if your contributions are going to be limited in this way.

However, if you are married, your non-working spouse also can contribute up to $2,000 to his or her IRA. That's a total of $4,000. In addition, if your children are employed, each of them can have their own IRAs. For example, if you are employed, your spouse is a housewife, and your two children have summer jobs each earning over $2,000, then your family unit could put away $8,000 ($2,000 into four separate IRAs) a year for retirement.

Up to $6,000

Starting in 1997, there is a new program for self-employed individuals and small business owners who employ 100 or fewer employees. The SIMPLE retirement plan is open to employers currently without a plan, who have employees who earn at least $5,000 a year.

Employees can elect to contribute up to $6,000 a year (adjusted annually for inflation) to this plan. Usually, the employer will match dollar for dollar up to 3% of the employee's compensation. The SIMPLE retirement plan can be structured for each employee as an IRA or as a 401(k) plan.

Up to $9,500 (in 1997)

The next step up in contributions is a 401(k) Plan. It will allow a maximum of $9,500 to be contributed in 1997 to an individual account. (This maximum changes each year.) With this plan, employees can decide how much they want to contribute from their own pay. The employer usually does not need to provide contributions for each employee. However, to meet certain requirements and to encourage employee participation, the employer may make a matching contribution to the plan.

Up to $24,000 or 15% of Salary (in 1997)

The next level of contribution jumps to either $24,000 or 15% of salary (whichever is less). The maximum amount of employee compensation that can be used to determine this retirement contribution is $160,000 in 1997. The traditional Profit Sharing Plan and SEP fall into this category. With both of these plans, contributions may be made if profits exist, but the percentage of salary for all employees who qualify must be the same.

Up to $30,000 or 25% of Salary

The next level of contribution is either $30,000 or 25% of salary (whichever is less). Again, the maximum amount of employee compensation that can be used to determine this retirement contribution is $160,000 in 1997. A Money Purchase Plan fits this criteria except this plan carries a mandatory contribution level—thus eliminating any flexibility. As an employer, you could maintain some flexibility by combining two plans. You could integrate a Money Purchase mandatory percentage of 10% and a Profit Sharing variable percentage of up to an additional 15% to take advantage of the 25% maximum salary limit. In this way some flexibility remains with the variable profit sharing percentage.

The Target Benefit Plan also fits this criteria. The benefit of this plan over the Money Purchase Plan is that higher percentages (up to 25% or $30,000) can be contributed for older employees. Still, these contributions are mandatory, and an actuary must determine the dollar amount of the contributions annually.

The Age Weighted Profit Sharing Plan, as with the Target Benefit Plan, also allows higher contributions for older employees up to the $30,000 or 25% limit (whichever is less). The advantage of this plan is that these contributions are not mandatory, making this plan similar to a Profit Sharing Plan in flexibility. However, the overall contribution your business can deduct from taxes is 15% of all salaries combined. Although the oldest employees can still have up to 25% of their salary contributed, the *overall* contribution of the practice *cannot exceed 15% of all salaries*.

For example: Dr. Jones' practice has a total salary expense of $240,000 ($150,000 for Dr. Jones and $90,000 for all staff combined.) Dr. Jones is 57 years old, and his staff is considerably younger. Dr. Jones can contribute $30,000 as determined by an actuary for himself and $5,000 for the rest of his staff combined. The total retirement contribution is $35,000. This is less than 15% of $240,000 and therefore fits the criteria for the age weighted profit sharing plan.

Unlimited Percent of Salary

The highest level of contribution is only possible with a Defined Benefit Plan. This plan has no defined limit on the amount of money that can be contributed in any year for an employee. It is not restricted to a percentage of salary. An actuary will determine the amount of money to be contributed annually for an employee based on the amount of money to be paid at retirement. In other words, the benefit to be received at retirement is defined in advance in the plan document. An example might be 60% of one's highest monthly salary for life. The only limits are on the amount of benefit that can be defined. For 1997, this limit is 100% of an individual's current annual salary or $125,000 (whichever is less). As with the Money Purchase Plan and the Target Benefit Plan, these contributions are mandatory.

Non-Deductible IRAs

Read the following example carefully to see how Mike and Jodi compared the results of non-deductible IRAs versus a fully taxable account. (If Mike or Jodi contributes to a qualified retirement plan at work, they will not be able to deduct their contributions to their IRAs because of their tax bracket.)

Mike and Jodi will have $4,000 before taxes to invest each year. If this investment were tax deductible, then the entire $4,000 would be available to invest. However, if Mike and Jodi cannot take a tax deduction for their IRAs, taxes will have to be paid first. Mike and Jodi want to see what the benefit of a non-deductible IRA would provide for them.

In this example, Mike and Jodi will pay their taxes due (35%) on this $4,000 of earned income out of this amount. In this way, they will only have $2,600 to invest each year after paying the taxes (35% x $4,000 = $1,400; $4,000 - $1,400 = $2,600).

They are projecting that their Lifetime Investing Plan will have an average annual compounded return of 14%. They want to understand how much more beneficial it will be to invest in their IRAs to create a nest egg in 25 years compared to investing in the same mutual funds but not in a tax-deferred vehicle. For comparison purposes only, let's project their total marginal tax rate to be 35% now and in the future. Also, let's assume that all taxes will be paid from their taxable investment portfolio. Taxes will reduce the real return in this taxable account from 14% to 9.1% (65% retained after taxes times 14% total return). In the IRAs at the end of 25 years, the entire portfolio will be taxed at 35%, again for comparison purposes only.

Table 5.1 describes the actual calculations used on a Hewlett Packard 10B Business financial calculator to compare the various scenarios for Mike and Jodi. The details of using a financial calculator are described in chapter 7. The financial calculator symbols *PV*, *N*, *I*, *PMT*, and *FV* are explained in that chapter.

Calculations demonstrate that with a non-deductible IRA, Mike and Jodi could have $373,142 after taxes to spend at retirement. But, with a taxable account and all other variables being equal, they would have $243,856 to spend.

If Mike and Jodi did not contribute to a qualified retirement plan, their IRA contributions would be tax-deductible as well as tax-deferrable. With a tax-deductible IRA, Mike and Jodi's entire $4,000 would be available to contribute. If all other variables were held constant as in the previous examples, Mike and Jodi would have $539,065 after taxes to spend at retirement.

Non-Deductible IRA had a 53% greater net than the taxable account.
Deductible IRA had a 121% greater net than the taxable account.

Look at these numbers carefully. In this example, contributing to a tax-deductible IRA produced 121% more spendable cash at the end of 25 years than investing in a taxable account each year for 25 years. Again in this example, a non-

Table 5.1: IRA Calculations for Mike & Jodi

Non-Deductible IRA

PV = 0

N = 25

I = 14

PMT = 2,600

FV = $539,065

$539,065 - $65,000 ($2,600 x 25 years = $65,000 non taxable contribution over 25 years)

= $474,065

Net after taxes: 65% X $474,065 = $308,142 + $65,000 = $373,142

Taxable Account

PV = 0

N = 25

I = 9.1

PMT = 2,600

FV = $243,856

Net after taxes: $243,856

Deductible IRA

PV = 0

N = 25

I = 14

PMT = 4,000

FV = $829,331

Net after taxes: 65% X $829,331 = $539,065

---

deductible IRA still provided 53% more money at the end of 25 years than a taxable account yielded. In my way of looking at things, this is significant.

However, as I described earlier in this chapter, there is one factor that you must consider. All money in an IRA will be taxed as ordinary income when it is withdrawn. Money accruing in a taxable account only might be subject to long-term capital gains which may be taxed at a lower tax rate than ordinary income in the future. But, for comparison purposes, it is almost always better to invest in a tax-deferred vehicle for your retirement years than to invest in a taxable vehicle with all other variables being equal.

As you continue to read through this book, you will be faced with challenges and financial opportunities. There are a host of everyday problems that could interfere with your long-term financial goals. I look at these problems as traps, ready to ensnare the unsuspecting or uninformed. The next chapter may open your eyes to them. Take a chance, and read on!

Money Traps

I've discussed inflation and how it dilutes the purchasing power of the dollar. I've described both compounding and dollar-cost-averaging and how they enhance your ability to accumulate wealth. I've suggested that investing in a tax-deferred vehicle greatly improves the end result over investing similarly in a taxable vehicle. However, if you don't prepare yourself for several traps along the way, you could get stuck.

Traps can catch you off guard; they often can stop you dead in your tracks. However, the more aware you are of potential problems, the more prepared you will be to handle them quickly and effectively.

Some of these money traps may be obvious in their form and easy to anticipate. Others may be insidious and harder to pinpoint. Some traps only lessen the amount of money that is available for you to invest while others can devastate you financially.

Here are eight traps that are more insidious than obvious. Each trap is illustrated through a real life situation followed by a solution for that particular hurdle. In some of the examples, Mike and Jodi may appear to be like you and your spouse. Yet, in other examples, they may not. Identify any of these traps that are interfering with your financial life. If they are, take the necessary steps to make some changes.

Trap #1
Not Saving Three to Six Months of Living Expenses in a Safe Place

Real Life Situation: Mike and Jodi were comfortably earning what they needed financially from Mike's general dentistry practice to live the way they desired. Mike has been in practice for only four years. Unfortunately, an economic disruption occurred in their community creating a tremendous strain on most of its residents. Potential and existing patients put their dental needs on hold while their job security took priority. Mike's patients and cash flow were immediately affected by the downturn in the general business climate. What was once an excess of cash flow from Mike's practice was now a scarcity.

Unfortunately, they had not prepared themselves for any hard times since things had always been easy for both of them. Mike and Jodi were in a bind, and they needed to borrow money to make ends meet during this crisis. They borrowed the money; they felt the crunch; they endured the stress. They vowed never to allow themselves to be caught unprepared again.

Chapter 6

The Solution: Mike and Jodi need an emergency savings account which will become their *security blanket*. They should establish this separate account in a money market fund that offers check writing privileges, and they should name it *Mike and Jodi's Emergency Account*. (The reason I recommend a money market account rather than a savings account at a bank is because a money market account will earn interest that fluctuates with short term money market instruments. This variable interest rate will often be higher than the fixed-rate associated with a savings account.) Then they should place money into this account every week until they reach the level they have determined is right for their needs. Most professional financial planners recommend saving three to six months of living expenses in such an account. You will need to determine the amount that is right for you.

It is critical that Mike and Jodi only use this money if an emergency arises. If dollars must be withdrawn, Mike and Jodi must make it their priority to replenish it as soon as possible. However, when the amount of money in the account grows beyond the predetermined need, the excess can be withdrawn and used as needed. It could be spent on something consumable, or it can be invested for a future goal.

Trap #2
Getting into Excessive Consumer Debt

Real Life Situation: I referred to Justin Tyme in chapter 2 regarding credit card debt. This is such an important trap that I wanted to emphasize it again.

Mike's practice created for him a high income level and an excellent credit history which brought out all the plastic-credit-card-people. The credit card companies sent Mike and Jodi pre-approved credit cards which they quickly gobbled up. Easy credit made it too easy to *buy now* and *pay later*. That was exactly what Mike and Jodi did—they bought on credit. They didn't realize how quickly the bills could mount up. Unfortunately, they began to notice that they were taking money that was budgeted for other things to pay their credit card bills. In a short time they found that there wasn't enough cash to pay the minimum amounts due monthly on each credit card. They entered a dizzying spiral.

The Solution: Mike and Jodi must stop spending money frivolously. They need to think before they spend. They should consolidate their existing high interest credit-card-debt into one loan with only one payment. They should arrange a payment schedule with which they are comfortable and not strapped. Their ultimate goal should be to become free of all consumer debt. When purchasing items, they should either pay cash or use a credit card that they will pay off completely every month so that there will be no buildup of debt and no additional finance charges.

Trap #3
Indiscriminate Spending

Real Life Situation: Mike went to the shopping mall to purchase a new suit. He knew before he left home that the suit was all he *needed.* However, once he got to the store, his *needs* and *wants* got confused. He purchased an array of items that he didn't need and probably wouldn't use very often. He actually spent five times what he would have spent on just the suit.

The Solution: Mike needs to plan before he shops. If he really needs something, certainly he should go out and purchase it. Then while shopping for a specific item, Mike needs to stick to the task at hand. He must avoid the temptation of all the slick marketing displays that try to lure him into making unnecessary purchases. Over time, this type of spending behavior will be very costly and will drain important dollars that could have been invested for future needs.

Trap #4
Failure to Pay Yourself First

Real Life Situation: Mike and Jodi both knew that they needed to save for the future. They both discussed their future financial goals and had every good intention to do what they needed to do to prepare for financial independence. However, they came to the end of every month with barely enough money left to pay their regular expenses. They couldn't find any discretionary income to fund a regular investment program for retirement.

The Solution: Mike and Jodi must come to terms with their goals. Mike needs to decide if a qualified retirement plan for his office is the way to go or if some other method is more appropriate.

If Mike and Jodi are sincere about planning for retirement, they must determine how much they must save each month. Then, they must invest that amount of money in the proper financial vehicle.

To develop the discipline to save regularly, Mike and Jodi should consider their monthly investment as a bill to be paid the first of the month—every month. Just like they would not miss paying their monthly utility bill or mortgage payment, they should never miss paying their retirement bill to their retirement plan.

To assist Mike and Jodi, their mutual fund company could send them a reminder notice. Another option would be for Mike and Jodi to set up an automatic investment program with their mutual fund company by which a specified amount of money is drafted each month from their checking account. An even easier method with more

diversification would be to do everything through a discount broker. I get into this in chapter 13.

Whatever method is designed, the bottom line for Mike and Jodi is to pay themselves first. They must never let this critical investment for their future become *past due*.

Trap #5
Never Being Satisfied

The Problem: Mike and Jodi loved expensive things. They always wanted the best. They were impressed by the material possessions of their friends. They weren't trying to compete, but they saw how happy their friends were, and they wanted to be as happy. So, Mike and Jodi continued to purchase those things that they believed would make them feel good. In reality, however, Mike and Jodi never seemed to reach a point where they really felt good. Yet, they were sure that they would be satisfied someday after they finally purchased all the things that they really wanted.

The Solution: How sad! Mike and Jodi will never be happy if they don't change their values. They are caught up in the *rat race*, and they are trying to feel something internally that can never be satisfied by external possessions. They must learn that *enough is enough*. They must learn to be satisfied with the things that they already have.

First, Mike and Jodi must set some goals. They need to understand what their specific survival *needs* are. Then they can identify their comfort *wants* and luxury *desires*. From this breakdown, they can realistically differentiate between their needs, wants, and desires. They must learn to postpone some of their wants and desires to a time in the future when they can truly afford them. Practicing *delayed gratification* is also a form of maturity.

However, real satisfaction will only come to Mike and Jodi after they learn that what really matters in life is their love for one another, for family, and for friends. Although some possessions are important, they are only external. For Mike and Jodi, the non-material things must take priority. All the rest is nice but often superfluous.

Trap #6
Mixing Investments With Insurance

Real Life Situation: Mike had a whole life insurance policy that covered him for $1,000,000. The policy had a cash value element that grew slowly over the years. Mike's premiums were $11,470 a year.

His associate, Steve, was the same age as Mike. Steve owned a $1,000,000 term life insurance policy that only insured his life. It had no savings buildup. The premium for Steve's term life policy was $1,160 a year, and the premium stayed level for 20 years. Thereafter, it became a decreasing term policy.

Mike wondered why his premiums were so high and if he could improve his portfolio by investing elsewhere.

The Solution: The purpose of insurance is to shift risk to the insurance company. The purpose of investments is to accumulate wealth. The two don't mix well in my opinion!

If Mike wants to accumulate wealth, he should consider purchasing life insurance that only insures against his premature death. This is called *term* life insurance. The difference in cost between the term insurance premiums and the whole life insurance premiums could be invested in my Lifetime Investing Plan which has an excellent history of total returns. His wealth accumulation in the no-load equity mutual funds of my Lifetime Investing Plan should outperform the cash value buildup in the whole life policy. Furthermore, the accumulated cash in his investment portfolio would be his to do with as he wished at any time.

Trap #7
Spending Dividend, Interest, and Capital Gain Income

Real Life Situation: Mike and Jodi had a series of stocks that paid annual dividends. The dividends provided an annual yield of approximately 5% of the stock portfolio. When they received their dividend checks throughout the year, they treated them as gifts and immediately spent them. What were they missing?

The Solution: Mike and Jodi are missing the benefits of compounding. They should reinvest those dividend checks immediately either into additional shares of the stocks that are paying the dividends or into shares of a no-load equity mutual fund. Their stock broker can arrange for an automatic dividend reinvestment program that takes the responsibility of reinvesting the money away from Mike and Jodi. The power of compounding will make their portfolio grow exponentially.

Trap #8
Not Funding an IRA

Real Life Situation: Mike is thinking about setting up a qualified retirement plan through his office. Because of his tax bracket, he was told that neither he nor his wife could deduct any contributions they made to their IRAs if he also contributed to a qualified retirement plan. Therefore, Mike and Jodi are considering not funding their IRAs anymore. What is wrong with this picture?

The Solution: IRAs grow tax-deferred. Even if Mike and Jodi can't deduct the amount of money they place into their IRAs from current income, the money within the IRAs will continue to grow tax-deferred. That means that all interest, dividends, and capital gains within the IRAs can be reinvested without taxes being taken out currently. This allows compounding to work its wonders. No taxes are due until money is actually withdrawn from the IRAs. As money is withdrawn after retirement, it will be taxed as ordinary income.

Everyone who has earned any income should consider establishing an IRA—even if this contribution is non-deductible. (Go back to chapter 5 to refresh your memory about tax-deferred versus taxable investing.)

These are only a few of the possible money traps by which every one of us could get snared. You must always be on guard to protect yourself and your money. Remember, no one cares more about your money than you!

Take some time to think about those traps that are lying in wait for you. You are in the best position to know what they are and where they lurk. Write them down as you think of them. Refer to that list frequently. You will find that the hurdles you identify are actually the major elements out there that can get you off your financial track. If you are conscientious in identifying them, you will be able to overcome them.

Let's get down to making your financial goals a reality. Get your pencil handy, you will be making lots of notes. There is much to absorb in the next chapter which deals with setting financial goals.

Don't be intimidated by the length and detail in chapter 7. Read it in pieces. Digest it. Reread what needs to be reread. Don't forget to take some breaks along the way. It is well worth your efforts!

Financial Goals

Capital Accumulation

As basic as it may seem, capital accumulation, which is a prime financial objective for all of us, is not well understood. What is capital accumulation? What areas in our lives require capital accumulation? How do we go about accumulating this capital? And, how do we keep this capital safe?

Capital accumulation is the saving and investing of money in specifically identified accounts to be used in the future for defined purposes. How much must you save and for what purposes are your financial goals.

I have broken down capital accumulation into five specific accounts. Think of each account as a separate compartment— each having a specific purpose. See Table 7.1: Capital Accumulation.

Table 7.1: Capital Accumulation

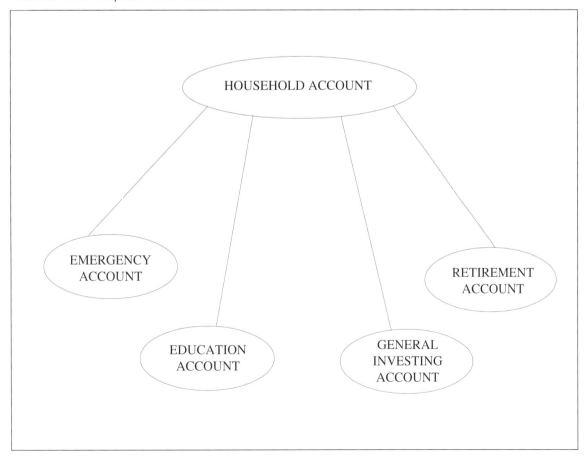

Household Account

This is most likely where you keep your money in order to pay your daily, weekly, and monthly expenses. This will usually be a checking account through a local bank that may or may not also be an interest bearing account. When you get paid, you will probably deposit the entire paycheck into this account and then write checks to disperse your money into other cubbyholes including the following four accounts: emergency account, education account, general investing account, retirement account.

Emergency Account

An emergency account should be started immediately! Its purpose is to handle unforeseen financial emergencies. For example, if you should become disabled, this money will carry you through your disability *waiting period* until your disability insurance takes effect. This account also could be a source for less serious but still unforeseen financial necessities such as deductibles for various insurance policies. The experts suggest that this account should consist of three to six months of living expenses.

Your emergency account must be a separate account, properly named, and invested in a safe, liquid vehicle. This means that your money in this account is not subject to loss or drop in value and that it is quickly and easily available when you need it. I recommend a money market fund invested only in government obligations. This will earn interest based on the treasury bill rate at any given time and is as safe as the solvency of the U.S. government. Necessary cash is available as quickly as it takes to write a check.

Almost all mutual fund companies (examples: Vanguard, Founders, Scudder, etc.) offer a government money market fund with check writing privileges within their family of funds. Usually a minimum of $1,000 is required to open such an account.

This fund then becomes your "security blanket". It helps you sleep at night! Therefore, this fund should only be violated if absolutely necessary, and, if used, it must be replenished to its original amount as soon as possible. However, when this account reaches a value that is worth more than your required number of months of living expenses, the excess can be redirected to other capital accumulation accounts.

Another option to consider in case an emergency of large proportion were to occur is to establish an open line of credit with your bank before you really need it. This is actually an agreement with your bank that you can borrow up to a certain amount of money (your line of credit) at any time by simply writing a check. You open such a line of credit the same way you would go about applying for a regular loan. The only difference is that you don't actually receive any money from the bank at this time. It doesn't cost you anything *until* you actually tap into your line of credit. If you exercise this option and borrow money on your line of credit, your repayment to the bank will be much like a repayment of any other bank loan with interest.

Education Account

Another type of capital accumulation is an education account. An education account is a savings or investment plan to accumulate a specific amount of money for your child's education. If you have children, you must estimate how much this sum should be. This is calculated from the costs for college today, anticipated inflation for the years ahead, and the total return you expect to receive from your investment. Later in this chapter I will discuss planning for college expenses in detail. (By the way, this does not only have to be for your child. Maybe you or your spouse would like to go back to school to further your education!)

General Investment Account

This account can be used for future, large purchases such as a down payment on a home, a boat, a vacation, etc. These funds are discretionary. Use them and enjoy them! But, while not being used, invest them to earn the highest return that satisfies your risk tolerance (more about risk in chapter 9). If this account is being saved for long term growth (over five years), the Lifetime Investing Plan should work well for you. However, once you reach the point when you need the money, then invest it more conservatively as you would your emergency account (i.e., in a government money market fund with check writing privileges).

Retirement Account

Time is of the essence for this account. This is where the miracle of annual compounding can be realized. Here's an example:

If you invest $10,000 into this account at the beginning of each year, earn 14% compounded annually, and do this for 20 years before you retire, then you will accumulate $1,037,684 by retirement! But, you must start early! If you follow this same scenario, but only do it for 10 years before you retire, then you will accumulate only $220,445! What a difference 10 years make!

All too often, this account is put off until it becomes very difficult to accumulate the wealth necessary for retirement in the time desired. In the example above, to accumulate $1,037,684 after 10 years investing at 14% would require an annual contribution of $47,072.

This account could be established within one of several retirement accounts so that your money will grow in a tax deferred environment. (i.e., IRA, SEP-IRA, 401(k), Pension Plan, Profit Sharing Plan, etc.) An IRA, of course, limits you to a $2,000 contribution a year.

I will go into depth later in this chapter regarding retirement planning.

Dealing With Financial Risks

There are risks which could get in your way as you prepare to reach your financial goals These potential hazards must be identified and handled appropriately.

Identifying these risks and taking the proper precautions are known in the financial planning world as *risk management*. There are four techniques of managing risk:

Avoidance of Risk

One way to eliminate risk is to avoid it. For example, if you don't snow ski, then you will avoid the risk of being disabled from a skiing accident.

Reduction of Risk

In order to reduce risk, you can take measures to prevent mishaps. If you do snow ski, you can take lessons from qualified instructors and use the proper equipment to try to prevent serious accidents from occurring.

Transfer of Risk

With this method of managing risk, your risk is actually transferred to another vehicle. Insurance is a means of transferring financial risk to an insurance company in return for a premium payment. If you snow ski and are involved in an accident, then your health insurance and possibly your disability insurance would cover most of your medical expenses and financial losses.

Retention of Risk

Another method of managing risk is to assume part of the risk. This can be done through the use of deductibles with your insurance. If you snow ski and break your leg, and have a $300 deductible on your health insurance, then you know that you will have to pay the first $300 before the insurance takes effect. By assuming a higher deductible or cost of the risk, you can lower your insurance premium and still maintain the proper coverage to prevent financial ruin.

Transfer Risk

The following five risks could create catastrophic financial losses to you and your family if not properly handled. Review these risks as a prevention checklist and consider insurance as the preventive means of transferring these risks to an insurance company.

Premature Death

Obviously this would bring your entire plan to a halt. Your family then would be thrown into a situation where there would be a loss of a steady income. To prepare for this potential devastation, the purchase of life insurance would protect your family by providing the necessary funds to maintain their standard of living if you should die. You will need to determine the proper amount of life insurance to purchase based on your current and future needs. Consider term life insurance which only insures your life and does not accumulate any cash value.

Illness

The cost of medical care could easily destroy anyone's savings. Health and major medical insurance is a must for any well thought out plan to reach financial independence. Also concider disability insurance to maintain a cash flow.

Remember that the purpose of insurance is to transfer the costs of catastrophic loss. Therefore, you shouldn't purchase insurance to cover every expense. If you did, the premiums would be out of sight, and the rationale for owning insurance would be misguided.

You should purchase your coverage so that you will pay for those expenses you can afford out of your pocket. These are called the deductibles of the policy. The real reimbursement from your medical policy is for those expenses that would be financially difficult or impossible for you to afford.

Property Loss

When you own possessions, you also have the risk of losing them. This could be due to accidents, fire, weather, theft, etc. Obviously, losing a $50 watch is not the same as losing a $5,000 watch. Property insurance is necessary, but, it is necessary only for valuable items whose loss would be costly to replace. When you purchase this type of insurance, consider purchasing *replacement value* insurance whenever possible. Replacement value coverage will pay for the replacement of the lost property which usually is higher than its depreciated market value.

Liability Loss

Each of us is exposed to possible liability claims made by others. We live in a litigious society. If someone trips on your front steps and breaks his leg, you are liable and can be sued! Property liability insurance is one means of transferring the potential financial crisis of liability lawsuits. Umbrella insurance is liability insurance that covers you above the usual limits of a standard liability insurance product. There are also many specialized types of liability insurance products for various businesses and professions.

Business Interruption

The overhead continues even if your business can't function. Consider what happened in Charleston, SC in September, 1989. Hurricane Hugo destroyed many dental practices. Unfortunately, some dentists did not have the proper business interruption insurance for perils both *on* and *off* premises.

Not only is it important to be covered for damage that occurs on your business property which could put you out of business, but it is also important to be covered for damage that occurs away from your business. For example, some policies will cover your business if it should burn down, but they may not cover your office if a major catastrophe occurs away from your office preventing customers from coming

to your business. Be sure you have business interruption insurance that insures you for perils arising both *on* and *off* your premises.

Although other risks exist, these five are the major ones to consider, and insurance is one of the best methods to transfer the financial burden which could result from each of them. A qualified insurance expert can help you identify your potential exposure to any of these risks and then recommend the proper type and amount of insurance you require. One caveat: Don't choose the first insurance agent you come across. Interview several; get some estimates; and then make your decision.

My Philosophy Is—S. I. M. P. L. E.

My philosophy of visualizing a financial goal and following through with it until it is reached is a simple process. However, like other life processes, the simple things often seem complex at first!

There is much for me to say and for you to understand with regards to financial goal setting. Take your time with the rest of this chapter. As I have already suggested, study it, and reread those sections that pertain to you. You should not feel compelled to complete this chapter with full retention after only one reading.

Refer to Table 7.2 and follow my acronym for **S.I.M.P.L.E.**:

Set your goal: You must first have a specific goal in mind before you can proceed. Your goal will be the basis for your plan, and your plan will serve as both a blueprint and a road map.

As a blueprint, it will show you what you will need as financial building blocks. Just as an architect relies on a blueprint to build a house, you will rely on your plan to construct your financial future.

As a road map, it will lead you to your final destination. Like all maps, there are many ways to travel to get to your destination. You can travel the road as outlined, or you can take side roads as necessary. The end result will be to reach your specific target. Not all roads, however, will lead to success. Follow those in your plan.

Your plan must be written out. It needs to be very specific. Why write down your plan? Studies have shown that individuals who write down their goals are more successful in reaching those goals than those who do not take the time to write them down. The reason probably lies in the fact that you think more about your goal when you write it and refer to it frequently. It's on your mind. You consciously and subconsciously direct your actions toward the achievement of that important goal.

To estimate how much you will need at retirement or for any other long-term goal is discussed later. It will depend on your anticipated expenses and other assets. Let's take a peek into Mike and Jodi's future planning (details come later in this chapter):

Mike and Jodi have decided that they want to accumulate $1.48 million in liquid assets so that they will be financially independent 25 years from now. With this in mind, they have written out their plan as follows:

Table 7.2: S.I.M.P.L.E.

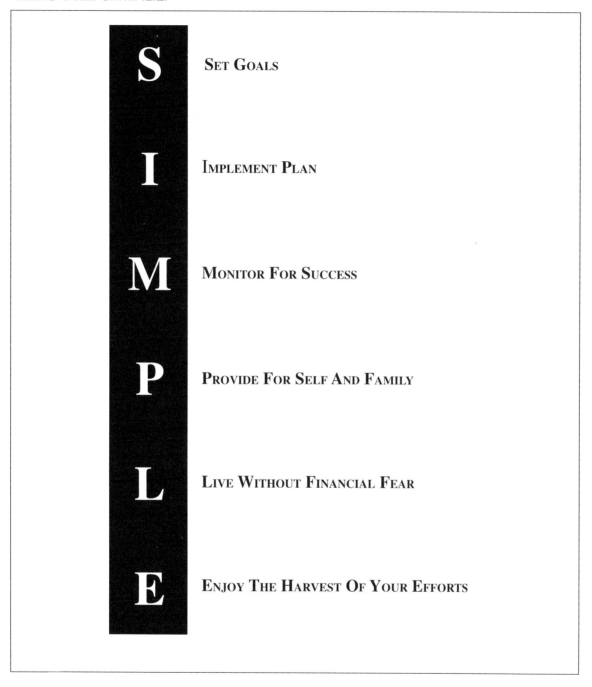

SET GOALS

IMPLEMENT PLAN

MONITOR FOR SUCCESS

PROVIDE FOR SELF AND FAMILY

LIVE WITHOUT FINANCIAL FEAR

ENJOY THE HARVEST OF YOUR EFFORTS

"We will invest $4,000 annually through our IRAs in no-load mutual funds based on the Lifetime Investing Plan. We plan to become financially independent in 25 years based on projections we have calculated. We will monitor our progress monthly and update our plan annually."

This plan now becomes law. Although it can be adjusted and even changed if necessary, it is their guiding light to follow.

Implement your plan: There is no chance of reaching any goal until you start. Although this appears obvious, the primary reason people fail to reach their financial goals is procrastination. They simply never get past the starting gate.

Start by doing some homework. This book will lay out a background and provide important research material for you to follow in order to implement your plan. Use it. Get the facts. Start today.

Monitor your plan: You will need to be sure your plan is staying on track. If it goes astray, and you are not made aware of it, you may fall short of reaching your goal within your projected time frame.

The best way to be sure your investments are on track is to know what your account balance should be at the end of each year from now until your retirement date or other long-term goal. (This is discussed in chapter 14.) If the balance at the end of any year is lower than what it should be, you will have the ability to make necessary adjustments right then. However, if the shortfall is allowed to compound uncorrected, then the discrepancy could mushroom into an unmanageable deficit.

Through the use of an inexpensive financial calculator, these yearly target balances can be easily determined. If the target balance in any one year falls short, you will have several options at your disposal. These options will also be discussed in Chapter 14.

Provide for yourself and your family: If you have been diligent in (1) setting realistic goals, (2) implementing your plan, and (3) monitoring its success, then you will have taken the proper steps to provide for yourself and your family. You cannot, and should not, depend on anyone or anything else to do this for you. No one cares more about your money than you. *No one!*

For example, the people who offer you financial advice are paid for their services. Often, their commitment to you ends with their last bill to you. Also, some of the brokers and agents who sell you financial products are primarily interested in their commissions, and rightly so! That is their business. You can't deny them that, and you also can't depend on them to make the right decisions for you.

Even programs that were set up for your benefit may not be around for you when you need them. An example is Social Security. By the time you retire, the rules of the Social Security game may have changed to such an extent that you would have to be labeled *poverty level* before you could receive any benefits. I don't know if this will happen, but it could. You shouldn't depend on Social Security to provide you with a meaningful source of income at retirement. Depend only upon yourself.

By creating financial independence through your Lifetime Investing Plan, you will be in control of securing your ability to provide for the needs and desires of your loved ones.

Live without financial fear: Did you know that most divorces in the United States are related to financial problems? Since most people never plan until it's too late, the stresses which build can become overpowering. Wouldn't it be satisfying to know that you have taken the proper steps early enough to avoid at least the financial pressures of preparing adequately for your retirement years?

I am sure you can find others in your community who demonstrate what a lack of proper planning can do to a family unit. You and your family can be above that. You will be able to live without the fear of financial stresses gnawing at your gut.

Enjoy the harvest of your efforts: Now you have reached financial independence. I define financial independence as the ability to live the lifestyle you have chosen from the money generated by your investments. In other words, your accumulated wealth will provide all the money necessary for you and your spouse for the rest of your lives.

Now is the time for you to enjoy the money you have saved. This is the harvest of your efforts over the course of your working lifetime up to this point. You deserve every penny of it. Your *investment plan* will now become a *withdrawal plan* which will be covered in chapter 16.

The word SIMPLE spells out my philosophy of investing for a lifetime. It takes you from where you are now to where you want to be. It also incorporates a way to maintain your chosen lifestyle for you and your spouse throughout retirement.

During the planning process, you will be using estimates to make predictions. Throughout the course of your plan, you must be flexible. Changes will need to be made. Nothing is, or should be, carved in stone. I believe investing does not have to be as complicated as others try to make it appear. I believe it should be SIMPLE.

Napoleon Hill's Personal Philosophy

No person in history has influenced the success of more individuals than Napoleon Hill. His most famous books, *Think and Grow Rich* and *Success Through a Positive Mental Attitude,* have application for anyone who wants to make things happen.

It all started with Andrew Carnegie, the steel magnate. Mr. Carnegie challenged Napoleon Hill to develop a philosophy of individual achievement. The project took Mr. Hill 20 years to complete.

The bottom-line-message after 20 years of analyzing the success of more that 500 of the 20th Century's greatest achievers is, "Anything your mind can conceive and believe, you can achieve." It all starts with a "burning desire."

Here are nine steps to make things happen in your life personally, financially, and professionally:

1. Determine your goal in life or your ambition, and then picture it in your mind so intensely that it becomes a part of your subconscious mind.
2. Get all the information you can about this goal, the requirements for it, and the possible compensation in happiness, contentment, and economic security.

3. Analyze all these facts and organize them into an order of accomplishment.
4. Set a definite time for the accomplishment of your goal.
5. Take immediate action to put these plans into effect. Do it today.
6. Be persistent with your plans. Don't let obstacles stand in your way.
7. Concentrate on a single step at a time to achieve your goal. You must walk before you can run.
8. Check yourself at intervals to see whether you are on the way, and adjust your plans as required by any circumstances over which you have no control.
9. Put this whole plan on paper, and make planning a habit.

Dabasir's Philosophy

History is a good teacher. Let's take a journey and go back 5,000 years. I'll take you to a time of great discovery.

In 1934, Dr. Alfred Shrewsbury, an archaeologist at Nottingham University, deciphered five clay tablets sent to him by Professor Franklin Caldwell from the ancient ruins of Babylon. They were dated to be approximately 5,000 years old. These five tablets disclosed the detailed plans of a person named *Dabasir* to pay off his debts and become financially independent. These five tablets divulged the essence of successful money management. More importantly, they described a philosophy of living fully. Five thousand years have passed, and no concept today can rival its foundation for creating financial independence and enjoying life's bounty.

I have summarized the three parts of Dabasir's philosophy below. As you read through it, it may sound overly simple and boringly basic. Don't be fooled! It is powerful!

Dabasir's Philosophy of Life

Plan for your future. Set aside at least 10% of everything you earn to keep for yourself. Think of this as your serious money for retirement. Don't invade it. Make it compound until retirement.

It's the consistent investment over time that makes the difference. Add to this the power of compounding as I've already illustrated in earlier chapters, and you have the greatest powers working for you.

Plan for your family. Live on 70% of everything you earn. Enjoy the harvest of your efforts. Intend to enjoy life and all it has to offer. But, don't spend more than 70% of what you earn!

Too often we get caught up in extremes. For instance, a dedicated dieter will never eat a piece of cake; a confirmed conservative will never listen to a liberal's point of view; a tightwad will never spend a whimsical dollar. Nonsense!

Life is meant to be enjoyed. You've earned your wealth. There is nothing wrong with using it to the fullest to satisfy your desires.

Plan for debt elimination. Use 20% of what you earn to reduce your debt burden. Repaying your loans with more than 20% of what you earn may not allow you to enjoy life as you should.

Again, extremes can get you into trouble. A debt-free life is a worthy goal. But, if all your efforts are focused toward debt reduction, you will miss out on all the splendor. Balance is the key here. You must stop and smell the roses.

As the story goes, Dr. Shrewsbury was enlightened by this ancient philosophy. Not only did he decipher the tablets, but also he was in dire need of its prophetic advice. You see, Dr. Shrewsbury in 1934 was personally on the verge of bankruptcy. However, after embracing this philosophy in his own life, he emerged from his potential financial ruin with direction and purpose. By 1937 Dr. Shrewsbury had repaid all his debts, had learned to enjoy life, and had begun a retirement plan.

The stories of ancient Babylon are intriguing. Babylon became the wealthiest city of the ancient world because its citizens were the richest people of their time. The Babylonians were clever financiers and traders. As best as can be determined, they were the original inventors of money as a means of exchange, of promissory notes, and of written titles to property.

George S. Clason was so enamored by the success secrets of the Babylonians, he wrote the modern day classic, *The Richest Man in Babylon*. This is a definite must-read-book! ...Very basic!...Very powerful!

You should take some time to think about goal setting. Your future is at stake. To do this right, you need to consider many scenarios. Don't feel rushed. To coin a phrase, *this is the beginning of the rest of your life*. Remember, investing is important but so is enjoying what life has to offer. Now for some specifics.

Long-Term Goal Planning

All long-term goal planning has one thing in common. The time horizon is more than five years away. Because of that, there is time to invest and allow various investment cycles to run their courses. (I describe the U.S. Business Cycle in chapter 8.)

In the rest of this chapter, you will learn (1) where to get additional help if necessary for your goal planning, (2) how to use a financial calculator to make projections into the future, and (3) how to plan for three specific long-term goals that many readers will need to consider.

The three goals that I'm going to describe in detail are: planning for college expenses, planning for retirement, and planning for long-term healthcare using investments as self-insurance. You should be able to take any other long-term goal that you have and fit it into one of these processes to make it work for you. Although I will introduce various investment vehicles, you will read in chapter 8 that my preference is no-load mutual funds.

Getting Additional Help

If you need some help in setting your financial goals and creating a financial plan, you need to know who is out there trying to *help* you and who is out there trying to *sell* you. Some of these people have no right to be doing what they do. It is critical that you know with whom you are dealing. Various letters after some peoples' names can compound the confusion. If you haven't taken the time to decipher all the titles and designations, I will help you put it all together.

The following professionals are eager to help you. Some work by themselves, some work for various brokerage firms, and some work behind the scenes where you may never meet them. But, before you seek out their services, know who they are, what they can offer you, and what they want from you! Their descriptions can be found in the LIP Gloss at the end of this book.

- **Registered Representative**.
- **Registered Investment Advisor (RIA)**.
- **Chartered Financial Analyst (CFA)**.
- **Chartered Financial Consultant (ChFC)**.
- **Certified Public Accountant (CPA)**.
- **Certified Financial Planner (CFP)**.

Fee-Only Certified Financial Planner

When you pursue financial advice, be sure you are paying for unbiased information. When you are purchasing financial products such as securities, insurance, annuities, etc., be sure you are not also looking for financial planning advice from the same person. Often, unbiased advice and the sale of commissional financial products are difficult to obtain from the same individual. There frequently can be a conflict of interest in this area.

My advice: Go to a fee-only Certified Financial Planner for advice. Their hourly rates vary tremendously based on geographical location, services rendered, and experience, but the average range is between $80 and $150 an hour. After you get their advice and personalized program, then go to the best salespeople you can find to purchase the products you need.

Assuming you believe that your financial planner should be a fee-only Certified Financial Planner, here is one way to find him or her. First, look in the Yellow Pages of your phone book under *Financial Planners*, and make a list of all of those with the CFP designation after their names. Then, contact the CFP Board of Standards to learn if these individuals are currently licensed by the CFP Board, if they have ever had their right to use the CFP designation revoked or suspended, and when they became certified (CFP Board of Standards, 1660 Lincoln Street, Suite 3050, Denver, CO 80264-3001; Phone (303) 830-7543; FAX: 303-860-7388). Next, make some telephone calls to these individuals. Ask if they are fee-only, and set up an appointment to interview them.

Here are several questions you should ask your potential financial advisor:
1. What is your education?
2. What types of clients do you have? (The purpose to this question is for you to engage a financial planner who has experience dealing with individuals like yourself—those with similar financial resources, goals, and philosophies.)
3. How are you compensated? Do you receive commissions?
4. Is your fee an hourly fee, a flat fee, or a fee based on total assets?
5. Do you provide monthly statements?
6. Do you receive referral fees from other individuals or organizations who sell financial products or services?
7. What percentage of your clients from three years ago are still with you?
8. Are you a registered investment advisor?
9. Can you supply me with four of your clients' names and phone numbers so I can speak to them regarding their experiences with you?
10. Will you personally handle my financial needs or will someone else in your firm be responsible for my account?
11. Have you ever been disciplined by a regulatory agency? Have you ever lost your license?

Also, be sure to request a copy of his or her *ADV Part II*. This is a document that the financial planner has filed with the SEC. It discloses information about the financial planner and any conflicts of interest. The planner is required to give this (or another document for disclosure that has been approved by the SEC) to you.

If you are going to use a financial planner or not, you want to make the planning process effective and meaningful. To help you with this, you should learn about the future value of money and how to use a financial calculator.

Future Value of Money and the Financial Calculator
What If...?

It is helpful to know what will happen later if a specific set of variables occurs now. The future value of money is simply the *what if* scenario of money over time. If a specific sum of money today is going to earn an interest rate over a period of time, what will it be worth at a designated time in the future? Or, if inflation is running at a stated percentage over a period of time, what will the U.S. dollar be worth at a specified time in the future? Or, if you want to have an amount of money at a certain time in the future, what amount of money must you invest now and what percentage return must it generate to reach that goal? These are questions relating to the future value of money. And, the easiest way to answer them is with a financial calculator.

The calculations that I have made throughout this book were done using a Hewlett Packard 10B Business financial calculator using the future value functions. A financial calculator is relatively inexpensive to purchase and easy to learn. The Hewlett Packard 10B Business financial calculator sells for approximately $35.

If you don't have a financial calculator or are not interested in purchasing one, you could have your financial planner or accountant do the numbers for you. Many software accounting programs such as Quicken let you do future value calculations. However, a financial calculator is a valuable, portable tool for many purposes. I strongly encourage you to own one and to learn its applications.

Variables to Future Value Calculations

There are five variables to future value calculations.
1. PV (present value): This is today's starting amount of money. If you are starting with nothing, then the present value is zero.
2. FV (future value): This is the amount of money you want at a specific time in the future.
3. PMT (payment): This is how much you will put into your investment at regular intervals. It is the dollar-cost-averaging part of investing. The PMT function key is also used to figure how much you will take out of your investment at regular intervals in a withdrawal program.
4. I (interest): This is the average compounded rate of return your investment will experience (or is expected to experience) at regular intervals over the course of a specific period of time.
5. N (number): This is the specific period of time over which your calculation is being figured. It is the number of intervals before you reach your goal (i.e., FV). It may be calculated in years, quarters, months, etc.

Each financial calculator has its own way of inputting numbers. My descriptions relate to the Hewlett Packard 10B. Be sure to read the directions of your financial calculator carefully. Also, be sure always to clear the registers before doing your next calculation.

For the HP 10B, the number of periods of payments in a year must be entered first. For annual calculations, enter 1 P/Y (one period per year). For monthly calculations, enter 12 P/Y (12 periods per year), and so on.

To help you visualize what happens to money over time, I am going to use two maps. (See Graph 7.3: Money Maps, BEGIN or END MODES.) The arrows pointing up refer to money going into your investment. The bullets (•) along the horizontal time line represent the beginning and end of each interest period. Numbers 1, 2, 3, etc. represent each successive time period. It could be monthly, quarterly, annually, or anything you need it to be. First you must understand the concept of BEGIN and END mode, then you need to understand the concept of *money going in* or *money coming out or available to come out* of the investment.

Graph 7.3: Money Maps, BEGIN or END MODES

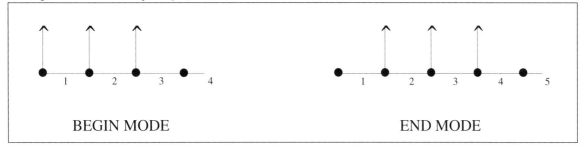

BEGIN MODE   END MODE

When Do You Make Payments?

The first map depicts what happens to money when it is put into an investment at the beginning of an investment period. This is known as the BEGIN MODE. (For example: money that is invested at the beginning of 1996 and earns interest for all of 1996 at the end of December, 1996.) The second map depicts what happens to money when it is put into an investment at the end of an investment period. This is known as the END MODE. (For example: money that is invested at the end of December, 1996, and does not earn any interest for 1996.) All financial calculators have a function key or keys to press to set the mode to either BEGIN or END.

Money Going In; Money Coming Out

I like to think of the calculator as your bank. When you put money into it, that is a *positive* event, and the numbers you enter into the calculator are positive (+) numbers. When you take money out of it or when there is a balance that is available for you to withdraw, that is a *negative* event, and the numbers you withdraw or are able to withdraw are negative (-) numbers. (This is my concept. Some people use the opposite signs but still get the same results.)

In Graph 7.4: Money Maps, Money Into or Money Out Of, the arrows pointing up representing money going into the investment have positive (+) symbols above them. Money coming out of the investment or available to come out of the investment are shown with arrows pointing down. They have negative (-) symbols below them.

Graph 7.4: Money Maps, Money Into or Money Out Of

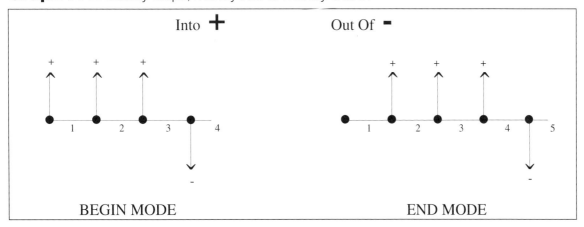

BEGIN MODE   END MODE

OK. I've probably lost you. Take your time to understand your financial calculator. It will be invaluable for future "what if" problems. Go back and reread some of my technical stuff and then continue along with me as I give you some examples. The examples will help clarify the negative and positive numbers that are displayed on the financial calculator. Follow the description of the problems below as well as their maps in Graph 7.5: Money Maps, Sample Problems.

Example of an Investment Plan

You have $1,000 to invest today. You will invest $100 a month at the beginning of each month for the next five years. Your investment will earn 12% annually but compounded monthly. What will you be able to remove from your investment at the end of five years? The answer to this is the function FV (future value).

Graph 7.5: Money Maps, Sample Problems

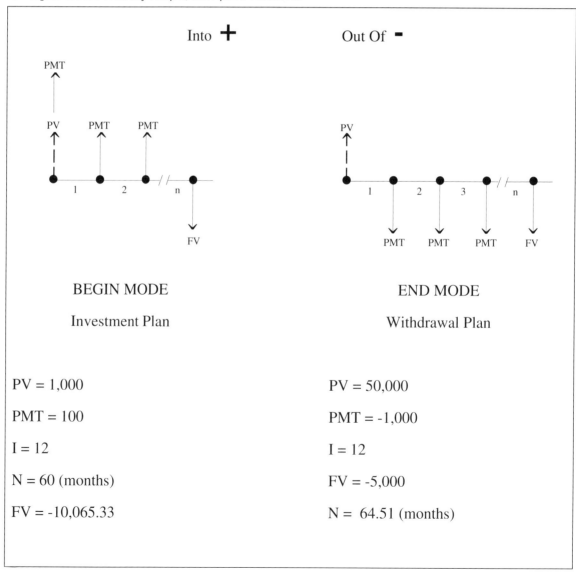

Into **+**   Out Of **-**

BEGIN MODE   END MODE

Investment Plan   Withdrawal Plan

PV = 1,000   PV = 50,000

PMT = 100   PMT = -1,000

I = 12   I = 12

N = 60 (months)   FV = -5,000

FV = -10,065.33   N = 64.51 (months)

The mode of the calculator is set to BEGIN. P/YR (periods per year) is set to 12. PV = 1000; N = 60 (12 monthly payments a year multiplied by five years); PMT = 100, I = 12; FV = the unknown. The FV is -$10,065.33. The FV is a negative number because you take this amount of money out of your bank at the end of five years.

Example of a Withdrawal Plan

You have $50,000 in your investment which is expected to continue to earn 12% annually but compounded monthly. You need to withdraw $1,000 a month from this investment at the end of each month. How long can you do this until the account is reduced to a balance of $5,000?

The mode of the calculator is set to END. Periods per year is set to 12 (12 P/Y). PV = $50,000; PMT = -1000 (It is negative because you are withdrawing this amount out of your bank.); I = 12; FV = -5000 (This is the balance that will remain in your investment, and it is negative because it is available for you to take out at the end of the time period.) N is the unknown and is equal to 64.51 months or 5.38 years.

Here are several future value problems to work out with your calculator. The answers are in Table 7.6: Answers To Future Value Problems.

Question #1: What will it cost in the future? If you need to live on $84,000 a year today, and you expect inflation to average 4.0% over the next 10 years, how much will you need 10 years from now to maintain the same standard of living? How much would you need 15 years from now to maintain your standard of living?

Question #2: How long will it last? You have $1,000,000 in your retirement account, and you want to withdraw $100,000 at the beginning of each year. You believe that your investments in your retirement account will continue to earn 8% adjusted for inflation. How many years will your nest egg last? How long will it last if you wanted to withdraw $150,000?

Question #3: How does inflation affect purchasing power? If you have $100,000 today, what will an inflation rate of 4.0% do to its purchasing power in 10 years? What will the purchasing power be in 15 years?

If you have $150,000 today, what will an inflation rate of 4.0% do to its purchasing power in ten years? What will the purchasing power be in 15 years?

1.Three Specific Long-Term Goals: Planning for College Expenses

When you plan for college expenses, there are three steps you must follow:

First, you need to know how much a college education is expected to cost. (I use the word *expected* because you can't be sure. There are many variables that could

Graph 7.6: Future Value Problems

Question #1: What will it cost in the future?

PV = $84,000

I = 4.0% (inflation)

PMT = 0

N = 10 years

FV = -$124,340.52 (The calculator shows this as a negative (-) number.)

PV = $84,000

I = 4.0% (inflation)

PMT = 0

N = 15 years

FV = -$151,279.25 (The calculator shows this as a negative (-) number.)

Question #2: How long will it last

Set the calculator mode to BEGIN since the withdrawals are to be taken at the beginning of each interest period.

PV = $1,000,000

FV = 0

PMT = -$100,000 / year (You must enter withdrawals as a negative (-) number into the calculator.)

I = 8% (inflation adjusted)

N = 17.54 years

PV = $1,000,000

FV = 0

PMT = -$150,000 / year (You must enter withdrawals as a negative (-) number into the calculator.)

I = 8% (inflation adjusted)

N = 8.85 years

---

change over time before the first college dollar has to be spent.) Second, you need to know in which investments you could invest to accumulate the necessary amount of money to meet future college expenses. Third, you need to determine if the investments should be in your name, in your child's name, in a custodial account, or in trust.

I'm going to review each step, then I'll suggest a method to minimize taxes on investment income.

Graph 7.6: Future Value Problems (continued.)

Question #3: How does inflation affect purchasing power?

PV = $100,000

I = -4.0% (This is a negative (-) number because it *takes away from* your investment.)

N = 10 years

PMT = 0

FV = -$66,483.26

PV = $100,000

I = -4.0% (This is a negative (-) number because it *takes away from* your investment.)

N = 15 years

PMT = 0

FV = -$54,208.64

PV = $150,000

I = -4.0% (This is a negative (-) number because it *takes away from* your investment.)

N = 10 years

PMT = 0

FV = -$99,724.90

PV = $150,000

I = -4.0% (This is a negative (-) number because it *takes away from* your investment.)

N = 15 years

PMT = 0

FV = -$81,312.96

How Much Will It Cost?

College costs are rising approximately 5% to 7% a year. The best method to determine current and future expenses is to contact several colleges or universities, and inquire about fees.

My suggestion is to obtain information from four separate types of schools. Get in touch with a large, state-supported institution; a small, state-supported institution;

a large, private institution; and a small, private institution. Ask to speak to the treasurer's office, and request the estimated current expenses for a four-year education. This should include tuition, housing, food, books, and other projected costs. Also find out the average percentage increase these costs experienced over the last five years. The office may even be able to give you an estimate of the price increases for the next few years. If the school does not have these statistics, your library may have some reference books on college tuitions.

Once you know the estimated cost for a four-year education for each type of school, you will need to project these figures into the future—to the year that you will begin paying the bills. If you wanted to be very exact, you could project the needs to each of the four years of college costs. However, for my example, I'll project all of the costs as a total to be accumulated by the first year of the college experience. To do this, you need a financial calculator; and you need to know today's costs, the average rate of increase, and how many years before your child will go to college. Here's an example that I'll use to demonstrate my ideas as you read through the rest of this section:

Mike has learned that a state-supported, small college in his home state costs approximately $40,000 today for a four-year program (all inclusive), and Mike's daughter will be entering college in 12 years. The average annual total expense for this school is expected to rise 5% a year. By using a financial calculator, Mike has calculated that the future cost would be approximately $72,000. (PV = $40,000; N = 12; I = 5; PMT = 0; FV = ? = $71,834.25)

Here is the form Mike used from Appendix I to figure his daughter's future expenses:

You should calculate the future costs for each of the scenarios I've suggested as it relates to your situation. Use the figures from a small state-supported school, a large state-supported school, a small private school, and a large private school. From these numbers you will get a good idea of the range of college costs and what your funding goals might be.

There is one caveat you need to consider. Many college students today take more than four years to complete their college undergraduate requirements. You may want to consider college costs for a five-year or even a six-year education instead of a traditional four-year stint. If you fail to calculate the correct number of years of tuition and other expenses that you might incur, you could end up with a significant shortfall.

Once you have decided how much you need to accumulate within a specific period of time, you can turn your attention to the type of investments to use and how much to put into them.

Funding the Expenses

There are many options to consider in order to prepare to have enough money when the time comes to pay the college bills. Here are seven options and how Mike can work with each one:

Table 7.7: College Expense Projection

Cost of college in future?

Cost of 4-year college today (**PV**): $40,000

Expected average percentage increase in costs until college begins (**I**): 5%

Number of years before college begins (**N**): 12

Required cash for 4-year college in N years (**FV**): $71,834.25

How much to save yearly?

Set calculator to BEGIN mode.

Current savings for college expenses (**PV**): 0

Number of years before college begins (**N** from above): 12

Expected after-tax return, compounded annually from investment (**I**): 12

Amount needed for 4-year college expenses from above (**FV**): $72,000

Annual amount required to invest at the beginning of each year (**PMT**): $2,663.79

- A mattress
- A savings account
- U.S. Government Savings Bonds
- A money market fund
- Zero coupon bonds
- Intermediate-term, no-load bond funds
- The stock market

A Mattress. This is not my recommendation, but it is an option. Mike could put cash under his mattress, but he will not earn any interest on his money. Also, this money would not be very safe. Fire or theft could totally wipe out his well-intentioned plan.

Chapter 7

From my previous example, Mike would have to save all $72,000 from his income sources and pay taxes on this income.

A Savings Account. This is a relatively safe place to accumulate $72,000, but the interest earned is minimal, and it usually stays fixed. If Mike's savings account at his bank earned 4% compounded annually, he would need to save $4,607.46 at the beginning of each year in order to reach his target of $72,000 in 12 years (PV = $0; N = 12; I = 4; FV = -$72,000; PMT = ? = $4607.46). He would have to pay income taxes on the interest earned each year even though the interest was reinvested into his account. His total out-of-pocket costs, not including taxes, would be $55,290.

U.S. Government Savings Bonds. U.S. Savings Bonds (Series EE) offer interesting tax advantages and flexibility. The purchase price of a bond is 50% of its face amount. The denominations are $50, $75, $500, $1,000, $5,000, and $10,000. There is a $15,000 purchase price limit per person per calendar year. Unfortunately, the interest rates are low and they vary every six months. Currently the interest rate is approximately 4.6%. Since the rates fluctuate, the exact time when the face amount is reached is not specified.

The interest accrues every six months for up to 30 years. Bonds issued after 5/1/95 earn interest for their first five years at 85% of the average six-month Treasury security. From five years through 17 years after purchase, these bonds earn interest at 85% of the average five-year Treasury security. After 17 years, another rate is quoted through year 30. After 30 years, the bonds stop appreciating in value. New rates are announced every May 1 and November 1. Call (800) 487-2663 for the current rates, and call (800) 446-7045 to receive additional printed information (Publication 550 and Forms 8815 and 8818).

If Mike were going to purchase EE bonds for college expenses, one method would be to purchase two $10,000 bonds and one $1,000 bond this year and to do the same for each of the next three years. Since the cost of each bond is half the face value, his cost would be $10,500 a year for four years. These bonds could be cashed in for each of the four college years as needed, yielding approximately $18,000 a year based on today's applicable interest rate.

One tax advantage of Series EE Bonds is that the interest is always exempt from state income taxes. Also, the federal tax can be deferred until the bonds are liquidated. In this way the interest compounds tax-deferred.

Another tax advantage is available if the proceeds are to be used for college tuition. You may be able to exclude the tax on the interest from the bonds if you meet certain eligibility rules (obtain Form 8815 and Form 8818 from the IRS):
- The bond holder's adjusted gross income is less than $57,300 if not married filing single, or less than $93,450 if married filing jointly or a qualifying widow with dependent child.
- The bonds were purchased on or after 1/1/90 and the bond owner pays tuition and required fees at a college, university, or qualified technical school

during the year the bonds are redeemed. Costs of room, board, and books are not treated as educational expenses.

- This exclusion applies to the bond holder, his or her spouse, or any legal dependent. Only bonds issued in the name of a person who was 24 years old or older on the first day of the month in which the bonds were purchased can be used for this education tax exclusion feature.

Still, another advantage is that the EE Bonds can be exchanged for HH Bonds, and the accrued interest in the EE Bonds would continue to be deferred. The HH Bonds pay a fixed rate of return every six months which is taxable on your federal income tax. HH Bonds can be held for up to 20 years. When the HH Bonds are redeemed, the tax-deferred interest from the EE Bonds becomes taxable on your federal income tax. The interest continues to be excluded from state tax.

A Money Market Fund. Money market funds (which I describe in chapter 8) pay the current money market rates which fluctuate daily. Currently, the average money market fund is paying approximately 5% annualized. At 5%, Mike would need to save $4,308.03 at the beginning of each year to reach the $72,000 target (PV = $0; N = 12; I = 5; FV = $72,000; PMT = ? = $4,308.03). Remember, he would have to pay income taxes on all interest income. His total out-of-pocket costs would be $51,696 excluding taxes.

Zero Coupon Bonds. This is a good way to provide a specific sum of money at a specific time in the future. Mike needs $72,000 in the future, but he only needs $18,000 in 12 years for the first year of college, $18,000 in 13 years for the second year of college, $18,000 in 14 years, and $18,000 in 15 years.

Mike could purchase zero coupon bonds today from a broker at a deep discount from their face value. These bonds are usually sold in increments of $1,000. Therefore, 18 bonds with a total face value of $18,000 could be purchased today and would be available at a specific maturity date (i.e., 12 years from now). The same could be done for maturity dates 13 years from now, 14 years from now, and 15 years from now.

If the yield to maturity were 6% for each bond, then the 12-year zero coupon bonds including commissions would cost approximately $8,960; the 13-year, approximately $8,450; the 14-year, approximately $7,970; and the 15-year, approximately $7,515.

Income taxes would be due each year on the interest accrued in the zero coupon bonds even though no interest was actually paid to Mike. If tax-exempt municipal zero coupon bonds were used, no Federal income tax would be due, but state income tax might be due. Mike's total up-front, out-of-pocket costs before taxes would be $32,895. (Tax-exempt municipal bonds are debt obligations of a state or local government. The proceeds go toward such expenses as roads, libraries, and government buildings.)

Intermediate-Term, No-Load Bond Funds. If Mike could not afford the up-front costs of zero coupon bonds or U.S. Savings Bonds, he could consider investing annually in an intermediate-term, no-load bond fund. (No-load funds are purchased directly from the fund company and do not charge a commission or load to you. I discuss no-load mutual funds in detail in chapter 8.)

It is important to understand that the total return for the bond fund can fluctuate greatly while the total return for zero coupon bonds does not if held until maturity. The total return for U.S. Savings Bonds does fluctuate to some extent. It is possible that when Mike needed the money from the bond fund, the bond market could be depressed, providing Mike with less accumulation than he projected he would have. Over the last 10 years, taxable bond funds averaged 8% a year, and tax-exempt municipal bond funds averaged 7%. (Tax-exempt municipal bond funds are exempt from Federal income taxes.)

At these rates, Mike would need to invest $3,513.00 into a taxable bond fund (PV = $0; N = 12; I = 8; FV = $72,000; PMT = ? = $3,513.00) or $3,761.63 into the municipal bond fund (PV = $0; N = 12; I = 7; FV = $72,000; PMT = ? = $3,761.63) at the beginning of each year for the next 12 years. He also would have to monitor these funds closely. As I indicated, it is possible that the bond fund might not do as well as anticipated, and Mike might need to add additional dollars to the fund along the way. It is also possible that the fund will do better than expected with the end result accumulating more money than projected. Again, appropriate taxes will be due on distributions that are reinvested. Capital gains taxes also might be due when Mike liquidates the fund shares. Total out-of-pocket costs, excluding taxes, would be $42,156 for the taxable bond fund and $45,140 for the municipal bond fund.

The Stock Market. The stock market offers the best overall returns but also the highest level of volatility and uncertainty. One of the easiest ways to invest in the stock market is through no-load equity mutual funds. The average U.S. equity fund over the last 10 years averaged 12%. (As you will read in cChapter 13 my Lifetime Investing Plan Portfolio from Jan. 1, 1985 to June 30, 1996 had an average compounded rate of return of 16.8%.) At 12%, Mike would need to invest $2,663.79 at the beginning of each year for 12 years to reach $72,000, and he will pay the income tax due on all annual fund distributions that are reinvested each year from other resources (PV = $0; N = 12; I = 12; FV = $72,000; PMT = ? = $2,663.79). He also will need to pay capital gains taxes after liquidating the fund once the college bills start rolling in. His total out-of-pocket costs would be $31,966 excluding taxes. I believe, however, that Mike could realize a higher total return if he used my Lifetime Investing Plan.(See Table 7.7: College Expense Projection to see how Mike used the *How much to save yearly* section to set up his calculations.)

You may have noticed that I have not included any form of cash value life insurance as an investment vehicle for college funding. There is a good reason for this although this is my opinion and not the opinion of all financial planners. I do not believe that the risk-transfer benefits of life insurance should be tied together with investments. In general, my philosophy is to purchase term life insurance if it is necessary to provide additional liquid assets for your family if you should die. The cliché, *buy term and invest the difference*, applies in most cases.

Who Owns the Investment?

Once you have chosen the investment that meets your needs, you will need to decide who is going to own it. Will it be you, your child, a custodian for your child, or a trust? Each has its advantages and disadvantages, and no one method is right for everyone.

Owned By You. If you owned the investment, then of course it would be yours to do with as you saw fit. You would not need to use it exclusively for your child if the situation warranted another use of the money. For example, it would be possible that your child did not want to go to college or was not college material after all of the financial preparations you had made. In this scenario, your investment could be directed toward some other useful purpose. All taxes that would be due from investment returns would be based on your marginal tax rate.

Owned By Your Child. If your child owned the investment, he or she would probably have less taxes to pay on the net gains because your child most likely would be in a lower tax bracket than you. However, if your child were younger than 14, the *kiddie tax* rule would take effect. This rule states that unearned income above $1,300 (1996 tax code) for a child is taxed at your marginal tax rate. Therefore, there would not be much benefit in giving income-producing assets to a child younger than age 14 if the unearned income were substantial.

Another problem has to do with legal capacity. In most states, a minor child is legally incapable of disposing of the asset. The reason for this is that a minor is allowed to *disaffirm* any contract entered into during his or her minority. Therefore, most people will not buy an asset from a minor because the minor could cancel the deal when the minor became an *adult*.

Another problem with giving your child the investment asset is that he or she legally could do whatever he or she wanted to do with the asset once he or she became an adult. When the time came for your child to go to college, you would have no control over the money in the investment if he or she decided to run off with a lover to Europe. Legally, the asset would be your child's. Your money would be gone—it's intended purpose never fulfilled.

Owned By A Custodial Account. One solution to the legal capacity problem is to place the investment assets into a custodial account. Custodial accounts are accounts that parents establish for a minor. Individual state law governs custodial accounts, and all states allow for the Uniform Gifts to Minors Act (UGMA). Cash and securities can be placed into this account easily. Some states have adopted the Uniform Transfers to Minors Act (UTMA) which is like the UGMA but also allows the transfer of real estate, personal property, and intangible property to the account.

There is usually no cost to set up either of these accounts, and you could transfer as much as $10,000 worth of assets a year into this account free of gift taxes. (This is called the $10,000 annual exclusion. It allows you to give up to $10,000 away to as many individuals as you wish every year without gift tax consequences. This is an excellent way to reduce your estate worth.) Your spouse could do the same, thereby allowing you and your spouse to provide as much as $20,000 jointly to each of your children each year without gift taxes being levied. If you and your spouse have three children, you could jointly give as much as $60,000 gift-tax-free every year.

The transfer is simple. You set up the account with a no-load mutual fund, for instance, and the account is titled in your name as custodian for your child under your state's UGMA (or UTMA). Technically, the property in this account now belongs to your child. This reference to the state UGMA (or UTMA) in the name of the account is all that is legally necessary to take advantage of the benefits of the UGMA and UTMA statutes.

The same problems with the kiddie tax exist as it would if the assets were in your child's name. However, you have more control over the assets until your child reaches the legal age for your state. It may be at 18, or it may be as old as 21. In any case, legally, the ownership of all of the assets will then belong to your child. Once again, he or she could run off with the proceeds if he or she so desired.

One benefit of the custodial account is that it usually cannot be attacked by either your creditors or your child's creditors. That provides some protection. However, once assets are distributed, creditors could come after them.

Owned By A Trust. A trust is a legal entity that holds assets given by a donor (you) for the benefit of a beneficiary (your child). A trustee (you or someone else) controls the assets within the trust and deals with the assets and its income as required by the trust document (which you and an attorney have drafted and which includes your wishes as allowed by trust laws). Most trusts must file income tax forms.

A special education trust has been set up by Congress and is called the *Section 2503(c) Trust*. The *2503(c)* refers to the section in the Internal Revenue Code that authorizes this unique trust. The primary feature of this trust is that assets transferred into it will qualify for the annual gift tax exclusion of $10,000. Just as with the UGMA or UTMA, you and your spouse can jointly give as much as $20,000 a year to each of your children, if you desire, into the 2503(c) Trust without gift taxes. The specific payout date of the trust occurs when your child reaches 21. However, you can arrange the trust in such a way to retain the assets beyond 21.

The 2503(c) Trust can be designed to give the trustee control even after the child reaches 21. This can be done by providing wording within the trust document which states that the trust will automatically continue to a designated older age, such as 25, unless the beneficiary makes a demand upon the trustee to receive all of the property and accumulated income at 21. Your child would have to be given a *window of opportunity* within three months after his or her 21st birthday to demand a distribution of the property from the trust. If he or she does not make such a demand within that time frame, the trust would continue until the age specified in the document. This window of opportunity may need to be made available every year after 21.

Taxes must be paid by the trust on all retained income. Also, a tax return will need to be filed for the trust annually. Although the kiddie tax rule does not apply, the tax brackets for trust income taxes are more condensed than those for individual taxpayers. (See Table 7.8: Comparison of 1996 Tax Rates for Individuals and Trusts.) As with custodial accounts, creditors usually cannot come after assets in the trust.

A Method to Minimize Taxes

I want to share a method with you that will allow you to invest for future education costs and also keep the tax bite to a minimum. The method incorporates income shifting from the 2503(c) Trust to the UGMA (or UTMA) account. Here is how to do it:

1. Establish a 2503(c) Trust for your child.
2. Fund the trust annually up to the maximum allowed ($10,000 per spouse).
3. Establish a UGMA account (or UTMA account).
4a. If *your child is younger than age 14*, distribute the first $1,300 of income from the trust to the custodial account. (For 1996, the kiddie tax will tax the first $650 at 0%; the second $650 at 15%.) All other taxable trust income is retained in the trust until the trust's tax bracket exceeds 15%. (For 1996, this is $1,500.)
4b. If *your child is 14 years old or older*, distribute all taxable trust income to the custodial account until your child's standard deduction is reached. (For 1996, this is $4,000.) All other taxable trust income is retained in the trust until the trust's tax bracket exceeds 15%. (For 1996, this is $1,500.)
5. Taxable income above the 15% bracket earned by the trust assets are either distributed to the custodial account or retained by the trust depending on which tax bracket will generate the least tax.

Taxable income that is generated by your child from other sources will affect the tax consequences that I have described earlier. This method gets somewhat technical, but it may save significant tax dollars. Be sure to discuss this idea with your accountant to see if it is dollar-wise for your specific needs.

I have provided an overview to help you plan for your child's college expenses. In the future, Congress may legislate a special IRA from which you could withdraw funds for educational expenses without incurring the early withdrawal penalty of 10%. The benefit of such an IRA would be that the assets within the special IRA would grow tax-deferred. This would allow the power of compounding to significantly increase the growth potential of your portfolio. The disadvantage would be that

Table 7.8: Comparison of 1996 Tax Rates for Individuals and Trusts

For Married Taxpayers Filing Joint Returns

Taxable Income

Over	But Not Over	Rate
0	$40,100	15%
$40,100	$96,900	28%
$96,900	$147,700	31%
$147,700	$263,750	36%
$263,750	-	39.6%

For Single Taxpayers

Taxable Income

Over	But Not Over	Rate
0	$24,000	15%
$24,000	$58,150	28%
$58,150	$121,300	31%
$121,300	$263,750	36%
$263,750	-	39.6%

For Individuals Filing as Head of Household

Taxable Income

Over	But Not Over	Rate
0	$32,150	15%
$32,150	$83,050	28%
$83,050	$134,500	31%
$134,500	$263,750	36%
$263,750	-	39.6%

For Trusts

Retained Income Rate

Over	But Not Over	Rate
0	$1,500	15%
$1,500	$3,600	28%
$3,600	$5,500	31%
$5,500	$7,500	36%
$7,500	-	39.6%

withdrawals would be taxed as ordinary income, not as capital gains. This could be a real financial concern if the tax on capital gains is significantly lower than the tax on ordinary income in the future. But, this is only an idea floating around Washington. There are no bills pending that include this provision. So, in the meantime, good luck with your planning process.

2. Retirement Planning

Retirement planning is also unique. It involves planning for many years into the future. It first involves planning for a specific amount of money to be reached at a specific time in the future (your retirement date). Then, it involves planning for that sum of money to generate an income for you and your spouse for the rest of your lives.

Look at Table 7.9: Yearly Savings to Accumulate $1,000,000. See the difference a few percentage points can make? If your goal were to have a $1 million nest egg in 20 years, you would need to save $17,460 a year if you could earn 10% compounded annually. However, if you could earn 18% compounded annually, you would only need to save $6,820 a year. Therefore, it is not only necessary to commit to an annual investment program over the course of many years, but it is also important to obtain the best total return that your risk level will allow. The sooner you begin the process, the better. (In this example, investments are made at the end of each year.)

Table 7.9: Yearly Savings to Accumulate $1,000,000

Years to Retirement	10%	12%	14%	16%
40	$2,260	$1,304	$745	$424
35	$3,690	$2,317	$1,442	$892
30	$6,079	$4,144	$2,803	$1,886
25	$10,168	$7,500	$5,498	$4,013
20	$17,460	$13,879	$10,986	$8,667
15	$31,474	$26,824	$22,809	$19,358
10	$62,745	$56,984	$51,714	$46,901
5	$163,797	$157,410	$151,284	$145,409

Years to Retirement	18%	20%	22%	24%
40	$240	$136	$77	$44
35	$550	$339	$209	$129
30	$1,264	$846	$566	$379
25	$2,919	$2,119	$1,536	$1,113
20	$6,820	$5,357	$4,202	$3,294
15	$16,403	$13,882	$11,738	$9,919
10	$42,515	$38,523	$34,895	$31,602
5	$139,778	$134,380	$129,206	$124,248

Now look at Table 7.10: Life Expectancy. This table gives you an idea of your average additional life span based on your current age. For instance, if you are a 55-year-old male, your life expectancy is another 21.7 years. If you are a 55-year-old female, your life expectancy is another 25.5 years.

After retirement, money can come to you from various sources. It can come from employee sponsored defined benefit plans and defined contribution plans, personal savings and investments, IRAs, and Social Security. You will need to estimate your retirement assets from each of these areas so that you can begin planning today for your future needs.

As I will describe shortly, Social Security is not something to count on in the future. If you are close to retirement however, you should contact the Social Security office to determine what your retirement benefits might be. You will need to call (800) 772-1213, and request the form for *Earnings and Benefits Estimate* (Form SSA-7004).

Planning must begin as early as possible. You must take control of your own destiny or your retirement lifestyle could be in jeopardy.

Deficiencies in Retirement Portfolios

Several studies have shown that Baby Boomers (those born between 1946 and 1964) may be forced to accept a significant reduction in their standard of living after retirement because of a lack of proper planning. Some studies suggest that most individuals nearing retirement have retirement savings that are far short of where they would need to be for these new retirees to maintain their present lifestyles.

These reports suggest that most Americans who will be retiring in the future will struggle to simply make ends meet—an experience last felt during the Great Depression. And, all Americans are at risk—from college graduates to those about to retire.

To put the past several decades into perspective, the savings rate in the United States has been decreasing from 8.7% in 1975 to a low of 3.9% in 1994. Individual and family savings are simply not keeping pace with future needs, and the prospects are unsettling.

My recommendation is not to depend on someone else to provide for your retirement bliss. Some people have depended on Social Security to take care of them. I believe that could be a disaster. Consider what is happening to the Social Security System.

Social Security Countdown

Our contributions to the Social Security System were only meant to help with, not to replace the need for, a retirement income. But for many of us, Social Security may not even help in the future.

The reason is that we are living longer—much longer than was expected. In 1930, the remaining life expectancy for a 65-year-old male in the United States was 11.8 years; for a woman, 12.9 years. Today, the remaining life expectancy for a 65-year-

Table 7.10: Life Expectancy

MALE	AGE FEMALE	LIFE EXPECTANCY ADDITIONAL YEARS	MALE	AGE FEMALE	LIFE EXPECTANCY ADDITIONAL YEARS
25	30	47.4	65	70	15.0
26	31	46.5	66	71	14.4
27	32	45.6	67	72	13.8
28	33	44.6	68	73	13.2
29	34	43.7	69	74	12.6
30	35	42.8	70	75	12.1
31	36	41.9	71	76	11.6
32	37	41.0	72	77	11.0
33	38	40.0	73	78	10.5
34	39	39.1	74	79	10.1
35	40	38.2	75	80	9.6
36	41	37.3	76	81	9.1
37	42	36.5	77	82	8.7
38	43	35.6	78	83	8.3
39	44	34.7	79	84	7.8
40	45	33.8	80	85	7.5
41	46	33.0	81	86	7.1
42	47	32.1	82	87	6.7
43	48	31.2	83	88	6.3
44	49	30.4	84	89	6.0
45	50	29.6	85	90	5.7
46	51	28.7	86	91	5.4
47	52	27.9	87	92	5.1
48	53	27.1	88	93	4.8
49	54	26.3	89	94	4.5
50	55	25.5	90	95	4.2
51	56	24.7	91	96	4.0
52	57	24.0	92	97	3.7
53	58	23.2	93	98	3.5
54	59	22.4	94	99	3.3
55	60	21.7	95	100	3.1
56	61	21.0	96	101	2.9
57	62	20.3	97	102	2.7
58	63	19.6	98	103	2.5
59	64	18.9	99	104	2.3
60	65	18.2	100	105	2.1
61	66	17.5	101	106	1.9
62	67	16.9	102	107	1.7
63	68	16.2	103	108	1.5
64	69	15.6	104	109	1.3

old male is 15.0 years; for a woman, 18.2 years. By 2070, the projected life expectancy at age 65 will rise to 18.5 years for men and 22.3 years for women.

Since the U.S. Social Security System provides a pay-as-you-go retirement program, decreasing numbers of workers will be paying for increasing numbers of retirees. In 1950, there were 16 Social Security taxpayers for every one recipient of benefits. Today, there are 3.2 workers for every recipient. In 2010, the projected ratio drops to 2.9 workers for each recipient. By 2060, the ratio is an unsustainable 1.8 workers for every recipient.

The Old Age, Survivors and Disability Insurance trust fund, OASDI trust fund, is the source of dollars to provide the benefits as mandated by the U.S. Congress. It is currently running a $22 billion surplus. But, with the baby boomers moving into the retired ranks in 2010, the OASDI will run a $23 billion deficit by 2015. This deficit will then explode to $145 billion in 2025!

There are several solutions to the dilemma that are being considered and discussed among government officials. Here are some options which have been proposed:

- Increase payroll taxes: It is estimated that it will take a rise of 6% above the existing 15.3% payroll tax to make a difference. However, this burden on employers is projected to cost the U.S. economy over 4,000,000 jobs because employers will downsize to offset the expense of the additional tax. With fewer employed, the need to increase taxes even more becomes a vicious cycle.

- Cut Social Security benefits to upper income elderly beginning at $40,000 incomes: This is known as "means testing." The argument is that the system was designed to assist those in need so that their retirement would not lead to destitution. Those individuals who have a significant source of income are certainly not destitute and therefore are not in need of help.

- Raise the normal retirement age by two months a year until reaching age 70: Already the law states that retirement age will rise from 65 to 67 over the next 25 years. The farther away the legal retirement age becomes, the less the government will have to pay out in benefits.

- Reform benefits: Again, if there is less to pay out for benefits, there will be more money in the system.

- Eliminate cost-of-living increases in payments to recipients: This will hurt the retired individual who really needs to make ends meet in an inflationary environment.

- Privatize some of the system: Individuals may be able to invest some of their social security taxes in mutual funds for their own benefit.

The bottom line regarding all of these plans is this: Don't count on the Social Security System to provide any benefits to those who have significant means of financial support at retirement. The consensus seems to be to do whatever is necessary to keep the program afloat. That means higher taxes, lower benefits, and an increasingly higher legal retirement age before benefits can be received.

No one cares more about your money than you! Be sure you are following a long-term investment plan for the future.

What Will It Cost To Retire?

The best way to determine how much you will need when you retire is to determine how much you would need to retire today. What did it cost you to live the lifestyle you enjoyed for the last 12 months? Go back to chapter 2 and get the necessary information from your Cash Flow Statement.

If this data is not available, keep a detailed record for the next 12 months of everything you personally spend—yes, everything. Don't forget your out-of-pocket expenses and such items as taxes and insurance. After adding all this together, the total is what it cost you to live for a year.

Next, adjust this annual expense. If there are additional expenses you believe you will incur during retirement, then add them to this amount. If, on the other hand, you believe that some expenses would not be necessary or would not exist after you retired, then subtract them from the total. For instance, you will not be putting money into your retirement account anymore. You also will not need to pay Social Security taxes or Medicare taxes anymore if you don't have earned income. (Your retirement income will come from your investments, and this is unearned income which is not subject to Social Security and Medicare taxes.) Now you have an approximation of what life will cost for 12 months living the lifestyle you desire as a retiree.

If you do not want to make these additions and subtractions from your current annual expenses, some economists suggest that your expenses at retirement will be approximately 60% to 70% of what they are today. This is obviously a gross generalization, but it is a basis from which to project into the future. Remember, all projections are just that—projections. They can be revised or even totally discarded at any time.

When do you want to retire? This is personal, and only you and your spouse can come up with the right answer. Will it be 10 years from now, 15 years, how many? The reason this is important to decide now is so you that can make intelligent projections taking inflation into account.

Inflation makes the dollar worth less and less as time passes. I have explained the dilution effect on the dollar in chapter 3. You will need to adjust your expected annual expenses based on an assumed inflation rate which will erode the purchasing price of the dollar between now and when you retire. In other words, it will cost more and more each successive year just to maintain the same lifestyle because of the ravages of inflation.

Assume an average rate of inflation that reflects a realistic projection for the future. Right now, inflation is at a cycle low. I don't believe it would be wise to use the current low rate of 2.8% to project into the future. Historically, the average rate of

inflation over the last 25 years has been 5.6% based on the Consumer Price Index. A more realistic rate to plan into the future would be at least 4%. Of course, you will need to revise your projections as time goes by.

Project your annual expenses into the future. You have determined what it has cost you to live for the past year. Now you need to project these expenses into the future taking inflation into consideration. You could use a financial calculator to get an accurate projection, or you could use Table 7.11: Inflation Adjustment (without calculator) to get an approximation.

To use the table, multiply your current anticipated expenses by the factor in the table that corresponds to:

1. How many years from now before you will retire, and
2. The anticipated inflation rate between now and then.

For example, assume your expenses for the last year were $80,000. After you added some additional things you wanted to enjoy during retirement and subtracted some expenses you believed would no longer exist, you came up with $50,000 as an annual need to retire. If you wanted to retire in 15 years, and you assumed a 4% inflation rate, then your first year's expenses at retirement would be approximately $90,000 ($50,000 x 1.801).

Ninety thousand dollars is considerably more than the $50,000 you would need today. Do you see where I am going with this discussion? If you fail to take inflation into consideration, you will fall far short of being able to live the lifestyle you desire. Also remember, you will need to increase your projected expenses by the inflation rate (in this example, 4%) every year during retirement.

Again, I must emphasize that these are only projections. Since the real accuracy of your projections depends on so many variables, the word *accuracy* is fairly inaccurate. Your projections are more like educated guesses.

Using the Financial Calculator

To get a more accurate projection of your future needs than the previous table can provide, and to project a plan to meet your future needs, you will need to use a financial calculator. The following detailed description will help you calculate all of your retirement projections using a financial calculator. Let's get into it. This is fun. It is also very enlightening.

I'll go through the four steps next. I'll also use examples from Jodi and Mike, our unabashed financial stars from previous chapters. Follow along in Table 7.12: How Much Does It Take?, to see Mike and Jodi's calculations.

1. Determine your current needs. Start with your annual expenses. Add to this those expenses that you believe will be included in the future, and subtract those expenses that you believe will not be included in the future. If you are not sure, you can use the

Table 7.11: Inflation Adjustment (without calculator)

Years before retire	Assumed Inflation Rate			
	3%	4%	5%	6%
1	1.030	1.040	1.050	1.060
2	1.061	1.082	1.103	1.124
3	1.093	1.125	1.158	1.191
4	1.126	1.170	1.216	1.262
5	1.159	1.217	1.276	1.338
6	1.194	1.265	1.340	1.419
7	1.230	1.316	1.407	1.504
8	1.267	1.369	1.477	1.594
9	1.305	1.423	1.551	1.689
10	1.344	1.480	1.629	1.791
11	1.384	1.539	1.710	1.898
12	1.426	1.601	1.796	2.012
13	1.469	1.665	1.886	2.133
14	1.513	1.732	1.980	2.261
15	1.558	1.801	2.079	2.397
16	1.605	1.873	2.183	2.540
17	1.653	1.948	2.292	2.693
18	1.702	2.026	2.407	2.854
19	1.754	2.107	2.527	3.026
20	1.806	2.191	2.653	3.207

Table 7.12: How Much Does It Take?

1. Current need per year = $50,000

    (retirement need in TODAY'S dollars)

2. Future Value of TODAY'S retirement need   (4 % inflation)

    PV = $50,000

    N = 25 years

    I = 4%

    PMT = 0

    FV = -$133,292

3. Determine inflation-adjusted return

$$= \left[\frac{1 + \text{rate of return}}{1 + \text{rate of inflation}} - 1 \right] \times 100\%$$

$$= \left[\frac{1 + .14}{1 + .04} - 1 \right] \times 100\%$$

$$= (1.096154 - 1) \times 100\%$$

$$= 9.6154\%$$

4. Nest egg required at retirement

    N = 40 years

    I = 9.6154%

    PMT = -$133,292

    FV = 0

    PV = $1,480,903.64

60% to 70% rule-of-thumb I mentioned earlier. To be conservative, you can project 100% or even more! The final dollar amount is what you think will be your yearly expenses at retirement (or whenever you want to reach financial independence) based on today's dollar.

Jodi and Mike have guessed that they will need $50,000 a year in today's dollars when they retire.

2. Determine what these needs will cost in the future based on the dilution effect of inflation. Here you need to make two decisions. First, you need to decide how many years from now you want to retire or to reach financial independence. Second, you need to estimate what the average inflation rate will be between now and that target date.

As I described in chapter 3, over the last 25 years, the inflation rate in the United States as expressed by the Department of Labor in the form of the CPI (Consumer Price Index) has been approximately 5.6%. Over the last 10 years it has been 3.7%. One can debate what is an accurate reflection of inflation. However, it is all academic since there is no guarantee that the future will duplicate the past. I will use a realistic inflation rate of 4.0% for the next 25 years in my examples.

I have emphasized that inflation is a factor that must be incorporated into future planning. Inflation makes things more expensive in the future. Therefore, when you project your expenses into the future, you must consider the cost of these expenses after inflation.

Using the financial calculator, the estimated cost to live the first year of retirement in today's dollars is the present value (**PV**). The inflation rate is entered with the **I** key. The number of years between now and when you retire is the **N** key. What this translates into after inflation has had its effects is the unknown factor—the future value (**FV**).

Jodi and Mike anticipate their yearly expenses to be $50,000 based on today's dollars. They will project this 25 years into the future using 4.0% as an inflation rate.

To enter numbers using a financial calculator, you will first press the appropriate number keys and then the appropriate function key (**N, I, PV, PMT, FV**).

For Jodi and Mike, they are: **25** is **N**, **4.0** is **I**, **50000** is **PV**, **0** is **PMT**, and **FV** is the unknown. (**PMT** is **0** because there are no payments going into the calculation or coming out of the calculation between now and retirement.) After entering the first four known variables in this fashion, press the **FV** key. The answer appears as -133,291.82.

Remember, the negative sign in front of the **FV** is a function of the calculator. Think of everything you put into your investment as a *positive* sign and everything you remove from your investment as a *negative* sign.

Jodi and Mike will require approximately $133,292 *the first year of retirement* 25 years from now to maintain their lifestyle of today.

Can you see why inflation is a critical ingredient to incorporate into your future planning?

3. Determine what you believe is reasonable to earn on your invested money, and then adjust it for inflation. Using my Lifetime Investing Plan, I believe it is reasonable to expect approximately a 14% average-compounded-return on your investments.

At the end of chapter 13, I summarized my LIP. From Jan. 1, 1985 through June 30, 1996 (11 1/2 years), the average compounded return rate for my hypothetical LIP portfolio was 16.8%.

Also, there are 311 no-load and low-load mutual funds monitored by Morningstar that have over 10-year histories as of June 30, 1996. Of those, 31 have average compounded annual rates-of-return of 14% or greater over the last ten years, are no-load, and are open to new investors. These are listed in Table 7.13: 14%-Plus Returns Over Last 10 Years.

You must adjust your expected annual rate-of-return for inflation. This adjustment takes into consideration what the real rate-of-return would be after the dilution effect of inflation is removed from the equation. The formula to calculate this is noted in Table 7.12. (If you were going to handle your investment during your retirement years differently than you are planning now, be sure to project the rate-of-return you expect to earn at retirement.) Here is how it works for Jodi and Mike:

In Mike and Jodi's example, the adjusted rate-of-return is 9.6154%. This adjusted return is necessary for the next step.

4. Calculate what you must accumulate in the future to live the lifestyle you have chosen for the rest of your life expectancy. Jodi and Mike have determined that in 25 years they will need $133,292 the first year they retire. That is approximately $11,000 a month. They will also need to increase that amount each year by the inflation rate in order to continue to live their desired lifestyle. Assuming they want their nest egg to last 40 years, here is how they can calculate what they must accumulate between now and retirement. (This calculation takes the inflation effect into account.)

Using the financial calculator again, you can determine what you will need to accumulate rather simply. Set the mode to BEGIN because you will take out your annual withdrawals at the beginning of each year.

N is the number of years your nest egg will last from the first year you begin retirement. Most financial planners recommend that you determine this number by adding 15 years or so to your life expectancy. You can use Table 7.10: Life Expectancy to determine how many years you have left to live based on actuarial statistics (gruesome but necessary). Some planners don't bother with this calculation and suggest you never deplete your nest egg. In this case, you could enter **100** for **N** to be very conservative.

I is the inflation adjusted rate-of-return you calculated in Step #3. It is important that you use at least four decimal places for accuracy in this projection.

PMT is the amount you will withdraw at the beginning of the first year of your retirement. Remember, this must be entered into the calculator as a negative number (-).

Table 7.13: 14%-Plus Returns Over Last 10 Years

through 6/30/96

source: Morningstar No-Load Mutual Funds

Name	Category	Phone #	10 yr.
Acorn	Growth	800-922-6769	15.0%
Berger 100	Aggressive	800-333-1001	15.8%
Brandywine	Growth	800-656-3017	16.9%
Clipper	Growth	800-776-5033	14.3%
Columbia Special	Aggressive	800-547-1707	16.0%
Dodge & Cox Stock	Growth & income	415-434-0311	14.3%
Fidelity Growth & Income	Growth & Income	800-544-8888	15.9%
Founders Growth	Growth	800-525-2440	15.2%
Founders Special	Aggressive	800-525-2440	14.2%
Gabelli Asset	Growth	800-422-3554	15.3%
Invesco Strategic Financial Services	Sector - financial	800-525-8085	16.2%
Invesco Strategic Health	Sector - health	800-525-8085	19.8%
Invesco Strategic Leisure	Sector - leisure	800-525-8085	16.7%
Invesco Strategic Technology	Sector - technology	800-525-8085	19.8%
Janus	Growth	800-525-3713	14.6%
Janus Twenty	Growth	800-525-3713	14.4%
Kaufmann	Aggressive	800-669-9181	18.7%
Lexington Corporate Leaders	Growth & income	800-526-0056	14.1%
Mairs & Power Growth	Growth	612-222-8478	14.6%
Managers Special Equity	Aggressive	800-835-3879	15.5%
Mutual Beacon	Growth & income	800-448-3863	15.2%
Mutual Qualified	Growth & income	800-448-3863	14.6%
Mutual Shares	Growth & income	800-448-3863	14.2%
PBHG Growth	Aggressive	800-433-0051	21.6%
T. Rowe Price New America	Growth	800-638-5660	14.1%
Safeco Equity	Growth & income	800-426-6730	14.4%
Strong Schafer Value	Growth	800-368-1030	14.8%
20th Century Giftrust Investors	Aggressive	800-345-2021	21.0%
20th Century Ultra Investors	Aggressive	800-345-2021	18.1%
Vanguard Specialized Energy	Sector - energy	800-662-7447	14.8%
Vanguard Specialized Health Care	Sector - health	800-662-7447	18.4%

FV is **0** because you will draw down your nest egg to nothing after **N** years. If you have decided not to deplete your nest egg during your life, you could enter **100** for **N** as I mentioned above.

Press **PV**, and you will get your answer. This is how much you must have in your retirement account when you retire if all of your other estimations stand.

Jodi and Mike plan to deplete their nest egg forty years after they begin retirement. After entering the proper numbers into the financial calculator, they determine that they will need to accumulate approximately $1.48 million by retirement to satisfy their projected future needs.

Your gross nest egg can be assembled from various assets. As I've already suggested, some sources of retirement income might be social security, defined benefit retirement plans, defined contribution retirement plans, personal savings and investments, your home, cash value from life insurance, and annuity contracts to name a few. You will need to determine the amount that you will depend on from your investments.

Wow! That is a lot of arithmetic! But, it gets you to the point where you have some educated idea as to where you are going and why. Remember, these projections are not carved in stone. They can be recalculated as your needs dictate. Don't ever feel that you cannot make changes. Everyone will and must make changes as time goes by. Be flexible but determined.

3. Self-Insurance for Long-Term Care

Long-term care planning incorporates strong emotional ties unlike the first two goals I've just described. Your decision to plan for the eventual need for long-term care must be made objectively. Here is the problem:

Fear sells. It's that simple. If one presents statistics in a compelling enough format, then one can hook almost anyone. Therefore, the buyer must beware.

One industry that preys upon the emotion of fear is the insurance industry. Don't misinterpret my message. Insurance is a critical part of managing risk. Yet, insurance companies can, and often do, present facts that only describe part of the picture. Although insurance companies aren't lying, they may be misleading at times. Here is a typical statement used by some in the long-term care (LTC) insurance business that uses facts to induce fear.

Twenty-four percent of people over the age of 65 stay in a nursing home for more than a year, use all of their money, and then are forced to go onto Medicaid. You wouldn't want that to happen to you, would you?

This type of rhetoric has created a burgeoning insurance market for LTC insurance. Today there are four million long-term care policies in force whereas there were only one million such policies five years ago.

The whole story about nursing homes and/or long-term care coverage must answer several questions. Some of these questions include: Who will *not* need nursing home coverage? How much does insurance actually cover? What will the insurance cost? Are all policies the same? What other options are available?

Who Will Not Need Nursing Home Coverage?

The *New England Journal of Medicine*, in an article by Kemper and Murtaugh, stated that men who are 65 today have a 67% chance of never requiring nursing home care. (*Lifetime Use of Nursing Home Care*, Vol. 324, No. 9, Feb. 28, 1991, pages 595-600.) Of those needing care, 19% will stay less than 12 months; 10% will stay one to five years; and 4% will stay over five years. Women age 65 today will have a 48% chance of never requiring nursing home care. Of those requiring care, 21% will stay less than 12 months; 18% will stay one to five years; and 13% will stay over five years.

How Much Does Insurance Actually Cover?

LTC insurance is like disability insurance. If you should need nursing home or in-home care later in life while the policy is still in force, the insurance will pay you usually a daily predetermined dollar amount for the period of time you need coverage up to the policy maximums. The premiums usually stay the same during the life of the contract. However some policies allow for premium increases along the way. The younger you are when you purchase these policies, the less expensive the premiums. Most policies are purchased 15 to 30 years before they are actually needed.

What Will the Insurance Cost?

Premiums are based on your age, your existing health, the benefit package you purchase, and the elimination period before coverage begins. The premiums you will pay for a LTC policy must be paid year after year to keep the policy in force. That's the cost of shifting the risk to the insurance company. There is nothing wrong with that. Naturally, if premiums are not paid, the policy terminates.

For example, if premiums were paid for 20 years and then the policy was dropped because either you or your surviving spouse could not afford to pay the premiums any longer, all premium dollars would be lost. If you needed coverage the year after the policy terminated, you would be out of luck. (There are some companies that provide nonforfeiture benefits which will return some of your premium dollars if you continue with the policy for a specific number of years. Of course, this type of policy is more expensive than one without this provision.)

Are All Policies the Same?

This is an ever changing market, and all policies are not the same. The National Association of Insurance Commissioners has drafted a model policy to act as a guide, but it is not mandatory for individual states to adopt this prototype.

If you feel the need to purchase a long-term care policy, here are some guidelines. Remember, this insurance usually does not pay for services. Rather, it general-

ly pays a predetermined daily rate directly to you. This may or may not cover your expenses for care.

Buy a policy that (1) has level premiums that can increase only to cover specified higher costs, (2) incorporates some type of inflation factor built into the benefits, (3) provides a waiver of premiums so that you will not have to continue to pay premiums while you are collecting benefits, (4) allows your own doctor to determine when you need care, (5) pays for in-home care as well as nursing home care, and (6) does not have *required hospital stays prior to receiving benefits* as a precondition to be eligible for benefits.

What Other Options Are Available?

There are other options to long-term care insurance. One option I prefer is to self-insure through investing.

Here is Mike's long-term care insurance scenario: Mike planned to purchase a policy that cost $3,600 a year, and he projected that he might need it in 25 years for a five-year duration. The policy provided a benefit of $100 per day which included a cost-of-living increase based on the Consumer Price Index. His total outlay for the policy would be $90,000 prior to making his claim in 25 years.

Then, during the five-year claim period, he would collect approximately $438,000 from the insurance policy to help offset his nursing care expenses. This incorporated a cost-of-living adjustment that brought the daily rate up to approximately $240 per day 25 years after the policy came into force.

In contrast, consider this self-insured scenario: Instead of purchasing the policy, Mike took the annual premium he would have paid for LTC insurance and divided it into monthly amounts ($3,600 ÷ 12 = $300) and dollar-cost-averaged into my Lifetime Investing Plan (details in chapter 13). (This selection is based on information you will read beginning in chapter 8.)

According to Morningstar, a research company that provides exhaustive statistics regarding mutual funds, the average growth fund on June 30, 1996 had a total annualized return of 15.1% over the last three years, 14.4% over the last five years, and 12.0% over the last 10 years. Over time, this asset category has been one of the best for total returns. However, my Lifetime Investing Plan had a total annualized return of 17.6%, 17.9%, and 16.2% over the same time periods.

If Mike were dollar-cost-averaging $300 per month for 25 years into my Lifetime Investing Plan and only averaged 14% compounded a year, his long-term care account would be worth approximately $818,000 at the end of 25 years. Taxes would be due annually on all distributions. Also, at the end of the 25 years, cashing out the fund would trigger capital gains taxes.

The significance to self-insuring in this manner is that you have the luxury of using the investment money for either LTC expenses or anything else you want.

Here's the catch with LTC insurance. If you did not need nursing care, you would receive no benefits. You would have lost all of the premiums. It is true that you would have had the insurance if you needed it, but it is also a statistical fact that you probably would not have made a claim.

Being self-insured is an entirely different story. No matter what you decide to do, money will be there for you to do whatever you want with it. Of course, the risks are that you do not start early enough to accumulate enough liquidity, or that the funds do not perform as expected, or that you lose your motivation and do not continue to dollar-cost-average into your plan.

To take this one step further, you can arrange for tax-deferred compounding by investing in a variable annuity that has minimum fees. Variable annuities allow you to put after-tax-dollars into various *sub-accounts* which will compound tax-deferred. These sub-accounts are basically like mutual funds, and you can choose the asset categories of the sub-accounts in which you wish to invest as required by the Lifetime Investing Plan. You only will pay taxes on that portion which you withdraw during retirement that was tax-deferred. Two examples of low-fee variable annuities which offer several excellent sub-accounts are Nationwide's Best of America at (800) 848-6331 and Jack White's Value Advantage Plus Variable Annuity at (800) 622-3699.

You will have several options with your long-term care investment program. If you did not use this money for nursing care, you could withdraw the cash and spend it. Better yet, you could convert it into an immediate annuity and receive benefits for life. Even better, you could set up a charitable remainder trust (See chapter 17).

Planning for long-term care is challenging. Insurance products exist to assist with the financial obligations of such care. However, insurance can become a gas guzzling engine that takes your dollars and gives little in return. For many individuals, self-insuring as I have described is a much more viable option. For some individuals, a combination of insurance and investments may be the answer. The younger you are, the more desirable an investment program will be. Of course, the older you are, the more expensive a long-term care policy will cost.

You should consult with a qualified long-term care insurance professional to determine what direction might be best for you, but be ready to be sold something. Have your goals firmly in front of you so you don't get sold what you don't want. Also, as I mentioned earlier in this chapter, a fee-only Certified Financial Planner could give you unbiased guidance before you seek the services of a salesperson.

OK. So you've set some financial goals, and you know what you need to invest to get where you need to be. But, in what should you invest to reach these goals. My suggestion begins to unfold in the next chapter.

The Stock Market and No-Load Mutual Funds

"Stocks appear to have arrived at a permanently high plateau. Take heed because we now have entered a new era of valuation."

These remarks were proclaimed by a prominent Yale economist. Opinions like these from knowledgeable men must not be dismissed—especially from men with topnotch credentials. These predictions were made by Irving Fisher. The year, however, was 1929! The stock market crashed shortly thereafter!

No one can predict the future. Some think the market will always move up. Some think the market will crash. Some don't think! The correct answer in my opinion is simply that it is important to invest for the future.

Investing is defined as using capital to create more money. It connotes the idea that the safety of your investment dollars is most important. This is in contrast to *speculation* which implies far more risk or *gambling* which is the extreme of speculation.

My philosophy is based on investing in ways that make good sense to me utilizing investment vehicles which I can understand. I want to be able to control my investments; I want to be able to take out my cash when I want it; and I want to be comfortable with the historical performance of the investment. If my philosophy and yours are in sync, then the ingredients for success are ready.

A Short Quiz

Here are some questions you might want to answer. It's a superficial little quiz that can give you an indication of how much you know about investing in general. The answers are at the end of this quiz. Don't worry if you don't know the answers or if you have some misconceptions. The remaining chapters should set you on the right path.

1. Over any 10-year period of time during the 20th century, which of the following types of investments do you think gave the highest rate of return?
   a. Stocks
   b. Bonds
   c. Savings accounts
   d. Certificates of deposit
2. When an investor diversifies his investments by investing in various asset categories, does his risk of losing money increase or decrease?
   a. Increase
   b. Decrease

3. Is the following statement true or false: "A no-load mutual fund involves no sales charges or other fees."
    a. True
    b. False
4. What is the most important first step to take before developing an investment plan?
    a. Request a prospectus
    b. Set your goals
    c. Learn how the stock market works
5. Which of the following best describes mutual funds?
    a. Mutual funds only invest in stocks and bonds
    b. Mutual funds pay a fixed rate of return on your investment
    c. Professional managers use the money received from many investors to invest
6. When interest rates go up, what usually happens to the prices of bonds?
    a. Bond prices go up
    b. Bond prices go down
    c. Bond prices stay about the same
7. How do you think most full-service brokers and financial planners are paid? Are they mainly paid:
    a. Based on the quality of advice they offer and how much their clients earn?
    b. Based on the amount and type of investments they sell to their clients?
8. What types of stocks make up the Dow Jones Industrial Average?
    a. High technology growth stocks
    b. Stocks of established companies with a history of paying dividends
    c. A combination of 500 of the largest companies in the United States.

Answers to questions: 1. a, 2. b, 3. b, 4. b, 5. c, 6. b, 7. b, 8. b.

Over the years, Salomon Brothers, Inc. has investigated many investment vehicles and their long-term results. They have looked at housing, U.S. farmland, stocks, bonds, certificates of deposit, gold, silver, diamonds, oil, old masters paintings, stamps, foreign currencies, and Chinese ceramics to name most. They have consistently found that the U.S. stock market ranked among the best of all investment vehicles over the long-term for total returns.

In addition, the stock market is easy to follow. It is easy to understand (as I will show you), and equities are easy to liquidate (to sell for cash quickly). To make life easier, there is a specific vehicle within the stock market that leaves the professional responsibility of management and stock selection in the hands of those who do it for a living. I am referring to mutual funds.

As I take you through this section, you will learn about the stock market and specifically no-load mutual funds. You will get a feeling for the cyclical nature of all investments. You will read about various methods of investing in no-load mutual funds, and you will be exposed to a powerful tool that will help you to determine how expensive (overvalued) or inexpensive (undervalued) the overall stock market is at any time.

The Stock Market
What Is It?

The stock market is a general term that refers to the organized trading of securities. Securities consist of stocks, bonds, convertible bonds, options to purchase or sell, and stock warrants. A stock exchange is a marketplace where the actual transactions in these securities occur. The beginnings go back to 1531.

The first European stock exchange was established in Antwerp, Belgium in 1531. The first exchange in England was formed in 1773. In the United States, the first stock exchange was the New York Stock Exchange, founded in 1792.

The issuance of stocks and bonds is a result of necessity. Companies need money to operate and expand. They can earn money by generating profits in their business. But, if more money is necessary, they can obtain the extra cash by either borrowing it or selling ownership in their business.

Corporations can issue bonds in exchange for cash. Bonds are certificates of debt. The corporation borrows money from an investor, pays interest on the borrowed money, and then returns the principal at a specified date in the future.

Stocks, on the other hand, are certificates of ownership. They represent a piece of the total corporation. In the initial offering of stock, the company exchanges stock certificates for a sum of money. Money is transferred into the corporation from the investor, and the investor then owns a portion of the company along with certain rights. The company does not have to pay any principal back to the shareholder. The company often pays dividends to shareholders, but it does so as a result of profits.

New issues of stocks and bonds come on the market through an investment banker such as Merrill Lynch, Morgan Stanley, or Salomon Brothers to name a few. The investment banker underwrites the issue which means that the banker gives the corporations a guarantee of success in selling the stocks or bonds. The banker also agrees to retain any of the securities which are not sold. This initial public offering is called the primary market.

Once these new issues are in the hands of the public, anyone can trade them back and forth. This is called the secondary market. These securities are traded through various exchanges and over-the-counter. The issuing companies do not receive additional money from the continued trading of their stocks or bonds. The motivation for the existence of this secondary market is profit.

Stocks and bonds are usually bought with the hope that their value will rise and a profit will be realized or that a certain stream of income can be realized in the form

of dividends. Stocks and bonds are sold with the anticipation that their value will go down or because of a need to liquidate and raise cash.

The changing price of a stock or bond has no effect on the actual value of the company's assets. Although the health and earnings of a company will affect the value of a security, the security can react to many other factors that are completely unrelated to the company itself. It is the potential for gain in the secondary markets that makes investing a viable means to accumulate wealth over time.

Why Does It Work?

The market works because it is an auction house. Buyers looking for bargains and sellers looking for cash make the market function. But, the markets are cyclical.

If the stock market moved in the same small increments day in and day out, it would be easy for you as an investor to jump in at any time to take advantage of the advances. Likewise, any losses would be gradual over time, and you could exit the market as you saw fit. But, the market doesn't work that way.

The market is cyclical. That means that there are extended periods of time when the market is rising, and there are extended periods of time when the market is falling. These patterns repeat themselves with varying amplitudes, frequencies, and durations. The U.S. Business Cycle, which I describe in detail later, is an example of such a repeating pattern. However, there are surprises along the way.

These surprises are a result of a market that is episodic. This means that there are very short periods of time when there are great bursts in price levels both to the upside and to the downside. These *spurts* to the upside and *drops* to the downside create sharp blips in amplitude.

Drops occur without much warning. For example, on October 19, 1987, the S&P 500 Index crashed 57.86 points or 20.5% of its value in just one day! Spurts also occur without much warning. For instance, the first weeks of 1996 saw a huge rise in the price of gold stock funds.

When you investigate the *average compounded rate-of-return* for a fund or for an asset category, the episodic bursts in price (both up and down) are averaged over the time period of the statistic. The statistic makes it appear that you could have invested at any time during that time frame and that you would have received the stated average compounded rate-of-return. This is not so!

If you invested before a spurt, you did well; if you got in after the spurt, you did less than ideal. Likewise, if you invested just before a drop, you suffered; if you got in after a drop, you participated in a buying opportunity. Unfortunately, the fact is that it is impossible to participate in every spurt and to avoid every drop. The exact timing of these spurts or drops is elusive. (This is one reason why dollar-cost-averaging works so well.)

There are external forces which drive the market. Although investors have no control over these, you can become familiar with how they work.

What Drives the Market?

If you were driving down a mountain road and momentum was pushing your car faster and faster, you would probably notice that the car behind you was following in lockstep. If you felt the need to slow down, you would apply foot pressure on the brake, and your car would decelerate. The car behind you would see your red brake lights, and it also would begin to slow. Once you got to the bottom of the mountain, and the road then began to wind itself up the side of another steep hill, you would need to put your foot on the gas pedal this time just to keep the car moving forward. Again, you would notice that the car behind you was following your lead.

Metaphorically, your car is the stock market; the gas and brake pedals are the forces which are manipulated by the Federal Reserve System; the car behind is the economy.

The Federal Reserve System is made up of the Federal Reserve Board of Governors, a network of Federal Reserve Banks located throughout the country, and the Federal Open Market Committee (FOMC). The Board of Governors consists of seven members appointed by the President of the United States and confirmed by the Senate. The United States is divided into twelve districts, with a Federal Reserve Bank located in a city in each district. There are Federal Reserve Bank branches in 25 additional cities. The FOMC is made up of the Board of Governors, the president of the Federal Reserve Bank of New York, and four other Reserve Bank presidents.

The long-range goal of the Fed is to keep monetary growth and credit large enough to meet the needs of an expanding economy, without generating an unreasonable increase in prices.

When the Fed lowers interest rates, it increases the money supply and thereby stimulates the economy. Here is how the Fed presses on the gas pedal:

1. **Lower the Federal Funds Rate:** The Federal Funds Rate is the interest rate charged by banks with excess reserves at a Federal Reserve district bank to banks needing overnight loans to meet reserve requirements which are set by the Federal Reserve Board. The Federal Funds Rate is the most sensitive indicator of the direction of short-term interest rates since it is manipulated daily.
   When short-term interest rates are lowered, it is cheaper to borrow money. When money is cheaper to borrow, more money is put into circulation. When more money is in circulation the money supply increases.

2. **Lower the Discount Rate.** The Discount Rate is what it costs banks to borrow money from the Federal Reserve. Lower rates encourage banks to borrow from the Fed. As the banks in turn loan these funds, the money supply is increased.

3. **Lower the Reserve Requirement.** Commercial banks are required to hold a certain percent of their deposits on reserve which cannot be loaned to customers. When the Fed reduces the percent required to be held by the com-

93

mercial banks, these banks will then have more money to lend. This allows the money supply to expand.

4. **Buy Government Obligations.** Government obligations are in the form of Treasury Bills. When the Federal Reserve "buys" these securities, it "puts" money into the reserves of the banking system. This action eventually increases the supply of money.

When the Fed raises interest rates, it decreases the money supply and thereby depresses the economy. Here is how the Fed puts on the brake:
1. **Increase the Federal Funds Rate**
2. **Increase the Discount Rate**
3. **Raise the Reserve Requirements**
4. **Sell Government Obligations**

Going back to the mountain road, if you slammed your foot on the brake pedal, the momentum of the car behind you might not have time to judge its stop. It could plow into the rear of your car.

Likewise, when the Fed tightens money too much or too quickly, the momentum of the stock market and the economy might hit a non-moving vehicle and drop. That's the potential problem of the Fed acting haphazardly or abruptly.

The bottom line is that changes in the monetary policy as set by the Federal Reserve Board are transmitted throughout the economy via changes in short-term interest rates. These changes affect the money supply. The money supply affects the stock market. And, the stock market is often a precursor of future actions in the economy. All of these changes can be viewed over the long-term as a cycle—The U.S. Business Cycle.

The U.S. Business Cycle

The U.S. business cycle is an economic cycle. It develops as a wave (see chart) which falls during its contraction phase, reaches a bottom, rises through its expansion phase, reaches a top, and then repeats itself. These cycles have been identified over the past 200 years and tend to repeat themselves approximately every 42 months.

During the U.S. business cycle there are a series of events which usually occur in sequence. This order allows an investor an opportunity to prepare for the next anticipated event. While this sequence rarely varies, the actual magnitude of each event and the time span between events do vary and are not predictable.

For example, during one cycle, the S&P 500 Index may rise 120% from its previous low to a new high and stay in an uptrend for 2.5 years. In contrast, during another cycle it may rise only 45% from its low to high points and stay in an uptrend for only 1.5 years.

The cycle can be divided into six stages. Look at the chart, and follow along:

Chart 8.1: U.S. Business Cycle

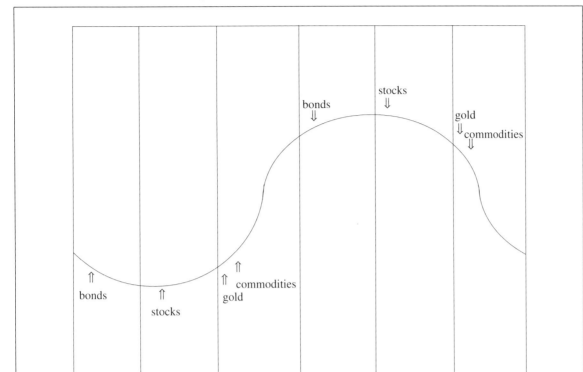

B = Bonds

S = Stocks

C = Commodities

Stage I: The Federal Reserve decides to stimulate the contracting economy by lowering the Federal Funds Rate. By reducing interest rates, the price of bonds rises. (This is an inverse rule. The technical explanation for this is that the yield to maturity is essentially kept the same between existing bonds and newly issued bonds.)

Stage II: The contraction phase of the economy seems to come to an end as the stock market ends its correction and starts rising.

Stage III: As the expansion in the economy moves forward, gold and commodity prices start rising. Hints of inflation may be entering the markets.

Stage IV: With signs of future inflation beginning to surface, the Federal Reserve decides to slow down the economy by raising the Federal Funds Rate. This causes bond prices to begin declining.

Stage V: The stock market loses its steam and begins to drop as the business cycle searches for a top.

Stage VI: The economic cycle is now in a contraction phase, and gold and commodity prices are falling. The contraction phase usually leads into an economic recession.

In a real life cycle, the wave takes on a more irregular pattern. The peaks and troughs for each event within the cycle are not always well defined. Sometimes, you can't identify a new trend until well after the turn.

It is important to realize that the financial world in which we all invest has some sense of sequential regularity. Individuals who try to time the stock market in order to buy and sell stocks will attempt to identify the turning points of each stage in the cycle. These turning points help identify which investments may be appropriate during the various stages of the business cycle. Knowledge of the cycle and its influence on specific investments may help investors using market timing to choose the right investments at the right time.

For example, if the cycle were just beginning its expansion phase, a market-timer might invest in aggressive-growth mutual funds. However, if the expansion phase of the cycle were beginning to reach its top after interest rates had already bottomed, the market-timer might *not* want to invest aggressively in growth stocks. The market-timer might consider inflation hedges which would benefit from rising commodity prices. If the contraction phase were actually creating a declining stock market, the market-timer might avoid stocks altogether, and temporarily move his or her investment portfolio into cash.

Martin J. Pring has written an excellent book describing the phases of the U.S. business cycle and how to invest throughout the cycle for maximum returns. For information regarding his book, *The All Season Investor*, call The International Institute for Economic Research at (800) 221-7514.

What Has the Market Done Over the Years?

The beginning of reliable statistics to examine the total return for the U.S. stock market can be traced back to 1871. Over this course of time, the market has had an upward bias even after being adjusted for inflation. Certainly there have been blips along the way—serious blips. But, the inflation-adjusted total return appears as a rising trend line over the last 125 years.

One dollar invested in 1871 into the overall stock market would have grown in purchasing power to $2,622 today. This is a 6.5% compounded rate of return above the rate of inflation. In contrast, one dollar invested for the same time period in Treasury Bills would have grown in purchasing power to only $10.51 today. This translates to an inflation-adjusted return of a mere 1.9%. A dollar invested in gold bullion would have virtually maintained its purchasing power.

This means that the stock market has been a shining star over the long-term, and Treasury Bills have proven to be only slightly better than a store-of-value. (Store-of-value refers to something that preserves its purchasing power by increasing in value to the same extent that inflation is decreasing its value.) The true store-of-value has been gold. For the most part, what could be purchased with one ounce of gold in 1871 still can be purchased with the same ounce of gold today.

These statistics argue that the stock market is the place to invest long-term. But, the blips along the way can be scary. There have been twenty-nine market downturns of 15% or more since 1871, with an average loss of 35%. The most severe loss was 89% following the crash of 1929. The least severe loss was 17% which occurred between January, 1960 and October, 1960.

How Can One Participate?

You as an investor can call a stock broker and purchase stock. If you do some homework by evaluating individual companies and the sectors in which they do business, you will be able to select several promising stocks which might be valuable investments.

Or, you could leave the stock picking to individual money managers whose full time jobs are to sift through the thousands of stocks available to U.S. investors and create a portfolio based on specific investment objectives. The best fund managers are at the helm of some of the best performing mutual funds today.

When I say best performing mutual funds today, I am referring to statistics that reflect at least the previous three-year period for that mutual fund. As you will see in chapter 12, my mutual fund selections are based on previous three- and five-year periods. It is imprudent to rate any fund or manager on the results of a single year's performance. The best investments still go through cycles, and any one-year period may catch the cycle in its down phase.

Mutual Funds

Mutual funds are my choice. Mutual funds are pools of money coming from you and me and many other investors. The fund manager then takes this money and invests it by purchasing various stocks and other securities for the portfolio. All expenses for the management of the fund are paid out of the total assets in this portfolio. The price of each share of the fund is equal to the value of the assets in the portfolio after all expenses have been paid divided by the number of shares outstanding.

For example, if the portfolio value minus expenses on a specific day is $50,000,000 and there are 10,000,000 shares outstanding, the price of one share is $50,000,000 ÷ 10,000,000 or $5 per share. This is called the net asset value (NAV).

At the end of every trading day, the fund reports its net asset value. The NAV is reported in almost all mutual fund financial sections of daily newspapers all across the country. If you wanted to buy or sell one share of that fund, the NAV is the value of that share for that specific day. Remember, this price changes daily.

There are two broad categories of mutual funds: load and no-load. There are close to 7,000 load funds and over 600 no-load funds.

Load funds have a sales commission added to the NAV of the fund which is a fee paid to brokers and agents who sell the funds. For every load fund there is usually a comparable no-load fund available. (There is also a category called *low-load* which refers to those funds which charge less than 3% commissions.) Some funds have back end loads which mean they charge a fee to sell the fund.

Some funds have *12b-1 fees* which are expenses for some of its distribution and marketing. However, 12b-1 fees do not come out of each investment when you purchase or sell shares as do load fees (discussed above). The 12b-1 fees, like other fund expenses, are subtracted from profits each day before the NAV is calculated at the day's close. Therefore, when you compare the NAV of one fund to the NAV of another, all fees and expenses including the 12b-1 fees are already accounted for before you make the comparison. So, if fees or expenses are excessive or detrimental to the performance of one of the funds you are comparing, then the better-performing funds will have higher NAVs. I will be describing how to choose the best performing funds in chapter 12.

No-load funds are the funds in which I invest. They are sold directly by the fund company, and there are no sales commissions added onto the NAV to be paid to a salesperson. Many also can be purchased through various discount brokers for no additional fee. Why pay the commission for load funds? There is one reason in my opinion.

If you need advice from a sales agent, then the sales agent deserves to be paid a commission for his or her advice. If the sales agent educates you and helps create your portfolio, he or she has earned the extra cost. However, if you do your homework, you will not need the advice of a sales agent to purchase your funds. Therefore, you should never need to pay the sales commissions of load funds since your due diligence will lead you to the right no-load funds.

There are two sources that I use to obtain the necessary information to make my mutual fund decisions. You should find both very helpful in your personal investment education process. One is the American Association of Individual Investors (AAII); the other is Morningstar.

The AAII is a non-profit organization which offers an excellent monthly journal and an annual guide to low-load & no-load mutual funds along with membership. The guide is called, *The Individual Investors' Guide To Low-Load Mutual Funds*. It is published every March. The AAII also offers a quarterly update for these funds. For information about membership, seminars, and publications, call the AAII at (800) 428-2244.

Morningstar has several publications, but I use their *No-Load Funds* monthly updates. This publication has a wealth of statistical and timely information concerning approximately 600 no-load and low-load funds. For information regarding

Morningstar's services and subscription rates, call (800) 735-0700. *Morningstar No-Load Funds* is available in the reference section of most libraries

Categories of Mutual Funds

Within all mutual funds, there are various asset categories or types of funds. The funds which make up each asset category invest a pool of portfolio money based on specific objectives. The objectives identify the types of investments in which the fund will invest (such as U.S. stocks, bonds, foreign securities, precious metals, etc.) as well as how aggressive or conservative its investment techniques will be (such as borrowing on margin, purchasing options, hedging, and selling short.).

Margin is the collateral someone puts up to back a loan. Borrowing on margin produces leverage because the customer deposits an amount of money with a broker as collateral and then borrows more than that to purchase various securities. For instance if a $500,000 loan is backed by a $300,000 margin, then the leverage is $500,000 to $300,000 or 5:3.

Options are the right to buy or sell an underlying security such as a stock, a commodity, or a stock index at a specific price at a specific time in the future. Since the option buyer must put up only a small amount of money to control a large amount of the security, options trading provides a great deal of leverage. Options to buy a security are called *Call Options* and options to sell a security are called *Put Options*. Call options make money when their underlying security rises in price. Put options make money when their underlying security drops in price.

Hedging is the practice of offsetting the potential of future loss. For example, if a stockholder thought that the U.S. market was going to drop sharply, he could purchase a *Put Option* on the S&P 500 Index. This will *hedge* some of that individual's U.S. stock portfolio for a specific period of time. Another example of hedging occurs when a foreign stock fund purchases foreign currency futures. This tends to offset the fluctuating value of its foreign stock portfolio which results from the foreign currency rising and falling in relation to the U.S. dollar.

Selling Short refers to the sale of a security that is not owned by the seller. The investor borrows the security certificate at the market price from a broker. This borrowed security must be returned to the broker at a later date. If the short seller can purchase the actual stock at a lower price later, he can return the borrowed certificate to the broker and will make a profit. If he must purchase the security later at a higher price, he will return the borrowed certificate to the broker and will have a loss.

For example, Fund X believes XYZ stock is going to fall in price. The fund manager instructs its broker to sell short 1000 shares of XYZ stock that is selling at $35 for a total sale price or $35,000. The broker then loans the fund 1000 shares of XYZ stock and the fund pays the broker $35,000 to secure the loan. The 1000 shares of the stock must be returned to the broker in the future. If the stock drops to $25 a share, the fund can purchase 1000 shares at $25 a share for a total price of $25,000. After returning the 1000 shares purchased at $25,000 to the broker, the fund will make a

profit of $10,000 ($35,000 - $25,000 = $10,000). However, if the stock goes up in price before the fund can repurchase it, then the fund will suffer a loss.

The following categories help to summarize what is available to the mutual fund investor. These categories are sometimes difficult to differentiate. Some funds also can fit into more than one category. In addition, one research organization may classify one specific fund as an aggressive growth fund, and another research firm may classify it as a growth fund.

Aggressive growth funds. The investment objective of this category is maximum capital gains. These funds invest primarily in stocks with significant growth potential as well as high risk. These funds also may use leverage by borrowing money to purchase securities and by trading in stock options and index futures. Many of these funds may concentrate their investing in specific industries or segments of the market. Usually the companies represented in this type of fund are small capitalized companies that do not provide dividends to its investors. They may do very well in bull markets (when prices are moving up) but may do very poorly in bear markets (when prices are moving down). These funds are specifically suited for the long-term investor (at least five years) who is not looking for current income or dividends.
Examples:
PBHG Growth (800) 433-0051
SteinRoe Capital Opportunity (800) 338-2550
Kaufmann (800) 666-9181

Growth funds. These funds are similar to the aggressive group just described except they usually do not engage in leveraging. In other words, they do not borrow money to purchase securities nor do they trade in stock options and index futures. They generally invest in growth oriented companies that are more mature and that may pay some cash dividends. They are also better diversified than the aggressive funds. As a rule, growth funds will move in the same direction as the general stock market in both bull and bear cycles. They usually demonstrate more appreciation in a bull market and more depreciation in a bear market than the general market indices.
Examples:
Founders Growth (800) 525-2440
Brandywine Blue (800) 656-3017
Janus (800) 525-3713

Growth and income funds. These funds will invest in securities of well established companies that usually pay high cash dividends. Income is an important objective along with long-term growth. These funds may be more stable than the general market but still duplicate the up and down trends.
Examples:
Safeco Equity (800) 624-5711

Fidelity Growth & Income (800) 544-6666
Vanguard Windsor II (800) 635-1511

Balanced funds. Within these funds, a large portion of the portfolio is devoted to stocks and bonds. Some funds may have a fixed allocation percentage (i.e., 40% bonds, 60% stocks), or some funds may allow the fund manager to switch between stocks and bonds based on the conditions in the marketplace. There is significant overlap between this category and that of growth & income. These funds provide a high dividend yield and are more stable than the general market.
Examples:
Fidelity Puritan (800) 544-6666
Evergreen Foundation Class Y (800) 235-0064
Lindner Dividend (314) 727-5305

Bond funds. As the name implies, these funds usually invest in fixed-income securities—bonds. This category is further subdivided into corporate, government, mortgage-backed, general, and tax-exempt bond funds. The date when bonds come due (maturity date) and the quality of the bonds determine the risk of the fund. Short-term bonds coming due within three years have much less risk and are therefore more stable than long-term bonds coming due more than 10 years from now. Intermediate-term bond funds fall somewhere in between. A portfolio of AAA rated bonds is less risky than one of BB rated bonds. Bond funds rarely offer growth potential.
Examples:
Vanguard Short-Term Corporate (short-term, taxable) (800) 635-1511
Fidelity Capital & Income (intermediate-term, taxable) (800) 544-6666
Strong Corporate (long-term, taxable) (800) 368-3863
USAA Tax Exempt Short-Term (short-term, tax exempt)(800) 531-8181
Vanguard Intermediate Municipal (intermediate-term, tax exempt) (800) 635-1511
Scudder Massachusetts Tax Free (long-term, tax exempt) (800) 225-2470

International bond funds. These fixed-income securities are from foreign companies and governments. There is more risk involved than with U.S. bond funds because of currency rate fluctuations and foreign government instability.

Examples:
Scudder International Bond (800) 225-2470
T. Rowe Price International Bond (800) 225-5132
Loomis Sayles Global Bond (800) 633-3330

Foreign stock funds. These funds invest in stocks of foreign companies. As with the international bond funds, there is added risk beyond U.S. stock funds because of government instability as well as currency fluctuations to a lesser degree. Foreign stock funds can be

subdivided further into developed market funds and emerging market funds. For example, developed markets include such countries as France, Germany, Japan, and Australia. Emerging markets include such countries as China, India, Poland, and Israel.

Examples:

(developed)

USAA International (800) 531-8181

Warburg Pincus International Equity (800) 257-5614

Acorn International (800) 922-6769

(emerging)

Lexington Worldwide Emerging Markets (800) 526-0057

Montgomery Emerging Markets (800) 572-3863

Robertson Stephens Developing Countries (800) 766-3863

Sector funds. These funds are industry specific. For example, there are funds investing only in health-related companies, or utilities, or financial institutions, or communications, etc. When one sector may be strong, another may be weak. These funds are much riskier than well-diversified funds.

Examples:

Invesco Worldwide Communications (communications)

(800) 525-8085

Century Shares (financial institutions)(800) 321-1928

Vanguard Specialized Health Care (health care) (800) 635-1511

T.Rowe Price New Era (natural resources) (800) 225-5132

Cohen & Steers Realty (real estate) (800) 437-9912

Lindner Utility (utilities) (314) 727-5305

Precious metals funds. By definition, these are actually sector funds. However, precious metals funds are the most volatile and therefore the most risky of all mutual funds. They deserve a separate category. These funds invest in mining stocks as well as precious metal bullion. Some precious metals funds also invest in other natural resources companies.

Examples:

United Services World Gold (800) 873-8637

Blanchard Precious Metals (800) 245-0242

Midas (800) 400-6432

Contrary-style funds. This is a relatively new category that is not recognized by all investors and is difficult for many research firms to categorize. It plays a very important part in my Lifetime Investing Plan as you will see. I will describe this category in detail in later chapters.

Examples:

Robertson Stephens Contrarian (800) 766-3863

Lindner Bulwark (314) 727-5305

Index funds. These funds invest in the stocks that make up specific market indices such as the S&P 500 Index, the Over-the-Counter Index, etc. Their purpose is to mimic the up-and-down trends of the indices they represent. They usually have much lower management fees than all of the other categories already described because there is little change in their portfolios. No attempt is made by the fund manager to time the market or choose the best performing stocks. However, the manager does balance the portfolio when necessary to maintain an accurate mirror of the index it represents. Examples:

Schwab Small Cap Index (800) 266-5623
Vanguard Index Trust-500 (800) 635-1511
Vanguard Total Bond Market Portfolio (800) 635-1511

Money market funds. Money market funds invest in short-term money market instruments. These instruments are turned into cash usually within a few days. They invest in repurchase agreements, government securities, certificates of deposit, and other highly liquid and safe securities. Money market funds act as a parking place for your money until it can be put to better use. That may mean you eventually will spend it on the things you need and want, or you will invest it in other ways when the time is right. The share value is held at a constant one dollar value. The percent return varies daily based on money market conditions. Most money market funds also provide check-writing privileges, providing you with a convenient way to instantly access your money. Almost all fund families offer a money market fund. All brokerage houses, both discount and full-service, offer money market funds. Also, there are money market funds that are taxable, and there are those that are exempt from federal income taxes.

Mutual Funds as Gifts

Mutual funds can satisfy many purposes. They are excellent investment vehicles as I have already described. They are also excellent gifts for those you cherish.

There are several good reasons to give financial gifts, and there are several good reasons to make those gifts no-load mutual funds. Here are some of my thoughts:

Benefits of Gift-Giving

1. You can give away $10,000 per year to as many people as you desire gift-tax free. This is called the $10,000 annual exclusion. As the donor, you don't have to pay a gift-tax, and the recipient does not have to pay income taxes. If you are married, you and your spouse can give a joint gift up to $20,000 gift-tax free.

2. Another benefit from the $10,000 annual exclusion is that you can reduce the value of your estate over time. If your purpose is to pass wealth onto your heirs, the least expensive way is to give away as much as you can gift-tax free

every year. The annual exclusion allows you and your spouse to reduce your estate by $20,000 per recipient each year. If you have three children, for instance, you and your spouse can reduce your estate by $60,000 a year.

By giving away assets that appreciate in value, you not only are reducing the value of your current estate, but you are also shifting current income and capital gains to someone else whose tax bracket may be less than yours.

For instance, suppose you had $5,000 in XYZ stock that compounded at 9% a year which included a 4% annual dividend distribution which was reinvested. Also, suppose you wanted to use this for your child, but you kept it for 10 years before giving it to your child.

The $5,000 stock portfolio would be worth $11,837 in ten years. You would have to pay income taxes on the dividends that were reinvested over the 10-year period at the time of distribution. When you finally sold the stock portfolio, you would have to pay capital gains taxes at your tax bracket before you gave the proceeds to your child.

To avoid paying taxes at your tax bracket on the current dividends of the stock portfolio and to avoid paying additional capital gains taxes on the appreciated value ten years later, you could give the $5,000 gift right away to your child. In that way the portfolio would appreciate outside of your estate. Your child would pay taxes at his or her tax level on both the reinvested dividends as they were distributed and on the capital gains after they were realized. Your child's tax bracket would probably be less than yours. Remember, however, the "kiddie tax" laws. (See LIP Gloss).

Benefits of No-Load Mutual Funds as Gifts

No-load mutual funds can be purchased for as much as you want or for as little as $250 through some fund families. It is easy for you or anyone else to add to the fund, and many funds allow as little as $50 to be added as additional purchases once the account is opened.

As gifts for children, no-load mutual funds can be given to your child outright or in trust or through a custodial account such as the Uniform Transfers to Minors Act (UTMA). These three methods were discussed in Chapter 7.

Funds are also excellent gifts for newlyweds. If you aren't sure what to get a newly married couple, consider a no-load mutual fund. As a matter of fact, newlyweds could let interested parties know of their favorite mutual fund, just as they let people know of their china and silver patterns. China breaks; silver tarnishes; but money invested in mutual funds can grow for a lifetime.

Methods of Investing in No-Load Mutual Funds

There are a few methods of investing in no-load mutual funds that I want to summarize. They can be used by themselves or they can be combined. My Lifetime

Investing Plan will combine three of the following four methods to produce a coherent approach that works well for most people.

Lump-Sum Investing

To begin your investing plan, you need to contact the fund, obtain a prospectus, fill out the simple application form, and return it to the fund company with your initial investment. This initial investment is actually the first method of investing known as lump-sum investing.

No matter how much you invest the first time, it is a lump-sum investment. It could be the minimum to open an account (example: $500), it could be a rollover or transfer from another investment (example: an IRA transfer from another qualified retirement account which was worth $100,000), or it could be whatever amount you wish to start your program of wealth accumulation.

After this initial investment, you could leave that amount of money in the account to compound, never adding another penny. However, to reach your financial goal, you most likely will want to fuel your account with additional contributions. The next method of investing will make it easy for you to commit to a regular investment program.

Dollar-Cost-Averaging

I described dollar-cost-averaging in chapter 4. It is the best way to invest because it takes advantage of market volatility, thereby allowing you to purchase more shares when the price is low. The beauty of this method is that it provides a disciplined approach to investing and allows compounding to work its astonishing results.

Let's assume your plan requires you to invest $250 at the beginning of each month into Fund XYZ. At the beginning of each month for the first five months, this fund has a selling price of $13.26, $12.97, $12.33, $11.95, and $11.78 respectively.

So, the first month your $250 will purchase 18.85 shares ($250 ÷ $13.26). The second month, 19.28 shares ($250 ÷ $12.97). The third month, 20.28 shares ($250 ÷ $12.33). The fourth month, 20.92 shares ($250 ÷ $11.95). And, the fifth month, 21.22 shares ($250 ÷ $11.78).

At the end of five months, you have invested $1,250, and you own 100.55 shares. The average price you paid was not the highest price of $13.26 per share, and it wasn't the lowest price of $11.78 per share. The average price you paid was $12.43 ($1,250 ÷ 100.55 shares).

For the next three months, the market begins to recover. You are able to purchase your shares at $11.85, $12.23, and $12.53. This adds another 61.49 shares to your portfolio for a total of 162.04 shares. You have now invested $2,000 over the course of 8 months, and the average price per share is $12.34 ($2,000 ÷ 162.04).

If you had invested the entire $2,000 in the first month of this eight-month investment period, you would have purchased 150.83 shares ($2,000 ÷ $13.26). Those shares would be worth $1,890 at the end of the eight months (150.83 x $12.53).

However, by dollar-cost-averaging in this example, you have more shares because you purchased more when the share price was low and less when the share price was high. At the end of eight months your 162.04 shares are worth $2,030 (162.04 x $12.53), not $1890.

This method works for any type of long-term investment program. It disciplines you to invest regularly, and it assists you in taking advantage of the *ups* and *downs* that are inherent in any market. It doesn't guarantee profits, but it does assure perseverance.

Table 8.2: DCA shows how dollar-cost-averaging works to average out the total cost of shares in the beginning of an investment program. For the first three months in this table, the investor put $100 monthly into his mutual fund. Shares were purchased at various prices. At the end of the three months, $300 was invested and 25 shares were purchased for an average price of $12 a share. In month four, another $100 was invested and 20 shares were purchased. Since the shares purchased in the fourth month were significantly less expensive than previous months, the average price per share for the four months was brought down to $8.89 a share. As you can see in this scenario, dollar-cost-averaging has helped to *average out* the cost of the shares purchased.

However, once the portfolio is significantly large, the continuation of dollar-cost-averaging does very little to impact the average price per share in the portfolio.

Look again at Table 8.2. The portfolio has grown to $40,000 over a period of time with a total of 4499 shares at an average price of $8.89 per share. When an additional $100 is invested, it only changes the average price per share by $0.02. Although dollar-cost-averaging has little effect on the average price per share after the portfolio has grown significantly, it does assure a disciplined approach to continued investing.

Asset Allocation

I will discuss this subject in much more detail in chapter 11. For now, it is sufficient to define it the way I will use it.

Asset allocation is the apportioning of investment dollars among various asset categories. The types of asset categories are usually chosen to offset one another's volatility. This helps to smooth out the overall volatility of one's portfolio and therefore reduces the overall risk of the portfolio. In my plan, I choose asset categories that are in the equity sectors of the stock markets from around the world. With asset allocation, the whole is conceptually more than the sum of its parts.

For example, in my Lifetime Investing Plan, I use five asset categories which tend to offset each other's volatility. They are: U.S. aggressive growth funds, U.S. growth funds, Foreign stock funds, Emerging foreign stock funds, and Contrary-style funds.

It is important that you stop for a moment and understand thoroughly what I am about to say.

Table 8.2: DCA

$100	@	$10.00 per share	=	10 shares	
$100	@	$20.00 per share	=	5 shares	
+ $100	@	$10.00 per share	=	+ 10 shares	
$300				25 shares	Average price per share $12.00
+ $100	@	$5.00 per share	=	+ 20 shares	
$400				45 shares	Average price per share $8.89

•••

$40,000	@	$8.89 per share	=	4499 shares	
+ $100	@	$5.00 per share	=	+ 20 shares	
$40,100				4519 shares	Average price per share $8.87

No matter how strong an individual company may be or how well a portfolio is assembled, when the overall stock market experiences a correction of any significance, all stocks will be affected to some degree in a negative way.

Reread this statement, please. This means that all stocks will have some degree of negative pressure placed on them when the overall market is having trouble. Because of this, my Lifetime Investing Plan will experience periods when its overall total return will be in negative territory. This is part of the risk of investing as I will describe in the next chapter.

Market Timing

The last method of investing with mutual funds which I will describe is market timing. This is defined as a means of deciding when to buy or sell mutual funds based on technical or fundamental indicators which try to identify the current trend (or

direction) of the stock market and the future direction it will take. These indicators help investors switch between equity funds, fixed-income funds, and money market funds based on whether their long-term price movements are expected to be either up, down, or sideways. I introduced some thoughts about market timing when I described the U.S. Business Cycle.

Some studies have shown that technical indicators such as a moving averages and trading-range breaks can improve investment results.

To calculate a *moving average*, the average price of a security or index is determined for a specific time period. This average price changes as each time period goes by. For example, a 200-day moving average is calculated each day for the previous 200 trading days. When the Dow Jones Industrial (DJI) Average is above its 200-day moving average, the market is considered to be in an uptrend, and an investor who is using market timing may want to be invested. When the DJI Average is below its 200-day moving average, an investor may want to move out of the stock market.

Trading-range breaks are when a price for a stock is able to move above a previous high or to move below a previous low. Here is an example. When the demand for XYZ stock has reached a point where its price breaks above its previous high that was set over the last ten weeks of trading, the price of the stock will tend to continue to move higher. In contrast, when XYZ stock's price falls below a previous low that was set over the last ten weeks of trading, the demand for the stock may have dropped, and the price of that stock may continue to decline. A market timer may use these price breaks as buying or selling indicators.

In my own personal portfolio, I include market timing as a means to take advantage of severely undervalued situations and as a means to avoid severely overvalued situations. Timing is far from perfect, and I have been successful at times and unsuccessful at other times when I have used it. This book *does not* include timing in the Lifetime Investing Plan. However, I want to share one timing concept that you can use for information. It deals with the value of the stock market at any time.

The Value of the Market

If you were going to buy a piece of furniture for your home, and it was so popular that the store could not keep it in stock, the chances are that the price tag would be full retail. As a matter of fact, it might even be above retail because the store would know that it could sell it for almost any price since the demand was so great.

On the other hand, when that piece of furniture had enjoyed all the buyers who wanted it, and the store's supply of that piece accumulated on the showroom floor, the store would likely put it on sale just to get rid of it. The store might eventually sell the furniture piece for less than cost just to get it out of inventory. At that point, the furniture piece would still be what you wanted, but it would now be at a rock-bottom price. When would be the best time to buy the furniture? Of course you're right— when the price was at rock-bottom prices. That would also be the best time to buy the stock market—when it was at rock-bottom prices (undervalued).

To obtain a clearer picture of how overvalued or undervalued the general United States stock market is, the S&P 500 yield can be compared to the risk-free interest rate of the 13-week U.S. Treasury Bill (also called the three-month or 91-day Treasury Bill). I call this the Relative Value Ratio (RVR).

When the treasury bill coupon yield is low compared to the S&P 500 yield, the market is at bargain prices. When the treasury bill coupon yield is high compared to the S&P 500 yield, the market is expensive. The RVR is calculated by dividing the 13-week U.S. Treasury Bill coupon yield by the S&P 500 Index yield.

The coupon yield is the annualized rate of return you earn on the purchase price (which is a discounted price) for the treasury bill. For example, assume a 5% 13-week treasury bill with a face value of $10,000 would cost you $9,875 today. To compute the coupon yield, you would first divide the difference between the face value ($10,000) and your purchase price ($9,875) by the purchase price ($9,875). The result would then be multiplied by 365 ÷ 91 (365 days in a year divided by the life of the Treasury Bill). Then multiply this by 100 to get a percentage. After you make the calculation for this example, you will find the yield on this investment to be 5.08%.

$$\frac{\$125}{\$9,875} \times \frac{365}{91} \times 100\% = 5.08\%$$

Barron's Financial Newspaper (a weekly newspaper) is a quick source to obtain these numbers from the *Market Laboratory* section every week. The S&P 500 yield is in the column, *Indexes' P/Es & Yields*. The 13-week treasury bill coupon yield is in the column entitled, *Money Rates*.

Example (2/9/96): 13-week treasury bill coupon yield = 4.88%
     S&P 500 index yield = (dividends paid ÷ S&P 500 index) = 2.18%
     relative value ratio = 4.88% ÷ 2.18% = 2.24

If you want to keep track of the RVR, you can use Table 8.3: RVR to record the data.

For the last 30 years, the relationship of the yields of the S&P 500 Index and the 13-week treasury bill has been very accurate in defining the periods of time when the stock market has been at bargain prices (undervalued) and when it has been at expensive prices (overvalued). When the RVR has been below 1.70, the U.S. stock market has been relatively undervalued and a real bargain. When the RVR has been above 2.15, the market has been relatively overvalued and expensive.

From 1968 through the end of 1994, there were eight times when the RVR was below 1.70 and seven times when it was above 2.15. All undervalued signals preceded stock market rallies which eventually rose to an overvalued situation. Six of the seven overvalued signals preceded a market downturn which eventually fell to an undervalued level. This represents a 93% success rate in identifying a change in trend.

Table 8.3: RVR

$$\text{Relative Value Ratio} \quad = \quad \frac{\text{13-Week Treasury Bill}}{\text{S\&P 500 Yield}}$$

Date	13-Wk Treas. Bill	S&P 500 Yield	RVR

Date	13-Wk Treas. Bill	S&P 500 Yield	RVR

What the RVR does not tell you, or me, or anyone else, is *when* the overvalued or undervalued condition of the market will correct itself!

In early 1995, the RVR registered its eighth overvalued signal since 1968. Although the RVR only gave a weak overvalued signal which hovered around the 2.20 area for most of 1995, the U.S. markets were relatively strong. For example, the S&P 500 Index had a total return of approximately 38% for all of 1995.

In 1996, the RVR was rising. As of July, 1996, the RVR reached 2.31. Also in July, many of the U.S. markets demonstrated signs of entering some type of a correction. Only time will tell how deep this correction will be.

For example, in July, 1996, the NASDAQ Composite Index experienced a correction of approximately 20%. The NASDAQ is the National Association of Securities Dealers Automated Quotation system. Primarily, this system provides brokers and dealers with price quotations for securities that are not listed on an organized stock market exchange (i.e., over-the-counter). The NASDAQ Composite Index is a broad-based index of over 4,000 over-the-counter securities which are considered speculative and very volatile.

The essence of this ratio is that you, the investor, may want to become cautious and conservative when the RVR is above 2.15 and aggressive when it is below 1.70.

Again, I'm not suggesting that you *time* the market. But, if you were in a position to add a large sum of money into the market, and the RVR were severely undervalued, you might want to emphasize an aggressive stock fund. If, at the other extreme, the RVR were severely overvalued, you might be more conservative with that large sum of money and simply park it safely in a money market fund. Then you could either dollar-cost-average into the stock market or wait until the RVR returned to a more normal range before entering the stock market.

Again, no matter what you do with this statistic, it helps you understand the inherent value of the overall U.S. stock market at any time. At least you know how expensive or inexpensive your purchases actually are compared to historical standards.

Benchmarks of the Market

What is the market doing?. Well, that depends. Different perspectives will produce different conclusions about how well or poorly the stock market is performing. The reason for this is that there are various indices that monitor different segments of the stock market. In order to determine how the market is doing, you first need to know what part of the market you are questioning. Then you need to know what specific indices are designed to describe that particular market sector.

For a description of many of the market indices and the market segments they monitor, check out Lifetime Investing Plan Glossary (LIP Gloss) at the end of the book and look under "Benchmark."

Investing in the stock market using no-load mutual funds makes good sense to me, but there is volatility in the marketplace. This is the risk of investing, and you need to know how it affects your investments. You guessed it; the next chapter addresses risk.

Risk

If you look over the edge of a cliff which has a vertical drop of 1,000 feet, your risk of falling is minimal if there is a guard rail. Remove the rail, and your risk increases. Stand on one foot at the very edge, and you're tempting fate. Let a gust of wind blow from behind, and it's all over!

What does this have to do with investing? Everything!

Risk is a part of life when investing. Risk is a measure of the chance of losing. The greater the risk, the greater the chance of loss.

Risk could be called the great inhibitor. The word fosters fear and anxiety deep within the depths of an investor's gut. Its existence must be understood, but it is not singular. It wears many hats.

There are market risk, purchasing power risk, interest rate risk, reinvestment rate risk, business risk, and financial risk. For foreign stocks, there are additional risks such as country risk and exchange rate risk. That's a great deal of risk to sort through. Fortunately, most risk is already factored into the price of an individual security. However, surprises in the risk arena do occur, and could cause the bottom to fall out. It's the potential surprises which must be considered before you can feel comfortable about any individual investment you make.

You can minimize risk by understanding certain measurements and then by taking certain precautions. Remove the safety nets, and the chances of loss increase. Worse yet, let something unforeseen happen when you are in a vulnerable investment, and you can lose almost everything!

Risk not only affects your investments, it also affects your inner being. For instance, if you invest in something that is riskier than you thought it would be, you might find it difficult to sleep at night. Your entire psyche can (and will) be affected if you take on more risk than you can handle.

With this in mind, it seems to me that a healthy approach to investing would be to learn how to evaluate the potential risks of any investment before investing. In general, a potential investment first must meet your risk tolerance; second, meet your goals; and third, enhance your overall portfolio.

As I've already explained, I believe that no-load mutual funds are the best vehicles for investing in the stock market. There is a great amount of statistical data at your disposal to assist you in making the proper choices from the mind boggling 600-plus no-load mutual funds available. You will learn how to select these funds in chapter 12, but you already know that by now.

Volatility

Volatility is the daily up and down fluctuations (or sharp swings) in the stock market. The degree of volatility is the magnitude and frequency of these moves. Altogether, this determines the relative risk of a particular investment. The disadvantage of volatility is that there is the real chance of losing principal. The advantage of volatility is that the potential for gain is greater than a guaranteed return.

Disadvantages

Volatility can make an investor nervous. If an investor must deal with more risk than he or she is prepared to, then the investor may bail out of the investment at the wrong time. An investor should never purchase an investment that does not meet the criteria of one's time frame, goal, and risk level.

Another disadvantage is that there is no guarantee that a stock fund will return to a previous high price level. In other words, you can lose money.

Advantages

Volatility allows the investor to benefit from dollar-cost-averaging. Historically, the long-term trend of the stock market is up. By investing the same dollar amount at regular intervals, the investor is able to purchase more shares when prices are low.

Volatility is also one of the main reasons an individual invests in the stock market. Investors are rewarded for the higher risk they accept. On average, risky investments return more than safe investments.

Risk and Total Return

I want to share the results of a study conducted by Morningstar and reported in the May 27, 1994 issue of *Morningstar No-Load Funds*. The editor reported what I believe to be profound.

The study showed a powerful relationship between a specific fund's past risk and its future risk. Even though the study included drastic market changes from the beginning of 1984 through the end of 1993, the riskiest funds tended to stay the riskiest, and the safest funds tended to stay the safest throughout the period. There was little change in the risk measure from year to year while there was great variation in a fund's total return from year to year.

The most exciting fact to come from the study was that a fund's historical risk level was an excellent predictor of future total returns. In a bull market, the riskier funds enjoyed the highest returns. In contrast, in a bear market, the riskier funds sustained the greatest losses, but the best of the riskiest funds produced the highest overall returns over the long term. That's the essence of this study, and that's an exciting concept.

Now, the task at hand is to determine which of the riskiest funds have been the best performers in the past. Although there is no guarantee that these funds will continue to perform the best in the future, the study by Morningstar indicates that there is a very high probability they will over the long-term. My Lifetime Investing Plan incorporates the results of this study in its cookbook formula.

Types Of Risk

Risk can be divided into two major areas: systematic and unsystematic. Systematic risk cannot be eliminated by diversifying. It can be thought of as a risk that is part of the *system* of investing. It tends to affect all securities to some extent, rather than being unique to a particular company. This type of risk includes market risk, purchasing power risk, interest rate risk, reinvestment rate risk, foreign country risk, and exchange rate risk. Unsystematic risk can be eliminated by diversifying. This risk is unique to a particular company and includes business risk and financial risk.

Systematic Risks

Market Risk. The market is guaranteed to do one thing—fluctuate. The up-and-down movement of prices is an inherent characteristic of the marketplace. All stocks demonstrate this volatility. In bear markets, when the overall trend and psychology of the marketplace is down, even the best stocks whose fundamentals have not changed may suffer to some extent. This is a very important concept to understand, and there is no way to avoid it unless you do not invest in the equity markets.

Purchasing Power Risk. Rising inflation makes the purchasing power of the dollar decrease over time. (Review chapter 3.) The risk of losing purchasing power occurs when inflation exceeds your after-tax total return from your investments. Since there is always some degree of inflation, there is therefore always some degree of loss of purchasing power over time. The only way to offset this risk is to have an investment portfolio that has a positive return after it is adjusted for inflation.

Interest Rate Risk. Interest rate trends often drive the market. When interest rates are trending down, the equity markets become more attractive and rise in price. Inversely, when interest rates are trending up, the equity markets become less attractive and fall in price. All stocks in all sectors can be affected by interest rates. Therefore, diversifying will do little to offset this risk.

Reinvestment Rate Risk. This risk refers to the dilemma faced by an investor with cash to invest after interest rates have declined. This is particularly important to bondholders with periodic interest payments to reinvest, but also it can affect stockholders who wish to reinvest dividends or capital gains. However, as interest rates are declining, stocks often are becoming more attractive in general.

Foreign Country Risk. Individual foreign countries may have unstable governments, economies based on only a few commodities or industries, or runaway inflation. Their stock markets might be illiquid. Or, their political systems could be subject to scandals and upheavals. Even the healthiest companies within an adverse environment like this could suffer.

Exchange Rate Risk. This relates to the potential loss resulting from changing values of foreign currencies. Here's an example of several scenarios of fluctuating currencies:

If the Japanese stock market were absolutely flat, and the Dollar-to-Yen rate was stable, then U.S. investors in a Japanese mutual fund would see no appreciable change in the value of their fund.

If the value of the U.S. dollar were to drop 10% against the Yen, and the Japanese market continued to remain flat, then the U.S. investor actually would see a 10% rise in the value of his Japanese fund because the value of the Yen appreciated 10% in relation to the U.S. dollar. In this case, the true value of the Japanese market did not change at all, but the share value to the U.S. investor increased in dollar terms.

The reverse is also true. If the dollar were to strengthen 10% against the Yen, and the Japanese market remained flat, the U.S. investor would experience a 10% loss in the value of his Japanese fund solely as a result of the currency exchange rate. This represents the currency risk.

In the real international world, the currency exchange rate fluctuates as well as the underlying value of that country's stock market. When the U.S. dollar is weakening against a foreign currency and that country's stock market is appreciating in value, a U.S. investor will enjoy huge gains. In contrast, if the dollar were strengthening and the foreign market were declining, a U.S. investor would suffer severe losses.

Look at Table 9.1: Exchange Rate Risk. It describes what happens to a U.S. investor's return when the U.S. dollar is either going up (▲) or down (▼) *and* the actual foreign country's stock market is going up (▲) or down (▼) as denominated in its own currency.

For example, if the U.S. dollar is rising (▲) the same percentage against a foreign country's currency as the foreign country's stock market is rising (▲) based on its own currency, then the U.S. investor would not see any movement (—) in the price of his stock fund. It would be a wash.

If the U.S. dollar is rising (▲), and the foreign country's stock market is rising (▲▲) much greater based on its own currency, the U.S. investor would see some gain (▲).

Finally as an example, if the U.S. dollar is falling (▼), and the foreign stock market is rising much greater (▲▲) based on its own currency, then the U.S. investor would enjoy significant gains (▲▲▲).

Unsystematic Risks

Business Risk. A company's success is influenced by many factors one cannot control. These include inexperienced management, poor products, and weak market-

Table 9.1: Exchange Rate Risk

If... US $ is:	And... Foreign Country's Stock Market (based in its currency) is:	Then, US Investor's Return is:
⇑	⇑	—
⇑	⇑⇑⇑	⇑
⇑	—	⇓
⇑	⇓	⇓⇓
⇑	⇓⇓	⇓⇓⇓
⇓	⇑	⇑⇑
⇓	⇑⇑⇑	⇑⇑⇑⇑
⇓	—	⇑
⇓	⇓	—
⇓	⇓⇓	⇓

ing to name a few. Also, the company may not be well established or properly capitalized. Its operating costs may be extremely high. In addition, its stock may be illiquid.

Forces that bear on one industry may not affect another industry. For example, while the communications industry may be affected adversely by government regulations, the healthcare industry could be booming.

Investors can reduce company risk by diversifying among various companies that represent various industry sectors.

Financial Risk. Debt creates financial risk. Excessive debt can make it difficult for a company to repay its obligations, especially if sales decline in an economic downturn for the company. If sales declined significantly, leaving insufficient profits to pay its creditors, a company would be faced with bankruptcy if debt holders foreclosed on the firm's assets.

Chance of Loss in Overall Stock Market

Studies have been done by Norman Fosback at the Institute for Econometric Research. The Institute did a comparison of the chance of losing money in the U.S.

stock market over different time periods from 1871 through 1994. Their model invested equal dollar amounts in all of the stocks of the New York Stock Exchange which provided a well diversified index of stocks. The results were enlightening.

For example, if you only invested during any one-year period between 1871 and 1994 into this diversified mix of stocks, your chance of losing money was 30% on average. If you invested over any three-year period, your risk dropped to 16%. When your time frame increased to five years, the chance of loss declined to 11%. For time horizons of 10 years, the risk fell to only 1%. Then for all time periods above 10 years, the chance of loss was practically 0%!

If you experienced a loss during any one-year period, the average loss would have been 13%. However, if you held a diversified stock market investment for a minimum of 10 years, the average loss (if there were a loss) would have dropped to less than 2% over that period!

Therefore, if your time horizon were over 10 years, your chance of loss in a diversified portfolio of stocks would be almost negligible. Then, if you did experience a loss, the average loss would be very slight. Remember, however, this is for a diversified portfolio of stocks. An individual stock could lose or gain significantly more than the average.

Graph 9.2 depicts the chance of loss your portfolio might experience over time. If your portfolio actually had a loss, Graph 9.3 depicts the percentage of loss your portfolio would suffer over time.

Tools to Identify Risk

You may not be interested in actually using the technical data I am going to describe. Or, you may prefer to leave the choice of funds to your financial advisor. No matter how involved you become with these tools, my Lifetime Investing Plan will set up a process of selecting funds in a cookbook, easy-to-use style. If you are not interest in statistics, then pick up your playing pieces and move onto chapter 10.

Four specific pieces of information can unlock the mystery of a fund's historical risk. It is critical for you to understand that these statistics are based on past performance. There is no guarantee that future performance will duplicate past performance! These statistics are: Standard Deviation, R-squared, Beta, and Alpha.

Standard Deviation

The Standard Deviation (SD) is a statistic which quantifies past volatility. It identifies the variation of a fund's total return above and below its average return. It can be described as 1 SD (Standard Deviation), 2 SDs, 3 SDs. A variation around the mean of *plus or minus* 1 SD has occurred 68% of the time; *plus or minus* 2 SDs occurred 96% of the time; and virtually all variations occurred within *plus or minus* 3 SDs (Graph 9.4: SD). (You can use a financial calculator to determine a standard deviation.)

Graph 9.2: Chance of Loss

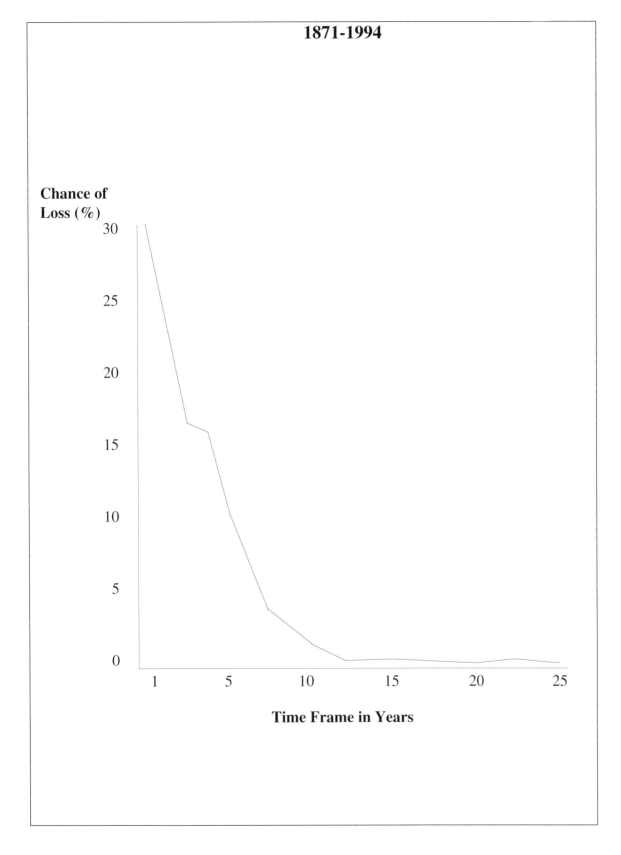

Time Frame in Years

Graph 9.3: If Loss, Average Annual Loss

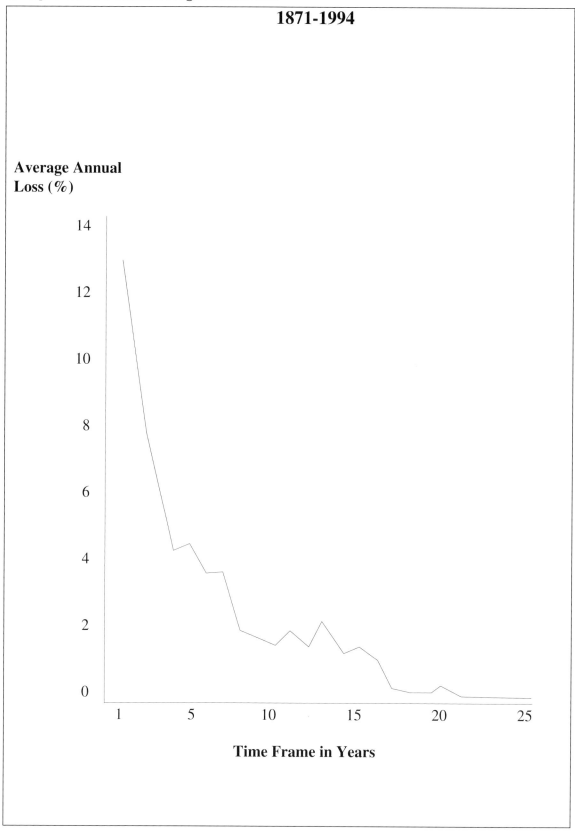

Graph 9.4: SD

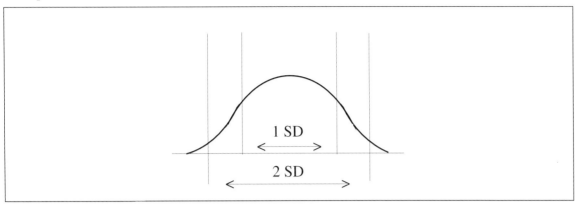

Here's an example:

ABC Fund over the last three years had an average total return of 12.0% and a SD of 5%. XYZ Fund had an average return of 26.0% and a SD of 13%.

ABC Fund varied between 7% and 17%, 68% of the time; between 2% and 22%, 96% of the time; and between -3% and 27% almost 100% of the time.

XYZ Fund varied between 13% and 39%, 68% of the time; between 0% and 52%, 96% of the time; and between -13% and 65% almost 100% of the time.

As you can see, the higher the SD, the greater the historical fluctuation around the mean. Although XYZ Fund has the potential for outstanding returns, it also has the risk for serious losses. While ABC Fund still can produce excellent returns, its downside risk is much less ominous than XYZ Fund. Therefore, from a volatility perspective, ABC Fund might be the better choice.

With the Standard Deviation, you can project a fund's range of performance and its potential for loss into the future. However, as I already stated, there is no guarantee. Furthermore, if a fund's performance does not respond in a typical bell-shaped deviation as shown in Graph 9.4: SD, the SD will not be valid. For instance, if the fund's real performance were skewed to the left or skewed to the right, you could not use this tool to make accurate predictions about the range of performance of the fund.

R-Squared

Some funds move as the market moves; some do not. The S&P 500 Index is generally used as the benchmark index for the U.S. stock market, and other stock funds are compared to the movements of this index. As the S&P 500 Index moves up, some funds almost always move up. On the other hand, some funds appear to have no correlation to the movements of the S&P 500 Index; these funds respond differently. R-squared is a mathematically derived statistic (known as the coefficient of determination) which helps to relate how closely a particular fund moves in relation to its benchmark index. This statistic also can relate one asset category to another.

If all of a fund's movements were attributable to its benchmark index, its R-squared value would be 100. If 25% of a fund's movements were attributable to the

Graph 9.5: R-squared

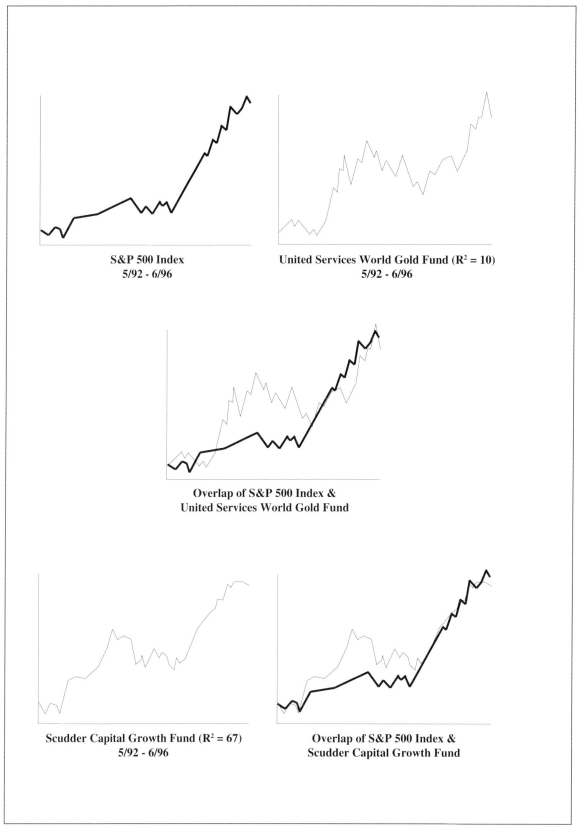

S&P 500 Index
5/92 - 6/96

United Services World Gold Fund ($R^2 = 10$)
5/92 - 6/96

Overlap of S&P 500 Index &
United Services World Gold Fund

Scudder Capital Growth Fund ($R^2 = 67$)
5/92 - 6/96

Overlap of S&P 500 Index &
Scudder Capital Growth Fund

benchmark, its R-squared would be 25. In this case, 75% of the fund's movements would relate to other variables affecting the fund. If the fund had no correlation at all with the benchmark index, its R-squared would be 0 or close to 0. In this case, practically all of the fund's volatility would be the result of factors other than the market risk associated with the benchmark index. This statistic is usually available for all funds which have been in existence for at least three years. (However, you could use a financial calculator to determine this statistic.)

Look at Graph 9.5: R-squared. The S&P 500 Index is compared to United Services World Gold Fund and Scudder Capital Growth Fund. The R-squared for United Services World Gold Fund is 10 because it only has 10% correlation with the S&P 500 Index. In contrast, the R-squared for Scudder Capital Growth Fund is 67 because it has 67% correlation with the S&P 500 Index. To better visualize these correlation factors, the graph of the U.S. World Gold Fund is overlaid on the S&P 500 Index so you can see how they move in different directions at various points in time. Also, the graph of Scudder Capital Growth Fund is overlaid on the S&P 500 Index so you can see how their movements are more closely correlated at different points. The importance of this concept is discussed in chapter 11.

You can see that when R-squared for a fund is high, it means that the fund has a strong correlation with the benchmark index. In this situation, there are two other statistics which have meaning: *Beta* and *Alpha*. It is important to note, however, that Beta and Alpha are not reliable statistics when the R-squared of a particular fund is low.

Beta

Beta measures a fund's relationship to the benchmark index. It measures the relative volatility inherent in a mutual fund against the volatility of the marketplace. It is therefore a measure of the overall market risk that a particular fund exhibits. It does not measure any volatility that is the result of other factors outside of market risk. This is important to understand as I will describe shortly.

By definition, the S&P 500 Index has a Beta of 1.00. If a mutual fund has a Beta of 1.00, it is expected to perform exactly as the S&P 500 Index. If the fund has a Beta of 1.10, it would rise 10% more than the S&P 500 Index and it would decline 10% more than the S&P 500 Index. If the Beta were 0.90, the fund would rise 10% less than the S&P 500 Index, but it would also decline 10% less. Look at Graph 9.6: Beta.

In Graph 9.6, funds X and Y move in tandem with their benchmark index. Fund X has 50% more volatility than the benchmark index, and Fund Y has 50% less volatility than the benchmark index. Therefore, the Beta of Fund X is 1.50, and the Beta of Fund Y is 0.50.

For well diversified stock funds that have high R-squared values, Beta is very useful. However, if one fund has a low correlation to its benchmark index, then the fund's Beta has little value because most of its volatility is a result of factors other than market risk.

Graph 9.6: Beta

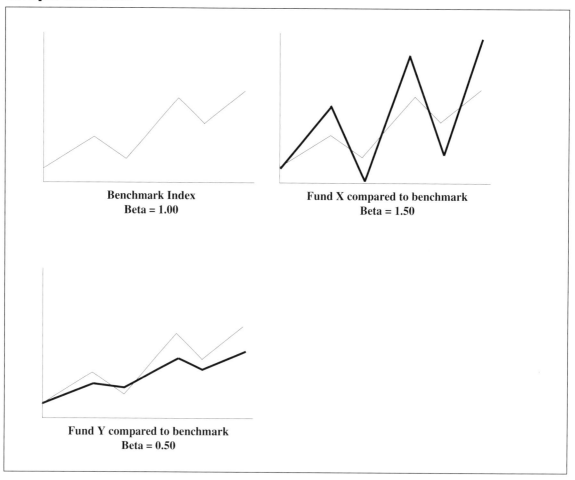

Benchmark Index
Beta = 1.00

Fund X compared to benchmark
Beta = 1.50

Fund Y compared to benchmark
Beta = 0.50

For instance, refer back to Graph 9.5: R-squared. United Services World Gold Fund has an R-squared of 10 relative to the S&P 500 Index. Although its Beta of 1.11 indicates only 11% higher volatility than the S&P 500 Index, this fund actually is one of the most volatile of all stock funds! The reason the Beta has little value in this situation is that there is relatively no correlation between this fund and the index to which it is being compared. Most of the volatility of United Services World Gold Fund comes from unsystematic risks, not market risk.

Alpha

Alpha is a measure of the difference between how a fund actually performs and how it is expected to perform. This measurement is based on the fund's Beta. When Alpha is positive, it indicates that the fund performed better than expected; when it is negative, it indicates that the fund performed worse than expected. (See Graph 9.7: Alpha.) The more positive the number, the better the performance; the more negative the number, the worse the performance. In essence, Alpha describes how successful the fund manager has been in investing the fund's assets.

Graph 9.7: Alpha

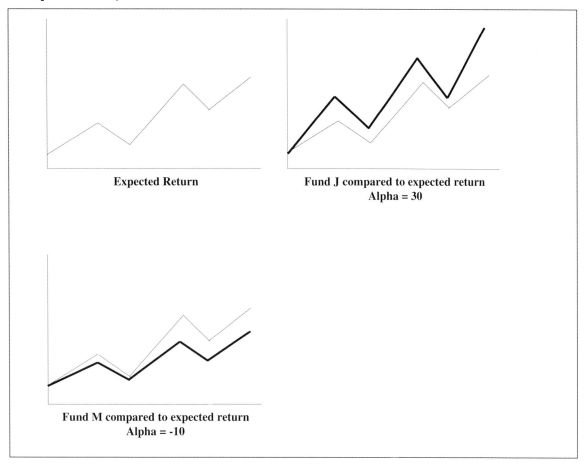

Expected Return

Fund J compared to expected return
Alpha = 30

Fund M compared to expected return
Alpha = -10

In Graph 9.7: Alpha, Funds J and M move in tandem with the benchmark index. Fund J has a management team that has produced better than expected returns, and Fund M has a management team that has produced worse than expected returns.

Once again, Alpha is based on Beta being accurate. If the fund reacts independently from the benchmark index as measured by R-squared, then both Beta and Alpha are not going to be significant statistics in your quest to determine overall risk for that fund.

In summary: The Standard Deviation will tell you how much volatility a particular fund has experienced in the past. A fund's rise and fall within 2 SDs will help you determine if your psychological makeup can tolerate the drops. If you are only investing in one or two funds, find the funds where the volatility is within your comfort level. In my Lifetime Investing Plan you will be investing in five different funds.

The R-squared will provide you with information on how closely correlated a fund is with its benchmark index. For stock funds, the benchmark is the S&P 500 Index. If the R-squared is high for a particular fund, Beta will suggest the degree to which the fund will move in relation to the benchmark index, and Alpha will disclose just how successful the fund manager has been in handling the fund's assets.

Chapter 9

All of these statistics for individual funds can be found in *Morningstar No-Load Funds* which is available in most libraries or by subscription as I have already suggested.

R-squared can also be used to relate one asset category to another. Funds from poorly correlated asset categories can be included in a portfolio; this will help to reduce overall volatility. My Lifetime Investing Plan uses this concept in the framework for the plan.

None of these statistics, however, mean anything until you relate them to how you feel deep inside. In other words, how much risk can you accept before you can't sleep at night? The answers are obviously very personal. The next chapter helps you turn introspective.

What Is Your Personal Investor Profile?

And the Winner is ...

The race to reach financial independence and lifestyle security isn't really a race at all. But, there is a necessary degree of perseverance required to reach these specific financial goals down the road. To be a winner, you need to know what *is* important.

Is it important to invest in the hottest deal in town? *No!* How many stories can you recall of the "hot stock pick" gone bust?

Is it important to seek out last year's best performer? *No!* Studies show that last year's stellar performing mutual fund could easily become this year's dog.

Is it important to wait until the ideal moment before investing? *No!* You can always find some reason not to get started. Procrastination is the number one reason for failure.

Then, what *is* important? Here is my answer: *Start Investing Now!*—simply, mechanically, and regularly. This *is* the critical ingredient.

For example, if you earn $75,000 a year in gross salary, and you plan to work 25 more years at that level, $1.875 million will pass through your hands, then into your pockets, and finally back out of your life. That's a lot of money.

Alarmingly, the facts suggest that 97% of the population will arrive at retirement age with less than an adequate nest egg to maintain their lifestyle. Yet, there is a simple and mechanical doctrine that could assure all concerned individuals that their retirement account could be substantial. It requires doing something slightly differently.

The basic formula for reaching financial independence is pictured in Table 10.1: Formula for Financial Independence. I define financial independence as that point when you can live the lifestyle you have chosen, financed from the assets you have accumulated, without the need for any additional income. Money put into a financial vehicle at regular periods of time and earning a specific rate of return will produce financial independence as long as you have patience and discipline and also allow compounding to work its wonders through reinvestment of all distributions.

If you keep on doing what you always have done, then you'll keep on getting what you always have gotten. Let's break that cycle just slightly. Take 10% off the top of your salary each month, and invest it. What do you think will happen?

Ten percent of $75,000 a year is $7,500. That's approximately $625 a month. Invest this monthly figure in a retirement account of some type such as a SEP-IRA, profit sharing program, 401(k) plan, etc.; and do it for 25 years at 14% a year com-

Table 10.1: Formula for Financial Independence

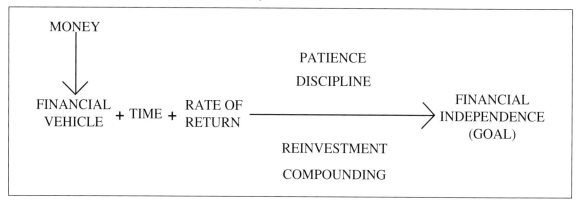

pounded monthly. (Again, I believe you can do this with my Lifetime Investing Plan.)

At the end of 25 years, you will have accumulated more than $1.7 million—almost as much as you earned in gross salary during the entire 25 years! What does this mean?

It means that although you had to work hard for 25 years to earn over $1.875 million, you could actually earn almost as much passively by simply and mechanically investing a small percentage of everything you took home. Amazingly, your life would move along as though you never had reduced your gross salary. You wouldn't miss the 10%. Slow but diligent investing wins.

Just as the tortoise beat out the hare, you could win the race for self sufficiency. You could be confident that the lifestyle you are creating would be secure for the rest of your and your spouse's lives.

The secret to winning the race in this scenario is straightforward.

- Invest 10% of your gross income every year.
- Invest in a vehicle that can provide the total returns you need to have.
- Invest over a long period of time to allow compounding to work its wonders.

If you followed these rules, you would never miss the 10% you took off the top. You would provide for yourself and your spouse, and you would live without financial fear. What a terrific game to play. What a terrific race to win. But, you need to get to know the investor inside of you before you can invest.

The Investor Inside of You

Do you know who you are as an investor? You need to know if you are to be successful. Here are some questions to help you get a grip on the investor inside of you. You may find that you have never been properly introduced to your inner-investor-self. Now is a great time to make the introduction.

Answer the following questions and then refer to the *Interpreting Your Answers* section immediately following. There are no right or wrong answers. You are who you are. This profile helps to bring your feelings to the forefront.

Personal Investor Profile
(answer *yes* or *no*)

1.   Investing and gambling are the same.
2.   I worry about things.
3.   I am comfortable with my decisions.
4.   I usually forget if I locked the door after I leave my home.
5.   I usually invest in those things recommended to me by my friends.
6.   I check the financial newspaper every day to see how well my investments are doing.
7.   Consider the following scenario and then answer accordingly:
     I have invested $10,000 in a good investment. At the end of 12 months, it would be hard for me to accept a loss of:
     A. I could not accept any loss.
     B. $100
     C. $500
     D. $1,000
     E. $2,000
     F. $3,000
     G. $5,000
     H. $7,000
8.   I believe that investment principal should never be jeopardized.
9.   I could add another $1,000 to my original investment of $10,000 even though its value is lower than when I started.
10. When the stock market is going down, I feel my financial goals are threatened.
11. I always buy things on sale.
12. I maintain a balance on my credit cards from month to month.
13. I am in control of my financial destiny.
14. I always have money to save at the end of each month.
15. My stomach gets "in knots" when I see my investment losing money.
16. My children place financial demands on me.
17. I usually invest in those things recommended to me by professional advisors.
18. Investing is a way of securing my financial future.
19. Money is more important to me than anything.
20. I have started a retirement program.
21. I look forward to buying expensive things.
22. I fear the future.
23. I understand that losses are part of investing.
24. I am impressed with wealth.

25. I earn enough money to live the way I want to live.
26. My goals include a bigger home and a more lavish lifestyle.
27. I never pay retail.
28. My spouse places financial demands on me.
29. I am in control of my life.
30. Planning for the future is fun.
31. I want to take personal control of my financial future.

Interpreting Your Answers

(Each number below refers to the question by the same number above.)

1. To reach your long-term goals, you need a system that works for you. You must understand that investing and gambling are not the same. If you fail to see the difference, then you probably would be better suited with fixed-income vehicles rather than stock market investing.

2. If you are the type of person who worries about everything, then the stock market might be an additional irritant to your emotional makeup. You certainly should be concerned when you invest, but if the degree of risk transforms your concern into worry, then your investments are one step beyond your risk level.

3. You need to believe in your decisions. You should act only after you have thought through your options.

4. If you constantly doubt that you have done something that you know you should have done, you may always second-guess your decisions. As an investor, you need to be comfortable with your final decisions to invest based on a well-conceived plan.

5. Your friends may have all the answers. But again, you must be comfortable with your own decisions if you are going to be a successful long-term investor.

6. It is good to be motivated and to monitor your investments so that you can make prudent decisions in a timely fashion. However, daily fluctuations in the stock market mean very little over the long-term.

7. This question directly identifies your comfort level of risk. Even though investing historically has produced an average total return of approximately 12% compounded annually, an investor must be prepared for temporary downturns. How deep of a downturn can you accept without it disturbing your sleep? This is an important concept. Since the stock market could participate in an average drop of 20% to 30% over the course of any twelve-month period, you must be able to accept at least this degree of a setback. If you can't, then on rare occasions the equity markets could cause you great anxiety.

8. If you believe that investing should be so safe that your principal is never at risk, then you should only invest in fixed-income securities of the U.S. government such as U.S. Treasury bills.

9. For investing to be successful, you need to understand the benefits of dollar-cost-averaging. When the cost of a mutual fund is lower than when you originally purchased it, this is a time when an additional investment will buy you even more shares at a lower price per share. Your investment plan will usually require you to invest regularly—no matter if the market is up or down.

10. As I discussed in comment #9, you must understand that the market *will* fluctuate. All statistics are reported as an average. Statistics are based on up cycles as well as down cycles. You can not invest without the market dropping at times. Based on historical averages, long-term investors have done well in the past.

11. This question may seem out of place. However, the stock market is not a place where you will always purchase shares that are greatly discounted. You must invest now. You should not try to time the overall market. Yet, it is always satisfying to purchase assets when they are selling for significantly less than their true value. (Refer to the Relative Value Ratio in chapter 8.)

12. You need to control your spending habits. To invest, you need money. If you are bogged down with debt because of excessive consumption spending, you will have a difficult time finding the money to invest. You must get your debt under control. Some of your most expensive debt (i.e., high interest rates) will be revolving credit card debt.

13. A positive attitude about where you are going financially is important. No one cares more about your money than you.

14. Having excess capital to invest is the fuel to make your financial goals unfold.

15. If you are uncomfortable about your investments, then you are more apt to sell at the wrong time. If your stomach gets in knots, then you are investing in a fashion that is more risky than you can tolerate. Either invest more conservatively or completely avoid the equity markets.

16. We all have financial demands placed upon us. But, are they more than we can handle without undue stress? Only you can manage your own stress. Perhaps your children must be made to understand what you can provide financially and what you can not. Evaluate your priorities and reduce your excessive spending where possible.

17. You must put your trust in others who have a degree of expertise. But, don't always take everything you hear as the gospel. After you get the facts, make sure you understand them and you see how they fit together to help you reach your goals.

18. Investing is definitely one way to secure one's financial future. You have to believe this completely to be a long-term investor.

19. Money is perfect for the things that money can buy. But, money cannot purchase the intangibles of life. Money should only work as your tool; money should never become your master. Put money in its place, and make it work

for you. As P. T. Barnum once said, "Money is a terrible master but an excellent servant."

20. The way to prepare for the future is to begin a retirement plan today. If you haven't yet, this book will show you how.

21. As I have reemphasized in these comments, acquiring material possessions in excess can get in the way of investing for the future. Learn that enough is enough.

22. You will only fear the future if you don't have a plan to control it. This book will help you free yourself of financial fear.

23. A basic tenet of investing is that you will experience losses during your investing life.

24. Too much reliance on money will put pressure on you to become more aggressive with your investments than your personality might allow. As I've already stated, you must not let money become your master. You must always be in control.

25. This is the essence of learning that enough is enough. Only in this way can you find the extra dollars to invest.

26. Your goals are *your* goals. If they are achievable and worthwhile to you, go for them. But, again, don't become overly consumed with only material possessions.

27. Sometimes when you are investing, especially with dollar-cost-averaging, you will pay higher prices for mutual fund shares than at other times. Don't try to guess the market. My Lifetime Investing Plan does not include timing the markets as I've explained earlier.

28. Just as with your children, you need to bring financial *needs* and *wants* into proper perspective. You only should do what you can afford to do. You always must be able to find the sources to make regular payments into your investment vehicles.

29. You are the only one to make it happen for you. Investing will be an extension of your personality.

30. Planning for the future should be fun. If you and your spouse embrace this idea as a challenge with exciting possibilities, it will be fun.

31. An answer of *yes* to this question means you will get a lot out of this book.

Good luck with all your financial goals.

Have you just been introduced to a total stranger, or did you know yourself all along? You should have a better understanding of what degree of risk you can tolerate in the stock market. The stock market is inherently risky. But, for long-term investing, which is what this book is all about, risk can be managed. As I describe asset allocation in chapter 11, you will begin to understand how my plan will keep risk to a minimum. But, and this is a gigantic *but*, risk will always exist. There is no guarantee that unforeseen events will not occur in the future. There is always the possibility of the market entering a severe downturn for a prolonged period of time. This potential must be accepted even if the probability is very low; otherwise, you should not invest in the equity markets!

Your ability to deal with various levels of risk is one of the building blocks of your personal investor profile. Two more concepts that help form your profile are attitude and time.

Attitude is opinion which exists in your mind. Time is fact which exists in reality. Attitude is subjective; time is objective.

Attitude

Earl Nightingale called attitude the "magic" word. By that, Mr. Nightingale meant that your attitude determines what you do and how you do it. Investors' attitudes about the stock market are one of the driving forces behind stock market moves, and an investor's attitude is constantly changing.

Investors may waver between greed and fear based on their attitude. The extremes of greed and fear cause stock prices to vacillate between overbought and oversold conditions. Prices fluctuate between these extremes at different rates. At times, the price of a stock moves slowly over a long period; at other times the price of a stock seems to explode in one direction with tremendous speed. The velocity of this change in price is called momentum, and investor psychology is actually at the core of stock market momentum.

You as an investor must realize that much of the movement in the stock market is due to the psychological forces of investors pushing the market in specific directions. Your personality as it translates into an investing attitude is in play with every other investor's personality. Although the psychology behind the market frequently has nothing to do with the inherent real worth of the companies, mass psychology does affect the price of stocks.

If you join the crowd, you lose your ability to think for yourself. You don't know what you are doing; you just follow the masses. The crowd seems to have all the answers even though the crowd is a stranger.

When investing, following the masses can be dangerous to your financial health. Group allegiance like this usually attracts three types of individuals—the greedy, the thrill-seeker, and the bragger.

The Greedy. Mass psychology is interesting. Every crowd has a leader, and the leader in an investing mob is usually *price*. Investors joining a market bandwagon usually do so because the market price is moving up dramatically or down dramatically. The greedy individual not only jumps aboard because of the potential "big win," but also because he or she has the excessive desire to win *more* and *more*. Of course, this individual joins in only after the majority of the move is over. Greed is attracting this market maven as the price is moving up, yet fear will eat into the same individual as

the price comes crashing down. This investor motivated simply by greed won't know what hit when the market turns against him or her.

The Thrill-seeker. Thrill-seekers are another type of investor lured into the mass movement. These investors are looking for excitement—the excitement of buying and selling with quick turnarounds and quick profits. The thrill of winning produces a great deal of entertainment, but the reality of losing creates a tremendous dose of stomach acidity. Constant action in the marketplace is what keeps this type of investor going. Who needs that kind of entertainment?

The Bragger. Members of this last group become so impressed with success that they can not keep it to themselves. These are the braggers. You can pick them out of any crowd. They are the ones who always hit the big winners. They never seem to have a loser. They always have the right investment, the right broker, and the hottest tip. Also, they are always ready to tell you and the rest of the world about their successes. The truth is that they usually have lost a bundle!

The greedy, the thrill-seeker, and the bragger are usually net losers, not only in investing, but also in life.

There is no reason to participate in this type of mass hysteria. Your attitude should be one of investing for a lifetime. Have *your* own plan of investment that *you* have researched. Understand *why* you are investing and *in what* you are investing. Have a plan to enter and a plan to exit. Leave the emotion completely out of the picture. By investing for the long-term, you also need the courage and confidence to stick with your plan throughout the ups and downs. If others are doing what you are doing, OK! If they are not, that's OK too!

Martin Pring, described in *Barron's Financial Newspaper* as a "technician's technician," has written an outstanding book, *Investment Psychology Explained* which addresses investors and their effects on the market. For information on this book, call The International Institute for Economic Research, Inc. at (800) 221-7514.

Time

When you invest, you are taking steps to reach a financial goal. This may be for retirement, for a child's college education, or for a major purchase. Whatever the goal, each one has a time frame which places certain constraints on your investing technique.

For instance, a planned retirement in twenty years gives you the opportunity to create your nest egg over the course of two decades. A college education that is five years away allows you just five more years to accumulate money before the first tuition bill comes due. Then, if you want to put a down payment on a home in two years, you only have that amount of time to make it happen.

My point is that there are different time frames for different goals, and you will invest differently for each one.

When you have 20 years to invest, you have the luxury of many years to be more aggressive and to take on more risk. You can do this because investing and economic cycles will repeat themselves several times over that holding period.

When you have five years before the first day of college, you still have time to invest. However, you won't have the ability to take advantage of more than one U.S. Business Cycle. (The U.S. Business Cycle is explained in chapter 8.)

When you only have two years before you need the money, you won't have any time to be on the wrong side of the market. In this case, your principal will require a great deal of safety.

What actually is happening inside your head is that you are comparing the risk of losing money against the number of years you have to invest and the total return you can expect from each investment. Your investing temperament may vary between growth-oriented for the long-term to risk-averse for the short-term, and that's how it ought to be.

This book is about long-term investing. For short-term goals up to two or three years, you only may be comfortable with money market funds, short-term bonds, or short-term bond funds. For intermediate-term goals from three to five years, you may lean toward balanced funds and intermediate-term bonds, or intermediate-term bond funds. For goals with time horizons over five years, you should find the Lifetime Investing Plan ideal.

If your profile allows for investing in the stock market, then let me put some more pieces of your brick foundation together in a way that reduces risk but still encourages better than average total returns. These are very special bricks, not the run-of-the-mill types.

CHAPTER 11

Asset Categories
and Asset Allocation

A basket of fruit may be made up of a banana, a pear, an apple, and some grapes. The basket has a variety of fruit, but it is still a basket of fruit. The basket of fruit could be called an asset category. If you added a wrench, a piece of wood, a book, and maybe an airline ticket, it no longer would be a basket of fruit, it would be a basket of unrelated objects. You could say that the basket was now made up of various asset categories.

An asset category is like the basket of fruit. The individual items in the basket may be different, buy they still have a common denominator. Like this basket of fruit, several diversified U.S. growth stock funds are made up of different stocks, but they are essentially all U.S. growth stocks. They all fit into one asset category—U.S. growth stock funds.

Asset categories therefore are separate entities that are similar unto themselves. Aggressive U.S. stock funds are an asset category; growth and income U.S. funds are an asset category; foreign stock funds are an asset category; precious metals funds are an asset category. Within each asset category there can be much diversification, but all of the funds within the category basically have strong relationships to one another by way of their investments.

The importance of an asset category is that each category has specific characteristics which make it either a good or poor investment. Each category relates to another as being highly correlated or poorly correlated. (Review R-squared in chapter 9.) Therefore, an asset category can be chosen because of its investment sector(s), its overall potential for return, and because of its degree of correlation to other asset categories.

Asset allocation is the art of putting unlike asset categories together. Each asset category has its unique qualities; each has little effect over the others. The basket which contains fruit, a wrench, an airline ticket, etc. is a basket of unlike objects. If each object represented an asset category, then the basket would become a portfolio holding various unlike assets. Your portfolio would metaphorically be this basket of unlike objects, and it would demonstrate asset allocation.

As I have described in chapter 9, risk is a major factor scaring investors out of the stock market. The lower the overall risk or volatility, the more comfort the investor will have. Asset allocation helps to reduce risk for the overall portfolio.

Asset allocation can combine volatile funds that move relatively independently of one another. The sharp moves in one direction of one fund can often be offset by the sharp moves in another direction by a different fund. The end result is a less volatile portfolio.

Smoothing Out Volatility

Asset categories that do not correlate well help to offset one another's volatility. In other words, when one *zigs*, the other may *zag*. Let me explain with several illustrations:

Graphs 11.1 and 11.2 show two funds—A and B:

Graph 11.1: Fund A

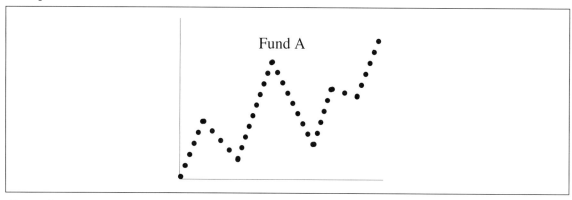

Fund A

Graph 11.2: Fund B

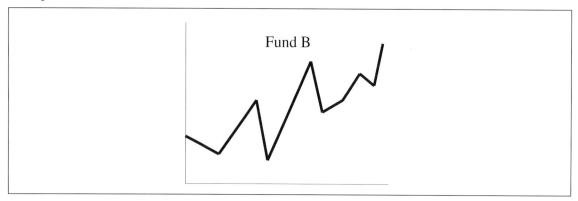

Fund B

Fund A and Fund B tend to move up over the long-term. Let's assume both report an average compounded return rate of 14% annually. Notice how A and B have sharp moves *up* and sharp moves *down*. The sharp swings are the volatility. When a fund's price has a spike *up*, you as an investor feel great, but when the price collapses, your stomach may become tied in knots. In fact, depending on both the depth and duration of the decline, you might bail out of the fund at the wrong moment. That's the problem with volatility—it makes you nervous. Even worse, it makes you sell out at a low point. What's the solution?

Graph 11.3: Funds A & B

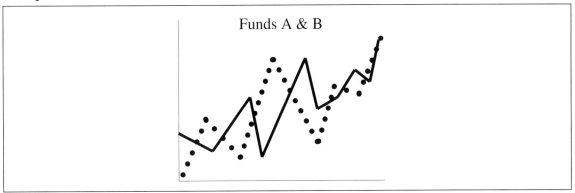

If you look at Graph 11.3, you will notice that Fund A tends to rise and fall at different times from Fund B. In other words, these two funds do not correlate well. Therefore, if you invested equal dollars into each fund at the same time, your portfolio would enjoy a blending of the two funds. Your portfolio would still receive the 14% compounded return, but you would not experience the uneasiness from extremes in volatility.

Graph 11.4: Smoothed Portfolio

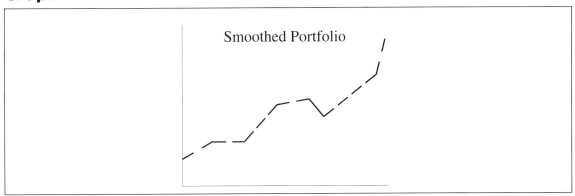

As you can see in Graph 11.4, the portfolio that incorporates both funds has its overall volatility greatly reduced. Through this type of asset allocation, an investor can participate in what might be considered aggressive vehicles yet still have an overall conservative equity investment plan. Since various asset categories are correlated differently to one another, the ideal asset allocation would be to combine those asset classes that historically have excellent long-term total returns and also offset each other's volatility.

For example, U.S. stock funds do not correlate well with foreign stock funds. Within U.S. stock funds, aggressive growth funds do not correlate well with growth funds. Within foreign stock funds, emerging markets funds do not correlate well with established country funds. Two other asset categories that do not correlate with any of these categories are precious metals funds and contrary-style funds.

Aggressive growth funds, growth funds, foreign stock funds, and emerging market foreign stock funds have excellent overall total returns. Precious metals funds do not have good overall total returns, but when they are in a bull trend, they have significant appreciation in value. There is very little data about contrary-style funds because they are so new and there are so few of them to study.

Rationale for Using Aggressive Growth Funds

Of the major asset categories (aggressive growth, growth, growth and income, balanced, bonds, foreign stock, emerging foreign stock, contrary-style), aggressive growth funds have had the highest average total returns over the last ten years. They also have one of the highest risk factors along with foreign stock, emerging foreign stock, and precious metals funds. In addition, they do not correlate well with the S&P 500 Index.

As I indicated in chapter 9, high risk funds tend to outperform the averages over the long-term according to Morningstar. Since the aggressive growth funds have had a high risk level as well as a high average total return over the last ten-year period, this is an excellent category to include in a portfolio.

Rationale for Using Growth Funds

Growth funds have a total return that is close to that of the aggressive growth category over the long-term. Their risk level is slightly below that of the aggressive category. Their correlation with the S&P 500 Index is approximately 65%.

Rationale for Using Foreign Stock Funds of Developed Countries

Foreign stock funds on average have low correlations with the S&P 500 Index. This makes them an excellent choice to help offset volatility. Their risk level is high, and their total return is slightly less than that of growth funds.

Rationale for Using Foreign Stock Funds of Emerging Countries

Emerging foreign stock funds have high risk levels and do not correlate well with either the S&P 500 Index or foreign stock funds of developed countries. They therefore offer excellent diversification to offset volatility. Because of their high risk levels, they have great potential for high returns.

Definition of Emerging Market. In 1981, the International Finance Corporation began tracking the performances of stock markets in emerging countries. These emerging countries were beginning their economic development and possessed at least one of the three following characteristics:

- The country has a low or middle per capita income. In 1994, the World Bank classified countries with less than $8,955 (U.S. dollars) of per capita gross income as an emerging country.
- The country has an economy that has not been industrialized. Such assets as adequate roads, telephones, and power generators are lacking.
- The country is underdeveloped in its financial infrastructure. The total market capitalization of the emerging country's stock market is only a small percentage of its Gross Domestic Product.

From these criteria, the International Finance Corporation found that 170 countries could be considered emerging countries as compared to 30 countries that were considered developed countries. Most of the emerging countries were located in Asia, Latin America, and Eastern Europe. Other emerging countries were located in Africa and the Middle East.

Largest Emerging Countries. China has more than 1.2 billion people and almost 3.7 million square miles of land. An example of how undeveloped this country is China which has one telephone for every 77 people. In the United States there is one telephone for every 1.3 people.

India has more than 900 million people with more than 1.2 million square miles of land. It provides only one telephone for every 131 people.

Investment Opportunities. The opportunity to make money in emerging countries is based on several factors. Higher returns on investment than from developed countries are possible because these developing economies are growing rapidly. Industries that are considered mature in the United States (like banking, construction, and telecommunications) barely exist in the emerging countries. Most of these countries depend on their exports for economic growth. Their low wages, highly skilled workers, and abundance of natural resources often provide the sources for a competitive edge.

Since the stock markets in the emerging countries are not efficiently set up, there are frequently stocks that go unrecognized by the investing public for a long time. When an astute fund manager can pick out these "sleepers" and include them in a fund's portfolio, there can be tremendous potential to the upside if the company continues to do well and the rest of the investing world discovers the stock.

However, along with the tremendous potential comes tremendous risk. It is not unusual for a market to be up 100% and then nose dive. For instance, the average emerging market fund was up as high as 85.6% in 1993, but down as low as -24.1% in 1994. For individual countries within the fund, the ups and downs are much more volatile.

The risks that encompass investing in the emerging asset category include more than just the volatility I've already described. There are also illiquidity, currency devaluations, and unanticipated political/economic developments. At times, it is difficult to sell thinly traded securities. When unexpected devaluations occur in a country's currency, major market sell-offs can occur. Also, political upheavals such as coups and drastic government policy changes can make an already illiquid market more helpless and vulnerable to collapse.

Rationale for Using Precious Metals Funds

Precious metals funds have the highest risk levels of all funds, but their total returns are not high. However, when they are in a bull market, they generate very high returns. Precious metals funds are often considered an excellent category when rising inflation is above normal levels. Their correlation with the S&P 500 Index and most other categories is extremely low which helps to offset other funds' volatility. This category of funds can be used instead of the Contrary-style category.

Rationale for Using Contrary-style Funds

An additional category which is relatively new is the contrary-style category. Very few funds can actually be included in this division. However, it offers several unique qualities.

Contrary-style funds have the ability to short overvalued markets, indexes, and stocks. Because of this, these funds offer the unusual ability to move in the opposite direction of other fully invested funds at important turning points in the markets. Contrary-style funds may also invest heavily in the precious metals sector. For these reasons, this category is an excellent replacement for the precious metals category.

Contrary-style funds do not guarantee they will be able to pick the turning points of the market. But, by investing in an opposite way from the masses when the market is statistically and historically overvalued, this asset category can offset the volatility of the more aggressive stock funds at the top of a bull market.

By objective, these types of funds attempt to achieve maximum long-term growth of capital. As I stated, they manage risk in their portfolios with put options and short sales. Usually, stocks of companies that represent out-of-favor asset categories or ones that are visionary in their thinking are prime picks for these funds.

I have metaphorically referred to your financial foundation as the laying down of bricks—quality bricks upon quality bricks. Only the best of available bricks will do. Chapter 12 describes the methods to choose the best no-load mutual funds for each of the asset categories. These will be the best of the best bricks.

How to Choose the Best No-Load Mutual Funds

No one can predict the future, and I don't want any reader to get the false impression that I can help you choose those funds that always will produce excellent results in the future. The best I can do for you (as I do for myself) is to help you identify those funds which have been historically excellent performers within their respective asset categories over a significantly long period of time—namely three to five years. These funds that also have the highest risk levels in their asset categories (see chapter 9 regarding the Morningstar study, May 27, 1994.)tend to perform well into the future, but there is no guarantee they will continue to perform well.

One fundamental factor which can change the reliability of a well performing fund is the replacement of a manager. When the management team is no longer in place, the fund is basically not the same fund from which the statistics were gathered. Another fundamental problem can develop when the fund gets too large and managing the tremendous inflow of cash becomes too difficult for the fund manager.

An excellent source to use to choose your funds is *The Individual Investor's Guide to Low-Load Mutual Funds*. This is published by the AAII. Membership in the AAII will bring this publication to you every March in addition to their monthly journal. Call (800) 428-2244 for information.

Using the *Guide*, go to the section called *Fund Performance Rankings*. There will be a listing of the funds in the major asset categories and their total returns for the last three-, five-, and 10-year periods. Also noted are their total risk ratings.

The three categories in the *Guide* in which I am interested for the Lifetime Investing Plan are aggressive growth, growth, and international stock. The *Guide* does not break down the international stock category into foreign and emerging markets. It also does not classify contrary-style funds as a separate asset category. However, I make this distinction for you in Appendix III because the Lifetime Investing Plan requires selections from the following categories: aggressive growth, growth, foreign stock, emerging foreign stock, and contrary-style.

To choose the best performing and riskiest funds, select only the no-load funds with the highest total returns in each asset category over the last three- and five-year periods. Do not include any low-load funds. The 10-year period is useful but not used in this exercise.

After you have narrowed your selection of funds for each category, then choose those funds from each category with a *category risk level* of *above average* or *high*. You will wind up with the best performing and riskiest funds over the last three and five-year periods. You only will need one or two funds from each category to use for the Lifetime Investing Plan.

Table 12.1: AAII Guide is a reprint of the aggressive growth pages in the 1996 edition of *The Individual Investor's Guide to Low-Load Mutual Funds.*

Table 12.1: AAII Guide reprint page from AAII Guide*

Aggressive Growth Funds
Ranked by 1995 Total Returns

Fund Name	Annual Return (%)				Category Risk	Total Risk
	1995	3yr	5yr	10yr		
Fidelity Sel Electronics	68.9	37.7	35.1	12.7	high	high
Fidelity Sel Air Transportation	59.5	17.7	19.0	11.1	high	high
INVESCO Strat Port—Health Sci	58.8	13.6	19.4	22.8	high	high
T Rowe Price Science & Tech	55.5	30.7	33.5	na	high	high
T Rowe Price New Horizons	55.4	23.9	26.2	14.4	av	high
Fidelity Sel Home Finance	53.4	26.1	39.1	21.0	av	high
Fidelity New Millennium	52.1	24.1	na	na	blw av	high
Fidelity Sel Computers	51.6	33.0	30.2	16.3	high	high
SteinRoe Capital Opportunities	50.7	24.3	26.2	14.3	av	high
Scudder Development	50.6	15.7	21.2	14.4	abv av	high
PBHG Growth	50.3	32.1	35.0	22.7	high	high
USAA Aggressive Growth	50.2	17.2	20.4	12.0	abv av	high
IAI Emerging Growth	49.5	19.8	na	na	abv av	high
Fidelity Sel Biotechnology	49.1	7.1	17.0	16.8	high	high
PBHG Emerging Growth	48.4	na	na	na	na	na
Fidelity Sel Defense & Aerospace	47.3	24.5	19.6	7.8	blw av	abv av
Warburg Pincus Emerging Grth	46.2	19.3	24.4	na	av	high
Twentieth Century Vista	46.1	17.2	22.3	17.0	high	high
Fidelity Sel Software & Comp	46.0	24.8	30.9	19.4	high	high
Fidelity Sel Health Care	45.8	21.9	22.4	20.4	abv av	high
INVESCO Strat Port—Tech	45.7	20.8	29.9	20.4	abv av	high
Fidelity Sel Technology	43.6	27.1	28.8	13.8	abv av	high
Robertson Stephens Value + Growth	42.6	28.7	na	na	abv av	high
Oberweis Emerging Growth Portfolio	42.5	14.7	26.2	na	abv av	high
WPG Tudor	41.1	13.0	17.2	13.1	abv av	high
CGM Capital Development	41.0	11.8	26.7	19.2	high	high
INVESCO Strat Port—Environm'l	41.0	6.0	2.5	na	av	high
Fidelity Sel Energy Service	40.8	19.6	6.2	4.9	high	high
Bull & Bear Special Equities	40.4	10.9	19.7	na	high	high
Fidelity Growth Company	39.6	16.6	20.4	16.9	low	abv av
Twentieth Century Giftrust	38.3	27.2	35.1	24.1	high	high
Fidelity OTC Port	38.2	13.3	20.0	15.7	low	abv av
Twentieth Century Ultra	37.6	17.3	25.0	19.8	abv av	high
INVESCO Dynamics	37.5	17.1	24.8	15.4	blw av	abv av
Evergreen—Class Y	37.1	13.6	17.4	11.8	low	av
Founders Frontier	37.0	15.7	20.3	na	av	high
Value Line Leveraged Growth	37.0	15.3	16.9	14.3	blw av	high
Kaufmann	36.8	20.8	28.6	na	av	high
Fidelity Sel Food & Agriculture	36.6	16.3	17.5	18.9	low	abv av
Cappiello-Rushmore Emerging Growth	35.9	15.7	na	na	high	high
Fidelity Emerging Growth	35.9	17.6	24.1	na	abv av	high
Baron Asset	35.2	21.5	22.3	na	blw av	abv av
Montgomery Small Cap	35.1	14.7	26.9	na	abv av	high
Salomon Brothers Capital	34.7	10.6	13.6	10.2	av	high
Berger Small Company Growth	33.8	na	na	na	na	na
T Rowe Price OTC	33.8	16.6	20.1	10.7	low	av
Fidelity Sel Multimedia	33.7	24.2	26.2	na	blw av	high
Marshall Mid-Cap Stock	33.7	na	na	na	na	na
SIT Growth	33.6	13.0	18.5	14.7	av	high
Strong Common Stock	32.4	18.1	25.6	na	low	abv av

* 1996 American Association of Individual Investors™, 625 N. Michigan Ave, Chicago, IL 60611; (312) 280-0170

Now you are ready to put the finishing touches on the best brick foundation that money can create. All of the loose ends will now come together. Chapter 13 is like a checklist to make sure you haven't forgotten anything that is important. It flows!

Table 12.1: AAll Guide reprint page from AAll Guide (continued)

Aggressive Growth Funds
Ranked by 1995 Total Returns

Fund Name	Annual Return (%)				Category Risk	Total Risk
	1995	3yr	5yr	10yr		
Fidelity Fifty	32.2	na	na	na	na	na
Fidelity Sel Medical Delivery	32.2	18.6	20.8	na	high	high
Loomis Sayles Small Cap	32.0	14.7	na	na	blw av	abv av
Founders Discovery	31.2	10.3	20.2	na	av	high
Dreyfus Special Growth—Investor	30.4	8.5	15.8	11.4	av	high
Chesapeake Growth	30.2	22.9	na	na	abv av	high
INVESCO Emerging Growth	30.0	15.5	na	na	av	high
Heartland Value	29.8	16.1	27.2	14.3	low	abv av
Dreyfus New Leaders	29.7	14.9	19.2	13.9	low	abv av
Columbia Special	29.3	17.1	22.4	18.4	low	abv av
Value Line Special Situations	28.9	13.7	14.4	8.4	abv av	high
Fidelity Sel Constr'n & Hous'g	28.7	13.0	19.3	na	blw av	abv av
Vanguard Index Trust—Small Cap	28.7	14.9	21.1	10.6	low	abv av
Fidelity Sel Consumer Products	28.3	14.1	17.4	na	blw av	high
Wasatch Aggressive Equity	28.1	18.3	21.1	na	blw av	abv av
Fairmont	27.9	16.6	20.5	8.6	abv av	high
Fidelity Sel Industrial Equipment	27.9	23.6	21.7	na	av	high
Schwab Small-Cap Index	27.6	na	na	na	na	na
Janus Enterprise	27.2	17.0	na	na	blw av	abv av
Fidelity Sel Leisure	26.9	18.1	20.5	14.8	blw av	abv av
Vanguard Explorer	26.5	13.6	20.9	10.4	low	abv av
Janus Venture	26.4	13.3	18.2	17.0	low	abv av
Safeco Growth	26.1	14.8	19.0	12.4	av	high
Fidelity Sel Environ'l Serv	26.0	4.2	3.7	na	av	high
Founders Special	25.6	11.5	19.7	15.8	av	high
Fidelity Sel Broker & Invest Mgmt	23.5	15.1	23.9	8.6	abv av	high
Legg Mason Spec Inv'mt—Primary Cl	22.5	9.7	16.2	12.5	av	high
Northern Small Cap Growth	22.5	na	na	na	na	na
GIT Equity—Special Growth	22.1	10.4	12.5	10.4	low	av
Fidelity Sel Paper & Forest Prod	21.9	18.1	20.0	na	abv av	high
Berger One Hundred	21.3	11.1	22.9	18.7	blw av	high
Twentieth Century Growth	20.3	7.1	14.7	14.2	blw av	high
Robertson Stephens Emerging Growth	20.2	11.6	16.5	na	high	high
INVESCO Strat Port—Energy	19.7	9.0	1.6	5.3	abv av	high
SteinRoe Special	18.7	11.3	16.1	14.7	low	abv av
Fidelity Sel Dev'ping Communic'ns	17.3	21.2	27.4	na	high	high
Caldwell & Orkin Aggressive Growth	16.5	9.8	na	na	low	av
INVESCO Strat Port—Leisure	15.7	14.2	22.9	18.2	blw av	abv av
Fidelity Sel Industrial Materials	15.3	14.8	18.2	na	av	high
Fidelity Sel Transportation	15.1	15.6	24.1	na	low	abv av
Merger	14.1	12.9	12.1	na	low	low
Fidelity Sel Automotive	13.4	10.2	21.1	na	blw av	high
Fidelity Sel Retailing	11.9	6.3	19.7	16.1	blw av	high
Crabbe Huson Special	10.7	18.5	21.0	na	blw av	high
Evergreen Limited Market—Class Y	10.3	2.6	12.4	10.5	low	abv av
American Heritage	-30.5	-14.0	8.2	na	high	high
Aggressive Growth Fund Average	**33.4**	**16.3**	**20.9**	**14.5**	**av**	**high**

Put it All Together— Lifetime Investing Plan

Dr. Van K. Tharp, a research psychologist in Raleigh, NC, has developed the *Investment Psychology Inventory*. His research has identified that a losing investor is frequently someone who:

1. Is highly stressed and has little protection from stress,
2. Has a negative outlook on life and expects the worst,
3. Has a great deal of conflict in his or her personality,
4. Blames others when things go wrong,
5. Is a crowd follower, and
6. Is impatient and wants action *now!*

Dr. Tharp goes on to suggest that the major problems most investors face are dealing with risk, coping with stress, resolving internal conflicts, overcoming emotions when investing, and making decisions. One solution, according to Dr. Tharp, is to adopt an investing program that gives you simple, mechanical rules on which to act—rules that you can recognize and feel good about. Dr. Tharp also adds that your rules must give you a positive expectancy and that you must practice sound money management.

Any tested investment plan which creates order in your investing life can help you become a successful investor. Order, when it comes to investing, involves buying *low* and selling *high*.

Buy Low—Sell High

This is an adage that has been used one too many times in the financial world, "Buy low; sell high." Every investment counselor says that this is what you should do. Every money manager tells you that this is what he or she can do for you. The reality is that it usually doesn't happen. Why?

The reason is that no one can know for sure that the low at which one buys is not going to be undercut by a lower low in just another week or so. Also, on the other end, no one can be sure that the high at which one sells is not going to be overcome by a higher high. More importantly, the low at which one buys may turn out to be a high if you sell at a lower low for a loss! (Did I confuse you with this gymnastic verbiage?) So, how can an investor buy low and sell high?

Conceptually you know, "If I could purchase an investment for a low price and sell it for a higher price, I would make money." Here is how the Lifetime Investing Plan helps you do just that.

Dollar-Cost-Averaging

While dollar-cost-averaging does not have any relationship to selling, it does assist with buying. The money you invest in a mutual fund will buy more shares when the price of the fund is low than it will when the price of the fund is high. The additional shares that you purchase at a lower price provide you with leverage. As the fund price eventually rises, you have more shares working for you, increasing the total value of your portfolio accordingly.

Annual Portfolio Balancing

Consider the following analogy. You have three buckets which fill with water at different rates. After a set period of time, each bucket has filled to a different level with water. If you poured water from the fuller-buckets into the less-full-buckets until all three water levels were the same again, you would be taking water out of the high buckets and adding it to the low buckets. Now, think of your mutual funds as collection buckets.

At the end of each year, each fund would be filled to a different level with dollars (total value of fund). One fund may be much fuller than another because it appreciated more than the rest. Sell some of the shares of this fund, and then purchase more shares of the less-full funds (i.e., those whose fund shares are selling at a lower price). By equalizing the total value of all of your funds in this way, you will mechanically take advantage of the investor's dream—you will be selling high and buying low.

By realigning your portfolio annually, you always will be taking some profits. When the sluggish funds start to outperform the others, you will have many more shares purchased at much lower prices appreciating in value. This leverage will help that fund fill with dollars (increase in value) rapidly. When it comes time to realign your funds again, you will have many more shares to sell at a higher price. (Selling funds in a taxable portfolio will trigger a taxable event. I will describe how to overcome this when balancing later in this chapter.)

Lifetime Investing Plan

Table 13.1 lists the eight steps which are the foundation of my Lifetime Investing Plan. You first saw them in the Introduction to whet your investing appetite. These steps bring together the concepts that I have presented up to this point and should create order in your investing life. For the remainder of this chapter, I will discuss each step. I will also provide an example of how this plan has worked over the last 11 1/2-year period. Then at the end of this chapter I will suggest a way to share the Lifetime Investing Plan with your friends and family.

1.   Select Best And Riskiest No-Load Funds From Five Asset Categories.

The five asset categories I have chosen for the Lifetime Investing Plan are Aggressive Growth, Growth, Foreign Stock, Emerging Foreign Stock, and Contrary-Style.

Table 13.1: LIP (Lifetime Investing Plan)

---

1.   Select the best performing and riskiest no-load mutual funds over the last 3- and 5-year periods from each of 5 distinct asset categories.

2.   Establish an account with a discount broker.

3.   Dollar-cost-average equally into each fund on a regular basis, ideally monthly.

4.   Once a year, determine if your current funds continue to satisfy Rule #1. If not, make the necessary changes.

5.   Equalize the dollar amounts in each fund at the end of the first 12 months of investing.

6.   Continue to Dollar-Cost-Average monthly for the next 12 months.

7.   Once every 12 months, repeat the process starting with Rule #4.

8.   As your need for income develops, liquidate a specific percentage of your portfolio equally across all asset categories, and move needed cash into a money market account.

How are asset categories chosen and why? Categories are selected that do not correlate well with one another, have better than average total returns over the last 10-year period, and have higher than average risk.

I evaluate most of these categories using the *Morningstar No-Load Funds* monthly newsletter. (Morningstar does not recognize contrary-style as a separate category because it is difficult to define and because there are so few funds to fit the category.) The newsletter is published in two sections every month. The first section, the *Summary Section*, has statistics regarding all of the funds in general. The second section, the *Analysis Section*, reviews in detail a segment of all of the funds monitored. Every fund has a detailed, full-page update once every four months.

In the *Summary Section*, the Performance Close-Ups subheading lists all of the asset categories and their total returns over the last three-, five-, and 10-year periods. I am concerned about long-term results, so I only use the 10-year data. The main reason for this is that I want to be sure several business cycles have been taken into account in the data. Since the U.S. business cycle is approximately four years long, the 10-year data will usually include at least two full cycles of volatility.

Another subheading in the *Summary Section* important to me is the Benchmark Averages. There is a great deal of information here, but my emphasis is on the Risk and R-squared statistics.

If you remember in chapter 9, I described a study that Morningstar reported where the riskiest funds tended to be the best performing funds over the long-term. In the Benchmark Averages, the risk levels of all major asset categories are listed.

The R-squared statistic in the Benchmark Averages refers to the correlation of the various asset categories to the S&P 500 Index (if it is an equity asset category) or to the Lehman Brothers Aggregate Bond Index (if it is a fixed-income asset category). A high number means there is a strong correlation to the Index; a low number means there is little correlation to the Index.

The Contrary-style category is unique as I discussed in Chapter 11. It has minimal correlation to each of the other four categories. In addition, when market risk affects all securities, this category has the ability to buck the trend or at least soften the blow. The reason is that up to approximately 25% of the assets in a contrary-style fund can be invested in short positions. An example are puts against the S&P 500 Index. When the market is dropping, the S&P 500 puts will be increasing in value.(Puts make money when their underlying security is declining in value.)

Selecting the best and riskiest no-load funds. The best performing and riskiest funds within each of the five selected categories are chosen. You could use the *Morningstar's No-Load Funds* or the *Individual Investor's Guide to Low-Load Mutual Funds*. I describe how to select these funds from the *Guide* in chapter 12.

Table 13.2 lists the two best performing and riskiest funds in each of the five asset categories that make up the Lifetime Investing Plan. The statistics are current as of June 30, 1996.

2. Establish Account

Once you've made a commitment to make my Lifetime Investing Plan your Lifetime Investing Plan, you must establish your account. You could open up an account with each individual mutual fund company with which you choose to invest. However, the easier and quicker way would be to use one discount broker to handle all of your transactions for all of your funds with just one phone call.

Most discount brokers offer no-transaction-fee funds, and this list is changing all of the time. The term *no-transaction-fee funds* mean that the discount broker charges you *nothing* to buy or sell these funds for your account or to reinvest all distributions.

Before you say that I must be crazy, let me tell you how the broker is compensated. The fund pays a small commission from its general expenses to the discount broker to handle all of this paperwork. This saves the fund time and money, and it gives the fund more exposure to the general investing public. Also, the discount broker makes money when you have cash parked in the broker's money market fund waiting to be invested.

Table 13.2: The Best Of Each Category

Over 3 & 5 Year Periods
Through 6/30/96

Category Name	Phone #	Risk	annual compounded total return (%) 6/30/96 3 yr.	5 yr.
U.S. Aggressive Growth				
PBHG Growth	800-809-8008	HIGH	35.3%	32.0%
SteinRoe Capital Opportunity	800-338-2550	ABOVE AVERAGE	33.8%	26.5%
U.S. Growth				
Founders Growth	800-525-2440	ABOVE AVERAGE	22.5%	20.8%
William Blair Growth	800-742-7272	AVERAGE	20.8%	18.8%
Foreign stock				
USAA International	800-531-8181	AVERAGE	14.1%	13.1%
Warburg Pincus Int'l Equity	800-257-5614	ABOVE AVERAGE	14.5%	12.5%
Emerging foreign stock				
Lexington Worldwide Emerging Mkts	800-526-0056	ABOVE AVERAGE	11.0%	9.3%
Montgomery Emerging Markets	800-572-3863	HIGH	11.6%	NA
Contrary-style				
(This category is relatively new and does not have long-term return data.)				
Robertson Stephens Contrarian	800-766-3863	HIGH	26.2% (1 Year)	
Lindner Bulwark	314-727-5305	HIGH	20.8% (1 Year)	

If the fund you want to use is not part of the no-transaction-fee list of funds, then the discount broker will charge a small fee to handle your transaction. This fee varies among discount brokers and is subject to change.

I am going to outline the steps to set up an account using a discount broker.(Look at Table 13.3). I list 13 discount brokers who offer no-transaction-fee mutual funds from various fund families. Call brokers to see which offer the services in which you are interested and get their most current list of no-transaction-fee funds. This list changes constantly. In my example below, I'll use Charles Schwab:

A. Call Charles Schwab at (800) 435-4000. (This is just an example. You should call various discount brokers to get their full range of services.)

- Request information on their mutual fund program.
- For tax-deferred accounts, request information for an IRA or whatever qualified plan over which you have control.
- For regular accounts, request information for a personal account.
- If you will be setting up an account for someone else, and you want to have control over the account, also request a *limited power of attorney form*. A limited power of attorney will give you permission to call the broker about the account and make telephone transactions to buy and sell for that account. If this form is not on file with the broker, you cannot make inquiries about the account and you cannot make any transactions for the account. (For Mike and Jodi, each has limited power of attorney over each other's account so that either one can call the broker to make the necessary changes when necessary for both accounts at one time.)

B. Complete the application form.

- Answer all questions.
- Select either the government money market (which is taxable for federal income tax but not for state income tax) or the tax-free money market (which is not taxable for federal income tax but usually is taxable for state income tax) in which to *park* cash. Usually, the tax-free money market will have a lower yield than the taxable money market.
- Be sure to *check off* that you want telephone switching privileges. This allows you to call the broker to request that your fund shares be sold and switched to the money market account and vice versa as you see fit.
- Be sure to *check off* that all interest, dividends and capital gains should be reinvested. This is offered by all mutual funds and brokers, and it makes compounding simple.
- Return the form to Schwab with your initial check to open the account.

C. Determine the mutual funds in which you are interested.

- Choose from those funds as I've described from the appropriate asset category.
- Call the broker and request a prospectus and a "statement of additional information." These are detailed documents. They will identify the fund's specific objectives, its style of investing, the risks involved, and the overall operation of the fund.
- Also request the most recent reports. These may be quarterly, semiannual, or annual. The reports will be more readable than the prospectus and the statement of additional information. They will generally have personal comments from the fund manager describing his or her opinions about market condi-

tions, how the fund is exploiting these conditions, and how the fund is expected to perform in the future. There will also be a discussion of the recent performance of the fund, a list of all the securities in the fund, and the fund's financial statement.

D. Read the prospectus, the "statement of additional information," and reports before investing (see Appendix IV)..

- You will learn the specific objectives of each fund as well as all the risks involved with the fund's particular style of investing from the prospectus.
- You will learn how the fund manager views the investing climate as well as which specific securities constitute the fund's assets from the annual or quarterly report.
- Remember, these funds are not being purchased alone. Only the appropriate ones will become a part of your total portfolio.

E. Tell Schwab what you want to do.

- Schwab is available by telephone 24 hours a day, 7 days a week as are many of the discount brokers.
- Tell them how much you want to switch from your money market account into each fund in which you wish to invest.
- Schwab as well as many other discount brokers offers many funds with no-transaction-fees. For all others, Schwab will charge a minimal transaction fee.

F. Begin an automatic investment program with Schwab.

- Every month, you should dollar-cost-average (described in chapter 4). Dollar-cost-averaging is the best way to invest over the long-term. It allows you to invest the same dollar amount regularly. You actually purchase fewer shares when the price is high and more shares when the price is low. For example, send Schwab $500 every month to be deposited into your money market account. When enough has accumulated, call Schwab and purchase shares for the mutual funds in your portfolio based on the percent allocation that you have indicated.
- You could arrange for Schwab to transfer a specific amount of money from your money market fund to each of your selected funds on a regular basis. This takes the burden off of you to remember to make the transfers. But, you will still have to remember to make regular deposits into the money market fund at Schwab.

G. Transfer other accounts to Schwab.

- Call Schwab and request a transfer form if you want to put other similar types of accounts under one roof.

- Once you fill out the form and return it to Schwab, Schwab will handle the entire transfer for you.

H. Monitor Your Results.

- In chapter 14, there are tables to help you track your mutual fund portfolio monthly. These tables will help you stay in tune with what your investment is doing for you. This type of motivation keeps you interested and alert— ready to make changes when necessary.

That's it. Schwab will send you a confirmation statement for each transaction. They will also send you monthly statements summarizing all activity in your portfolio.

3. Dollar-Cost-Average Regularly.

Refer to chapter 4 to review the concept of dollar-cost-averaging. For my Lifetime Investing Plan, I recommend monthly investing. The regularity of monthly investing helps reinforce the habit of investing as well as to take advantage of the market's volatility.

If monthly investing is not an option for you for whatever reasons, that's OK. But, try to determine the frequency that will work best for you, and stick to it. Your future financial goals are based on accumulating a specific amount of money. If you are using the Lifetime Investing Plan to reach your goal, then you should discipline yourself to dollar-cost-average.

Table 13.3: Discount Brokers with No-Transaction-Fee Funds

Broker	Phone Number	# of No-Transaction-Fee Funds	Broker Minimum Purchase	On-Line Trading Available
AccuTrade	800-882-4887	662	$200	yes
Barry Murphy & Co.	800-221-2111	330	none	no
Charles Schwab	800-435-4000	577	$1,000	yes
Fidelity Brokerage Services	800-544-8666	432	$2,500	yes
Jack White & Co.	800-233-3411	817	none	yes
Kennedy, Cabot & Co.	800-252-0090	196	none	no
Lombard Institutional	800-688-3462	385	$500	yes
Muriel Siebert	800-872-0711	474	none	yes
National Discount Brokers	800-888-3999	395	$5,000	no
PC Financial Network	800-825-5723	391	$5,000	yes
USAA Brokerage Services	800-531-8628	317	$2,000	no
Waterhouse Securities	800-934-4443	391	none	no
York Securities	800-221-3154	457	none	no

4. Annual Maintenance.

You need to do some housekeeping once a year. Pick a date each year, and determine if your current funds continue to satisfy Rule #1. It doesn't matter what date you choose, but be consistent. Make this mechanical, and stick with the same date each year.

If any of your current funds do not meet the specifications under which you chose it in the first place, consider replacing it. When you call your discount broker to balance your asset categories as I describe in #5 next, that would be the ideal time to tell the broker to sell the funds which are not meeting your rules and purchase the funds that do. (Remember, whenever you sell shares in a taxable account, there will be potential taxes to pay on the gains.)

5. Balance Asset Categories.

How often do you, or does someone else, perform normal maintenance on your car? You probably have a set pattern to do certain things to keep it running smoothly and in balance.

For example, if you were realigning your car's front end, you would go through the mechanical process of putting it back into balance. There's a similar type of balancing that you can do with your investment portfolio—especially since it is invested in no-load mutual funds. Mutual funds allow you to buy and sell fractions of shares with just a telephone call.

Following the Lifetime Investing Plan over the course of a year, you would dollar-cost-average into your funds based on the percentage breakdown already discussed. Also over the course of the year, some funds would have performed much better than others. Those that excelled would now be worth more than their ideal percentages would suggest, and those that lagged would now be worth less than their ideal percentages.

In order to balance your portfolio, you must take money out of the funds that had the greatest advances and reinvest it into the funds which weren't as successful. An added benefit to this process is that it forces you to sell high and buy low.

When you take money out of the best performing funds as I have suggested, you are selling shares that have appreciated greatly. Therefore, you are selling high. When you reinvest this money into the funds that are not performing as well, you are purchasing shares of those funds that are cheap. In this way you are buying low.

Selling high and buying low are the goals of all investing; yet, most investors fall short of reaching this goal. This simple method of balancing, however, will make it easier for any investor to mechanically sell high and buy low.

You can balance your portfolio anytime you wish. I recommend once a year. As an example, you may want to consider balancing your portfolio on the last Friday of every December.

When you set up your portfolio, try to use only those funds that the broker offers with no transaction fees. However, if you balance your portfolio with funds that

have transaction fees, the fees will usually be minimal, around 0.5%. You also may have taxes to pay on capital gains if your account is not within a tax-deferred retirement vehicle. Transaction fees and taxes that are paid out of the account will reduce the amount of investable dollars and thereby reduce the compounding effect within the portfolio.

Table 13.4: Example of Balancing helps you visualize how the process occurs.

Determining Gain. When you sell shares, your profit is based on what you paid for those shares. The purchase price and any commissions paid are called the cost basis of the shares. The generally accepted method to determine profit is that the first shares purchased are the first shares sold.

You must keep all of your statements from the discount broker. These will show when and how many shares you purchased and how much you paid for them. It will also show the same data when distributions were reinvested in your fund for additional shares. When you sold shares (both those that you actually purchased and those that were reinvested from distributions), the difference between the cost basis and their selling price would be your gain or loss. (If shares were held for more than one year, they would be long-term gains or losses. If shares were held for one year or less, they would be short-term gains or losses.) If there were any additional transaction fees when you sold the shares, this expense would be subtracted from your profit or added to your loss. Table 13.5: FIFO shows how to keep an ongoing record.

In this example, the dates for specific purchases and sales of fund ABC (a fictitious, no-load mutual fund) are recorded.

On Jan. 3, 1994, 500 shares were purchases at $10 per share for a total of $5,000. Then on Dec. 30, 1994, the fund declared a distribution of $0.80 per share. This $400 distribution ($0.80 X 5,000 shares) was reinvested at the current share price of $12 a share, increasing the portfolio by 33.33 shares to a total of 533.33 shares.

On Jan. 3, 1995, 200 shares of the portfolio were sold at $15 per share for a profit of $1,000. To determine the profit using the *first in/first out* method, you subtract the price of the first 200 shares purchased (200 shares X $10 per share = $2,000) from the sale price (200 shares X $15 per share = $3,000). $3,000 minus $2,000 leaves a profit of $1,000.

Another method that may be simpler for mutual fund shares is to use the average cost basis. (These shares must be held by the broker or the fund's agent.) Once you use an average cost basis, you must continue to use it for all accounts in the same fund.

In this example, you determine the average price of all of the shares you purchased and all of the shares that were reinvested from distributions. Add all of the purchase prices minus all expenses of all the shares when purchased and reinvested. Then divide this by the total number of shares owned.

Here is how it is figured. From Table 13.5: FIFO, the total purchase price is $5,400 ($5,000 plus $400). The total number of shares owned is 533.33 (500.00 shares plus 33.33 shares). The average cost basis is $10.13 ($5400 ÷ 533.33).

Table 13.4: Example of Balancing

The following example assumes there are five funds in a portfolio:

Prior to balancing, the portfolio is divided in this manner...
Fund A = $13,500
Fund B = $12,000
Fund C = $11,500
Fund D = $10,300
Fund E = $12,700

The total portfolio value equals $60,000.

The portfolio breakdown in this example is supposed to be...
20% for Fund A
20% for Fund B
20% for Fund C
20% for Fund D
20% for Fund E

After balancing, the result should be...
Fund A = 20% of $60,000 = $12,000
Fund B = 20% of $60,000 = $12,000
Fund C = 20% of $60,000 = $12,000
Fund D = 20% of $60,000 = $12,000
Fund E = 20% of $60,000 = $12,000

To accomplish this:
Sell enough shares to transfer...
$1,500 out of Fund A ($13,500 - $1,500 = $12,000), and
$700 out of Fund E ($12,700 - $700 = $12,000).

Purchase shares in the amount of...
$500 for Fund C ($11,500 + $500 = $12,000), and
$1,700 for Fund D ($10,300 + $1,700 = $12,000)

To determine your profit (or loss) subtract your cost price from your net sales price. From Table 13.5, your net sales price is $3,000 (200 shares X $15). Your cost basis for these shares is $2,026 (200 shares X $10.13). Your profit is $974 ($3,000 – $2,026).

Tax Problems? If balancing would cause a significant tax burden, here is an alternative method that avoids any taxable gains from balancing. Instead of selling shares to purchase others, you could invest new money monthly into those funds in your port-

Table 13.5: FIIFO

(First In, First Out)

_____

Fund Name

Purchase/Distrib				Sale				(Fee)	Profit
Date	$ Amt	NAV	# Sh	Date	$ Amt	NAV	# Sh		(Loss)
1/85	1,000	2.00	500.00	9/90	2,375	4.75	500.00		1,375
12/85	250	2.75	90.91	9/90	432	4.75	90.91		182
3/86	5,000	3.25	1,538.46	9/90	2,193	4.75	461.68		693

folio that were under represented by their lower percentages. For example, in Table 13.4 you would only invest in Funds C and D until their values as a percentage of their total portfolio where back to 20% apiece. Then return to dollar-cost-averaging into all five funds with equal amounts going into each fund.

Since you are working with a discount broker, the process is simple. One telephone call to the broker can take care of the entire balancing process. Sometimes, the agent on the line can do all of the math for you. It doesn't get much simpler than this.

If you have any transaction fees to pay, let the broker take them from the money you are transferring from one fund to another. Don't worry if the resulting percentage breakdown is not exactly to the decimal point. This is not an exact science. Rather, it is a practical method of balancing and taking profits.

6. Continue Regular Investing.

Whatever you had to do to balance your portfolio, you have done. Now, continue the perfunctory task of dollar-cost-averaging. You can accomplish this by sending your money regularly to the discount broker and directing him or her to divide it accordingly among your funds in the five asset categories.

If you are not selling funds because of tax reasons, and you are investing more money in those funds that were weaker performers as I described in Step 5 under *Tax Problems?*, then you will need to keep a record of your regular investments during the year until each of your funds represents 20% of the total value of your portfolio.

7. Repeat Process Starting with #4.

Twelve months now have gone by, and you are ready to start all over again. Do your homework to evaluate the quality of the funds that are in your portfolio. Do the maintenance as described in Step 4, and let the cycle repeat.

8. Liquidate When Needed.

There comes a time when you need to use the money you are investing. In order to use it, you need to liquidate it properly.

Think about liquidating only what you will need for specific periods of time. If you need cash in one year, begin to sell shares over the next twelve months and place the proceeds into a money market account. When you do sell shares, sell an equal dollar amount from each asset category. This is like dollar-cost-averaging in reverse.

For example, if you need $60,000 in one year, begin to sell enough shares monthly to raise approximately $5,000 (i.e., $1,000 from each asset category). Transfer the $5,000 into a money market account at the brokerage house. After twelve months, you will have approximately $60,000 plus the interest earned in the money market account.

In the same example, you could consider selling enough shares to net $60,000 at one time (i.e., $12,000 from each asset category), especially if you believe the U.S.

Table 13.6: Hypothetical LIP

YEAR		Aggressive 20th Century Ultra %	Value	Growth Founders Growth %	Value	Foreign T.R. Price Int'l Stock %	Value	Emerging Lexington Emerging %	Value	Contrary Vanguard Gold & Prec. Metal %	Value	PORTFOLIO VALUE
1985	A		1,000		1,000		1,000		1,000		1,000	
	B	26.1%	1,261	28.7%	1,287	45.1%	1,451	26.7%	1,267	-5.0%	950	6,216
	C		1,243		1,243		1,243		1,243		1,243	
1986	A		2,243		2,243		2,243		2,243		2,243	
	B	10.2%	2,472	19.7%	2,685	61.2%	3,616	20.6%	2,705	49.8%	3,360	14,838
	C		2,968		2,968		2,968		2,968		2,968	
1987	A		3,968		3,968		3,968		3,968		3,968	
	B	6.6%	4,230	10.0%	4,365	7.9%	4,281	0.2%	3,976	38.7%	5,504	22,356
	C		4,471		4,471		4,471		4,471		4,471	
1988	A		5,471		5,471		5,471		5,471		5,471	
	B	13.3%	6,199	4.8%	5,734	17.9%	6,450	10.5%	6,045	-14.2%	4,694	29,122
	C		5,824		5,824		5,824		5,824		5,824	
1989	A		6,824		6,824		6,824		6,824		6,824	
	B	36.9%	9,367	41.7%	9,670	23.7%	8,441	28.1%	8,742	30.3%	8,892	45,112
	C		9,022		9,022		9,022		9,022		9,022	
1990	A		10,022		10,022		10,022		10,022		10,022	
	B	9.3%	10,954	-10.6%	8,960	-8.8%	9,140	-14.2%	8,599	-19.9%	8,028	45,681
	C		9,136		9,136		9,136		9,136		9,136	
1991	A		10,136		10,136		10,136		10,136		10,136	
	B	86.4%	18,894	47.3%	14,930	15.8%	11,737	24.2%	12,589	4.3%	10,572	68,722
	C		13,744		13,744		13,744		13,744		13,744	
1992	A		14,744		14,744		14,744		14,744		14,744	
	B	1.2%	14,921	4.3%	15,378	-3.4%	14,243	3.8%	15,304	-19.4%	11,884	71,730
	C		14,346		14,346		14,346		14,346		14,346	
1993	A		15,346		15,346		15,346		15,346		15,346	
	B	21.8%	18,691	25.5%	19,259	40.1%	21,500	63.4%	25,075	93.3%	29,664	114,189
	C		22,838		22,838		22,838		22,,838		22,838	
										Robertson Stephens Contrarian		
1994	A		23,838		23,838		23,838		23,838		23,838	
	B	-3.6%	22,980	-3.3%	23,051	-0.7%	23,671	-13.8%	20,548	-5.5%	22,527	112,777
	C		22,555		22,555		22,555		22,555		22,555	
1995	A		23,555		23,555		23,555		23,555		23,555	
	B	37.7%	32,435	45.6%	34,296		26,240		22,165	30.9%	30,834	145,970
	C		29,194		29,194	11.4%	29,194	-5.9%	29,194		29,194	
		PBHG Growth				USAA Int'l						
1996	A		30,194		30,194		30,194		30,194		30,194	
	B	15.1%	34,753	12.6%	33,998	12.9%	34,089	13.4%	34,240	15.9%	34,995	172,075

Business Cycle is at a peak for stock market investments. Another reason to sell all of the necessary shares at one time might be if the RVR (see chapter 8) is overvalued and warning of a stock market correction.

If this is your retirement account, and retirement is a few years away, you could consider liquidating enough shares to provide cash for three to five years. The proceeds of this liquidation could be placed in zero coupon bonds that come due one year from now, two years from now, and so on. This method provides liquidity for your cash flow needs as well as continued wealth accumulation within the balance of your Lifetime Investing Plan. (I will discuss more on options at retirement and withdrawals in chapters 15 and 16.)

Here is an example from our financial wizards, Mike and Jodi:

Let's assume they are ready to retire. They have accumulated approximately $740,000 in each of their IRAs. They know that they will need about $133,000 in their first year of retirement. Mike can sell approximately $66,500 worth of his mutual funds—about $13,300 from each of the five asset categories. The proceeds could be placed in a short-term bond fund within the IRA. Jodi could do the same thing with her IRA. Then, as they need the money, they can withdraw it from their short-term bond fund and deposit it in their checking account outside of the IRAs. The amount they will actually withdraw will depend upon how they arrange to take their series of substantially equal payments because they will be retiring before age 59 1/2. (I refer to this method of early retirement under Investing Options in chapter 15.)

Lifetime Investing Plan Over the Last 11.5 Years

Table 13.6: Hypothetical LIP details the hypothetical investment results using my Lifetime Investing Plan. This means that I applied the present rules of my Lifetime Investing Plan back 11.5 years. I used the following categories in 1985: aggressive growth, growth, foreign stock, emerging foreign stock, and contrary-style. For the contrary-style category, I used precious metals funds. When contrary-style funds became available in 1994, I substituted them for the precious metals funds.

To simplify this example, the same funds were used from the beginning of 1985, to the end of 1995 except when the precious metals funds were replace in 1994. These funds included 20th Century Ultra (aggressive growth), Founders Growth (growth), T. Rowe Price International Stock (foreign stock), Lexington Worldwide Emerging Markets (emerging foreign stock), and Vanguard gold and Precious Metals (contrary-style). In 1994, Robertson Stephens Contrarian Fund replaced the Vanguard gold and Precious Metals Fund. In 1996, PBHG Growth Fund replaced 20th Century Ultra, and USAA International fund replaced T.R. Price International Stock.

Also, money was contributed into each fund at the beginning of each year rather than at the beginning of each month. If contributions had been bade at the beginning of each month, dollar-cost-averaging would have benefited from the volatility in the

funds' NAVs that occurred from month-to-month. More shares would have been purchased when the prices dropped, and less shares would have been purchased when the prices rose.

In this portfolio, $1,000 was invested into each fund at the beginning of each year for a total of $5,000 per year. However, the compounded returns would be the same no matter what dollar amount was consistently invested. The total percentage return for each fund for each year is listed under percent.

Row A represents the fund's value at the beginning of each year after the annual contribution was made. *Row B* records each fund's value at the end of the year. *Row C* is the result of balancing the funds. Balancing was done immediately after the year's ending value as noted in *Row B*.

No taxes were subtracted from this example. You could think of this account as a tax-deferred account. It also was assumed that there were no transaction fees to be paid. As of June 30, 1996, the portfolio value was $172,075. (There is no *Row C* for 1996 because balancing will not be done until the end of 1996.) The average annual compounded rate-of-return from Jan. 1, 1985 through June 30, 1996 (11 years and 6 months) was 16.8%.

Sharing With Friends and Relatives

You should now have a good understanding of my Lifetime Investing Plan. You may want to share this with other people. You may want to think about forming an investment club. Investment clubs are nothing more than a group of people getting together to pool their talents and cash in order to invest as a group. This is a good way to share your knowledge and also to learn from others. It is also fun!

There is a sharing and learning experience that accompanies investment clubs. Individuals share their knowledge about their investment blunders and successes. Technical and fundamental techniques are debated and constructed. Individual members have homework assignments requiring some independent study which is reported to the group at subsequent meetings. The club's portfolio not only prospers, but each member becomes a better individual investor.

The National Association of Investors Corporation (NAIC) is a nonprofit organization which monitors about half of all clubs nationwide. There are over 13,000 clubs which are members of NAIC with over 300,000 individual members. These clubs range in size from 2 to 140 with the average club having 15 to 17 members.

To start a club is easy. Simply get together several people who are interested in investing as a group. These people need to have similar risk levels and time horizons. The club also must have a similar philosophy of investing. According to Barry Murphy, the NAIC's director of marketing, "Most clubs break up because of differences of opinions on what a club wants to invest in." The core to your investment club could be the Lifetime Investing Plan.

Together, the group will decide how much each member will contribute monthly to feed the portfolio. The average individual investment in NAIC member clubs is $32 per month. However, there are some clubs whose members invest $1,000 or more a month. This regular injection of fresh capital will allow the portfolio to grow using dollar-cost-averaging. By investing in growth oriented investments, using diversification, and reinvesting all dividends, income, and capital gains, the club's portfolio should realize sizable gains in the coming years.

Most clubs take on the business form of a limited partnership. They elect members to leadership positions and then divide the responsibilities. It is important to develop operating procedures for such items as withdrawals and admitting new members. Often, clubs are set up like mutual funds, with units that can be bought and sold. Your club also may want to buy a fidelity bond which will protect the club against fraud. (A fidelity bond is insurance coverage against losses due to employee dishonesty.) It is unfortunate, but it is possible for a club treasurer to embezzle some of the cash.

To obtain detailed information about starting an investment club, contact NAIC at (800) 428-2244.

Another organization providing meetings is the American Association of Individual Investors (AAII). The AAII has local chapters which do not function as an investment club but do provide a source of study and sharing of information. The AAII can be reached at (312) 280-0170 for more information.

To stay on track, you need a road map you can follow. AAA® gives you a Triptik® to guide you through the United States. I give you the *Monthly Portfolio Monitor* and *Annual Monitor* to guide you through your financial course. Turn the page, and check it out!

Monitoring For Success

The best way to follow your success is to have the proper tools to visualize where you are and where you are headed. I have developed two monitoring guides to assist you in this manner, the *Monthly Portfolio Monitor* and the *Annual Monitor*. As their names imply, one helps with your monthly progress and the other helps with the larger picture.

Monthly Portfolio Monitoring

This tool summarizes all of your portfolio activity at the end of each month. It provides a convenient place to keep score of your funds in each asset category.

The following legend will help you use this tool:

- **Date**—The last trading day of every month is used to monitor your total portfolio. However, when you rebalance your portfolio, you will enter the date before you rebalance and the date after you rebalance so that you will have an accurate picture of the shares held in each fund.

Aggressive Growth Fund—This is the place where you list the names of the funds that fit this category.

- **Shares**—This is the number of shares you own in this fund.
- **Price**—This is the closing price of the fund for the date indicated.
- **Value**—This is the dollar value of each fund for the date indicated.

Growth Fund—This is the place where you list the names of the funds that fit this category.

- **Shares**—This is the number of shares you own in this fund.
- **Price**—This is the closing price of the fund for the date indicated.
- **Value**—This is the dollar value of each fund for the date indicated.

Foreign Stock Fund—This is the place where you list the names of the funds that fit this category.

- **Shares**—This is the number of shares you own in this fund.
- **Price**—This is the closing price of the fund for the date indicated.
- **Value**—This is the dollar value of each fund for the date indicated.

Emerging Foreign Stock Fund—This is the place where you list the names of the funds that fit this category.

Date	Agg. Growth Fund	# Shares	Price	$ Value	Growth Fund	# Shares	Price	$ Value	Foreign Stock Fund	# Shares	Price	$ Value	NOTES
6/30/10	PG+G Growth	1260.83	27.52	34,753	Founders Growth	2044.38	16.63	33,998	USAA Int'l.	1853.66	18.40	34,059	

Table 14.1: Monthly Portfolio Monitor

Date	Emerg. Foreign Stock Fund	# Shares	Price	$ Value	Contrary Style Fund	# Shares	Price	$ Value	Total Portfolio Value	NOTES
6/30/96	Lexington Emerging	2822.75	$12.13	34,240	R.S. Contrarian	2189.92	$15.98	34,995	$173,075	

Table 14.1: Monthly Portfolio Monitor (continued)

- **Shares**—This is the number of shares you own in this fund.
- **Price**—This is the closing price of the fund for the date indicated.
- **Value**—This is the dollar value of each fund for the date indicated.

Contrary-style Fund—This is the place where you list the names of the funds that fit this category.
- **Shares**—This is the number of shares you own in this fund.
- **Price**—This is the closing price of the fund for the date indicated.
- **Value**—This is the dollar value of each fund for the date indicated.

Total Portfolio Dollar Value—This is the total value of all of the funds that make up your Lifetime Investing Plan.

At the end of each year, you will have a *total portfolio dollar value* that you can insert into your Annual Monitor under the heading *actual* for the appropriate *End of Year* date. (See Table 14.2: Annual Monitor.)

Annual Monitoring

You should set up an annual monitor for each of your financial goals. The Annual Monitor (Table 14.2) projects what the values of your portfolio account should be for a specific financial goal at the end of each year. It succinctly monitors where you are and where you should be. If you are off track, you will be made aware of that quickly.

I use annual monitoring rather than monthly monitoring to make adjustments for three reasons:
- Annual monitoring gives your investments time to do what they can do for you.
- Annual monitoring gives you plenty of opportunity to correct inconsistencies.
- Annual monitoring follows my concept of SIMPLE because more frequent adjusting would prove to be too cumbersome.

The following legend explains the terms of the Annual Monitor. Follow along with Jodi's Annual Monitor (Figure 14-2):

Goal—This is the amount of money you wish to accumulate at a specific time in the future for a particular financial goal. This is the FV button on the financial calculator. (Remember, this will be a negative (-) number in the calculator.)

Years to reach goal—This is the number of years you have to allow compounding and your plan to work for you before reaching your goal. This is the N button on the financial calculator.

Beginning value of portfolio—This is the amount of money, if any, with which you are starting. This is the PV button on the financial calculator and begins at the *End of Year "0"*.

Anticipated annually-compounded rate of return—There is no guarantee you will achieve this return. It is based on the historical returns of the funds you choose. It is always wise to underestimate this number. This is the I button on the financial calculator.

Table 14.2: Jodi's IRA Annual Monitor

Date _____

GOAL __$740,000_____

Years to reach goal __25_____

Beginning value of portfolio __$12,300_____

Anticipated annually-compounded rate of return __14%_____

Annual contribution __$2,000_____

End of Year	End of	Age	Target	Actual	Adjustments
0	1997	30		$12,300	
1	1998	31	$16,302		
2	1999	32	$20,864		
3	2000	33	$26,065		
4	2001	34	$31,994		
5	2002	35	$38,754		
6	2003	36	$46,459		
7	2004	37	$55,243		
8	2005	38	$65,258		
9	2006	39	$76,674		
10	2007	40	$89,688		
11	2008	41	$104,524		
12	2009	42	$121,438		
13	2010	43	$140,719		
14	2011	44	$162,699		
15	2012	45	$187,757		
16	2013	46	$216,323		
17	2014	47	$248,889		
18	2015	48	$286,013		
19	2016	49	$328,335		

Annual contribution—This is the sum of money you will be able to contribute, or the sum of money you must contribute, into your investment plan to reach your goal. You can invest this amount monthly, quarterly, or however you wish. For simplicity, the calculation is based on this amount being added annually at the beginning of each year. Set the financial calculator mode to BEGIN. Your first regular contribution will be invested at the beginning of year "1". This is the PMT button on the financial calculator.

Table 14.2: Jodi's IRA Annual Monitor (con't.)

End of Year	End of	Age	Target	Actual	Adjustments
20	2017	50	$376,582		
21	2018	51	$431,583		
22	2019	52	$494,285		
23	2020	53	$565,765		
24	2021	54	$647,252		
25	2022	55	$740,147		
26					
27					
28					
29					
30					
31					
32					
33					
34					
35					
36					
37					
38					
39					
40					
41					
42					
43					
44					
45					
46					

End of Year—All calculations are based on the value of the account at the end of the year. When determining the target value, this is the N button on the financial calculator.

End of: This is the end of the year you actually are targeting.

Age: This is your age at the end of the target year.

Target: This is the dollar amount your portfolio should be worth if you are on track with your goal. This is the FV button on the financial calculator.

Actual: This is the real value of your portfolio at the end of the target year. Get this number from your *Monthly Portfolio Monitor* under *Total Portfolio Dollar Value* at the end of each year. If you have a *Beginning value of portfolio*, this dollar amount is entered into the *Actual* column for the *End of Year "0"*.

Adjustments: This is the difference between the actual amount minus the target amount. If this is a negative number when you monitor this form annually, then you need to consider making an adjustment to your plan as I discuss after the following example.

Let's revisit Jodi and fill out her Annual Monitor for her retirement goal. Mike's IRA Annual Monitor will be an exact duplicate of Jodi's.

At the end of 1997 (year "0"), Jodi is starting with "$12,300". At the beginning of 1998, she will begin her investment program. To simplify the calculations, I'll assume that her annual investments of $2,000 are all deposited at the beginning of each year rather than divided over the 12-month period.

At the "end of year 1", Jodi should have $12,300 plus $2,000 plus 14% total investment return ($2,002) to equal $16,302. To determine the target balance, enter "1" and then press the N key; enter "12300" and then press the PV key; enter "14" and then press the I key; enter "2,000" and then press the PMT key. Press the FV key to get the "target value at the end of year 1" (-$16,302.00).

Do this for all 25 years. Simply press 2; press N; press FV; and you have the value at the "end of year 2". Press 3; press N; press FV; and you have the value at the "end of year 3", etc. You won't need to reenter the numbers for I, PV, or PMT. They are already in the calculator.

The Annual Monitor will fill in as shown in the example. That's all there is to it.

The blank Annual Monitor in Appendix I is for you to use. Save your table along with all of your other important papers. Each year, complete the *Actual* column and determine if you are staying on track. If not, adjustments may be necessary.

Adjustments Along The Way

As you progress toward your financial goal, your Annual Monitor will show you if you are on track. If you have more in your account than is targeted, consider this a cushion against future years which may not be as successful. If you have less than is targeted, you may need to make some adjustments. Here are some options to keep you on target:

You could add more to your plan to make up for the discrepancy. By monitoring your plan annually, you will be able to catch discrepancies early. If you are *down* an amount that is affordable for you to add to your account, do it. (If this is an IRA or other qualified retirement account, you are limited to the maximum dollars you can add per year. What you could do is open up a regular, non-tax-deferred account with your discount broker, or you could set up a variable annuity whose interest, dividends, and capital gains are tax-deferred and reinvested.)

You could switch to better performing funds. If any of your funds are not performing well, remember the rules for the Lifetime Investing Plan. Remove those funds which no longer fit the criteria to be chosen and replace them with the best performing funds that have the highest risk levels for the categories in question. If your account is not in a tax-deferred vehicle, then there will be tax consequences to consider when switching funds. However, your priority should be quality investment returns; taxes should hold second place.

Change dollar value of goal. Possibly you can decrease the projected amount of your goal. For example, if you are trying to accumulate $50,000 for a particular financial goal, but $40,000 would still work for you, then this may be a viable option.

Change the length of time to reach your goal. If you have some flexibility in your time frame, then you may want to extend your goal date. This additional time will give your plan added compounding power to grow toward your target value.

Let's look at Mike and Jodi again. Suppose at the end of year eight, Jodi only had $61,000 in her IRA; that would be $4,258 short of target. Since Mike's IRA was invested in the same manner, together they would be $8,516 short of being on target. Because they were already contributing their allowable maximum to their IRAs, they could not increase their IRA contributions. They didn't want to change their retirement goal; so fortunately they could find some extra money to invest. What they decided to do was to open a variable annuity with $10,000 and began to include that annuity into their overall LIP program for retirement.

There is a wonderful feeling of excitement and accomplishment as you progress toward your financial goals. Having a laid-out-course to help you picture exactly where you are and where you are going is motivating as well as practical. These two monitoring guides are the maps to your success.

One of the major goals you will realize eventually will be retirement or financial independence. My definition of financial independence is being able to live the lifestyle you have chosen solely from the cash flow you can generate from your investment nest egg. Chapter 15 looks at your options once you reach retirement.

Options at Retirement

If you are getting ready to retire, or you are just putting your thoughts together about what your options will be when you are ready to retire, then here are some of my thoughts for your consideration. First, there are retirement challenges that need to be addressed, then, there are investment decisions to sort through.

Retirement Challenges

Successful retirement just doesn't happen all by itself. It takes planning.

Think of retirement as a career change. Most of us spend many years studying and preparing for our current vocations. College, on-the-job training, and continuing education prepared us for the careers we have today. Retirement is just another career that requires preparation for success and satisfaction.

The bottom line here is to plan ahead for a broad range of considerations. Here are six areas that need your attention:

A. Financial

This area needs to be addressed as early as possible as I have emphasized up to this point. Until retirement, planning has been done to create a nest egg which could provide the necessary income to maintain a specific lifestyle for the rest of your life. After reaching retirement, you will not add additional money to the investment account. Now, a withdrawal program will provide a stream of cash to meet all living expenses while the remaining assets in the retirement account will continue to grow. This is discussed in the next chapter. Based on your projections, the withdrawal plan is designed to last a lifetime.

B. Legal

Unfortunately, you won't know how important legal documents or titling of property are until you or your beneficiaries need to use them. The following should give you some ideas.

Will. A will is a legally enforceable declaration of what a person wants done at death with his or her property and other matters. It may be changed or revoked at any time up until one's death. State law dictates the legal requirements which must be met in order for the will to be valid.

The importance of the will to your overall estate is that all of your assets will pass through the will and must therefore go through probate unless there have been other means of titling these assets prior to death such as life insurance trusts (described in chapter 17), jointly owned assets (*JTWROS* described later), living trusts (described in chapter 17), and outright gifts given over the course of a lifetime.

Probate is the process where the will is presented to a court and an executor is appointed to carry out the will's instructions. This takes time, costs money, and makes all of the assets in the will open to the public and to creditors.

Living Will. If you were to find yourself in a medical situation where your life was being prolonged solely by medical technology, you might prefer not to allow that compromised quality of life to continue. If you believe that you would prefer to control the medical care given to you while in such a disabled state, then you must make your wishes known before that occurs.

A vehicle to do just that is known as a *living will*. Basically, this document is a written declaration instructing a physician to withhold or withdraw life-sustaining medical procedures in the event of a terminal condition. A physician or health facility acting in accordance with the statutory requirements will not be subject to criminal or civil liability or deemed to have engaged in unprofessional conduct. A sample wording of such a document is displayed here. Again, consult your attorney to prepare your *living will* to meet your specific requirements.

Figure 15.1: Living Will Sample

Living Will

If the time comes when I can no longer take part in decisions for my own future, this statement and declaration shall stand as the expression of my wishes.

Statement

If there is no reasonable expectation of my recovery from physical or mental disability, I wish to be allowed to die and not to be kept alive by artificial means or heroic measures. I wish only that drugs be mercifully administered to me for terminal suffering, even if they hasten the moment of my death.

Declaration

I willfully and voluntarily make my desire known that my dying shall not be artificially prolonged under the circumstances stated below. I declare the following:

1. If at any time my attending physician has determined that I have a

Figure 15.1: Living Will Sample (continued)

---

terminal condition from which death is imminent, I direct life-prolonging procedures be withheld or withdrawn when the application of such procedures would serve only to prolong artificially the process of dying.

2. I wish to die naturally with only the administration of medication or the performance of any medical procedure considered necessary to make me comfortable or to alleviate pain.

3. If I am unable to give directions regarding the use of such life-prolonging procedures, it is my intention that this declaration be honored by my family and physician as my final expression of my legal right to refuse medical or surgical treatment and to accept the consequences for such refusal.

4. I understand this declaration fully, and I am emotionally and mentally competent to make this declaration.

Durable Power of Attorney. Before understanding the *Durable Power of Attorney,* you need to understand a *power of attorney.*

A power of attorney is a legal document which allows you, the principal, to grant another individual, an attorney-in-fact, the power to act legally on your behalf. This power can be granted either for very limited use or for very broad use. However, if you should die or become incompetent, the power given to the attorney-in-fact terminates immediately. Since incompetency is the most important reason for another individual to act on your behalf, a document needs to be created to survive your incompetency.

A *Durable Power of Attorney* is a special *power of attorney* which will survive your incompetency. It usually does not require any court proceeding or judicial supervision. In other words, the *Durable Power of Attorney* will immediately allow an individual or individuals to act on your behalf legally when you are not physically or mentally able to do so. However, as with a general *power of attorney,* if you should die, the *Durable Power of Attorney* will also terminate.

You may divide the powers granted under a *Durable Power of Attorney* as you see fit, and you may choose who will continue to handle your legal affairs. For example, your business partner could be granted powers over business decisions while your spouse could be granted powers over health care and other personal decisions. This legal document will also negate the necessity of petitioning a local court for appointment of a guardian or conservator to handle your assets.

Many powers may be granted under the *Durable Power of Attorney.* Some of them include:

- To collect and dispense money and checks
- To sue in your name
- To hire and discharge employees

- To borrow money
- To make business decisions
- To manage property
- To make gifts
- To create, amend, or revoke trusts
- To change beneficiaries of life insurance and retirement plans
- To deal with the IRS
- To make disclaimers
- To make health and well-being decisions
- To purchase and sell securities and other assets

Durable Health Care Power of Attorney. This is a very specific type of durable power of attorney. This also may be an important document for you to have It works in conjunction with a Living Will. It gives the individual you designate broader power to make healthcare decisions for you that include more than life-and-death decisions.

Titling of Property. There are nine legal methods by which property can be owned and titled. The types of assets requiring legal title include real estate, automobiles, mobile homes, boats, bank accounts, mutual funds, individual securities, and brokerage firm accounts. No asset can be titled in more than one way at the same time.

- *Separate Ownership*—When you own property solely, you have total control. Because your name is the only one on the title, it is easy to transfer, sell, or refinance the asset. You simply sign your name to the document. This property, however, has no protection from liens which can be placed against it by your creditors.
- *Tenancy in Common*—This is a form of joint ownership with at least one other person or entity such as a corporation, trust, or partnership. You have the right to sell, transfer, gift, or bequeath your interest to anyone you wish without the expressed permission of the other joint owners. However, in order to dispose of the entire asset, all joint owners must agree to sign. This can present a logistical problem if it is difficult to contact the other owners. As with separate ownership, creditors can place a lien on this property and force a sale to satisfy a judgment. Although the judgment can be against the other owners, the problem is that the jointly owned property is entirely at risk.
- *Joint Tenancy with Rights of Survivorship (JTWROS)*—This is the most common form of joint ownership. It carries the same advantages and disadvantages of tenancy in common with one major exception. When one of the owners dies, the decedent's share automatically passes on to the surviving tenants. Also, this transfer takes precedence over any will or trust document. The asset does not go through probate. This is critical to understand because

many people do not realize that their property is actually owned in JTWROS. If your intention is to bequeath this property or to maintain certain control over it, then ownership can not be JTWROS.

- *Community Property*—There are nine states that have a form of co-ownership of property known as community property, and they are Arizona, California, Idaho, Louisiana, Nevada, New Mexico, Texas, Washington, and Wisconsin. Community property is owned by both husband and wife and is subject to liens from creditors just as with the previous forms of ownership discussed. One major tax advantage of community property over other types of ownership occurs when one spouse dies. When either spouse dies, the *cost basis* of the entire property is *stepped-up* to the market value at the time of death. In JTWROS and tenancy in common, the *cost basis* of the deceased's portion of the property is the only portion that is *stepped-up*.

- *Tenancy by the Entirety*—This is joint ownership between a husband and wife and is allowed in many non-community property states. It functions much like JTWROS, but it only can be terminated by joint agreement of both spouses.

- *Custodial*—Minor children and incapacitated persons are not considered to have legal capacity and cannot enter into a binding contract. Therefore, accounts set up for these people must have a custodian named who can trade, buy, and sell assets in this account. A custodian does not personally own the asset for himself/herself; he/she oversees the asset for the benefit of another. These assets are usually exposed to judgments against the beneficiaries. Also, the custodian has a fiduciary responsibility to the beneficiaries and is legally liable for his actions.

- *Partnership*—Two or more adults can form a partnership and own property. The partners can be either general partners or limited partners. General partners are personally liable for any claims against the partnership. Not only are the assets subject to judgments, but each general partner is 100 percent liable for any legal actions against the partnership. On the other hand, limited partners are not personally liable for any claims.

- *Corporation*—A corporation can be formed by one or more individuals and can own property. The major benefit is that judgments against the corporation usually cannot be placed against the individuals. However, this is not always the case. The *corporate veil* does not always protect the corporate officers or employees from all liability.

- *Trust*—Property can be placed in a trust and administered by a trustee. The trustee holds title to this property for the benefit of another and thereby has a fiduciary responsibility. The trustee also has the sole right to manage, buy, and sell assets within the trust. A trust can be revocable (where the assets transferred into the trust can still be controlled to some extent by the individual setting up the trust) or irrevocable (where ownership and control of

the transferred assets are given up completely by the individual setting up the trust). In specific instances, the assets in the trust can be protected from creditors who have judgments against one who originally set up the trust.

C. Health Care

Generally at age 65, your primary insurance carrier becomes Medicare. To fill in some of the gaps in Medicare coverage, Medigap insurance is available for purchase. You need to become educated about both of these forms of insurance. Unfortunately, most individuals will remain financially vulnerable to the cost of healthcare beyond these coverages during their retirement years.

Medicare is a federal program which provides health insurance at minimal or no cost. To be eligible, you must generally be 65 years old and eligible for Social Security Retirement or Survivor's benefits, and/or receive Social Security disability benefits for at least 24 months, regardless of age. There are two primary coverages under Medicare, Part A and Part B. Part A is hospital insurance which covers inpatient hospital costs, some nursing facility care, and some care in the home. Part B is medical insurance and covers most outpatient care. There is no charge for Part A benefits, but there are monthly premiums to pay for Part B benefits.

Medigap insurance covers some of the gaps in the Medicare program. Medigap covers the deductibles and the coinsurance portions not covered by Medicare. However, many gaps still remain. In 1989, Medicare covered about 50% of all healthcare costs of persons 65 or older. Medigap insurance paid a total of approximately 6% of all healthcare costs for the same group.

You also need to consider the advantages and disadvantages of long-term care insurance. You may want to consider investing in the Lifetime Investing Plan that is earmarked for later healthcare needs. (I described this technique in chapter 7.) Such a plan could provide you with an adequate source of cash in lieu of, or in addition to, long-term care insurance.

D. Role Changes

Relationships ultimately will change during retirement. You may need to give some thought to becoming a caregiver to a loved one. Also, personal losses could have a serious impact. The loss of a spouse, a friend, or even a pet could change the entire lifestyle of an individual.

As each of us progresses through retirement, we must learn to become more independent of, rather than dependent on, others. Preparing ourselves for these potential role changes takes planning and frankness.

Remember Mike and Jodi? Let's move ahead to the point when they are in their 60s. They have had their ups and downs in life like everyone else. They have had to change some of their goals along the way and to deal with tragedies. One goal that they have accomplished is the security of knowing that each one can be a self-sufficient individual. They have shared equally in all of the financial and legal decisions they made. Each is comfortable with the investments and retirement plan they have created for themselves. If either one should die suddenly, the other is fully equipped to carry on with his or her life. Yes, it would be difficult emotionally, but, the understanding of what would need to be done is well established.

E. Living Arrangements

After retirement, you may decide to live somewhere totally different to fulfill your dreams, or you may need to move as a result of financial or health matters. Your options need to be clear, and the anxieties that could result need to be discussed.

For example, your home probably constitutes a large percentage of equity which increases year after year. What can you do with this equity to make it work best for you? There are several options:

1. **Nothing.** Simply live in the house and let the equity grow. It's not working for you now, but it is available when you may want it in the future (assuming your home's value does not decrease).

2. **Purchase another home of greater value.** In this way, you will not have to pay any capital gains on the appreciated value after the sale of your existing home. When you purchase your new home, the purchase price becomes your new basis. This actually amounts to a tax-free gain. You can reinvest these tax-free gains from home to home by purchasing more expensive homes after the previous one appreciates. There is no guarantee however that home values will continue to increase in value.

3. **When you reach 55 years of age, you can sell your home and not have to buy an equal value or more expensive home.** You are allowed a one time $125,000 capital gain exemption which is free of tax. Therefore, you could size down by $125,000 to a smaller home, pocket the $125,000 profit, and still pay no taxes on the capital gain of $125,000.

4. **Borrow the equity and invest it.** As long as the return on your investment is more than the cost to borrow the equity and any taxes you must pay on the invested return, then this makes sense. You could invest this money into the Lifetime Investing Plan and let it accumulate and compound. This investment could be earmarked as your self-insured, long-term care plan. If you or your spouse should need long-term medical care in the future, this source could assist you with needed cash. (I discussed this concept in chapter 7.)

5. **You can take a reverse mortgage.** This will allow you to receive a monthly, tax-free cash flow based on the equity in your home. The lender will eventually be repaid either in a lump sum payment from you or by taking possession of your home.

6. **You can establish a personal residence trust.** Through this vehicle, you can gift your home to your children. Your children will receive the home after a specified period of time, and your estate will save on estate taxes. Check with

your tax attorney to see if a personal residence trust makes sense in your situation.

F. Time Management

What will you do with your time? This may seem silly, but how will you spend your hours, your days, your years? The more hobbies you create in your pre-retirement years, the more choices you will have after retirement. Will you become a frequent traveler, or possibly volunteer your services to a non-profit organization such as SCORE, or become entrepreneurial and start a totally new business? Some retirees don't stop to think about such things and become bored and depressed with all the unfilled hours of their days.

Retirement is not the end of work. It is the opportunity to accomplish new goals in life and to live out your dreams. When planned for properly, these things can be accomplished without the need to continue working for a living. The six goals I have just described all come together to ensure the enjoyment of your golden years.

There are also several decisions that must be considered regarding your investment program. I've identified five options, but you may be able to think of a few more.

Investing Options
Option #1: Stay With the Plan

Continue with the plan as I have described in this book. It *is* a Lifetime Investing Plan. Your only change at retirement will be to begin withdrawing money regularly from your plan rather than dollar-cost-averaging into it as you have been. You could consider withdrawing a fixed-dollar-amount or a fixed-percentage of the total portfolio. You can even arrange with most discount brokers to have this withdrawal made automatically. In other words, the discount broker would automatically sell enough shares monthly to provide you with the fixed-dollar-amount or fixed-percentage that you have requested. The remaining invested assets in your portfolio will continue to grow.

When you sell shares to raise cash for your annual needs, sell approximately the same dollar amount or percentage from each asset category. This is like dollar-cost-averaging in reverse. Sometimes, the stock market will be depressed; at other times it will be booming. Just as you were not trying to "time" the market when you were creating your nest egg, likewise you should not try to "time" the market when you are withdrawing from it.

In chapter 16, I describe in detail how to project your withdrawals for the rest of your life.

Option #2: Relinquish
Management of the Plan

If you no longer wanted to deal with the management of your portfolio, you could hire someone else to do it for you. However, you would lose control of your money. You could, of course, teach someone else how to follow the Lifetime Investing Plan to the letter. But remember, no one cares more about your money than you!

Option #3: Purchase Zero Coupon Bonds

You could become much more conservative and decide to liquidate a portion of your portfolio and then purchase the necessary number of zero coupon bonds that come due at various dates in the future to meet your cash flow needs. I described zero coupon bonds in chapter 7 when planning for a child's college education.

For example, Mike and Jodi could liquidate enough of their portfolio to purchase zero coupon bonds coming due each year for the next five years. The face value of each year's zero coupon bonds would be for the amount of money they projected they would need for each of the next five years. The remainder of their portfolio balance could stay invested in the plan until they were ready to purchase another batch of zero coupon bonds spaced to come due each successive year for another five years, and so on.

Remember that zero coupon bonds are bought at a deep discount to their face value. No interest is received along the way although accrued interest is taxable annually if the portfolio is a taxable account. At the maturity date, their full face value is paid to the owner of the bonds.

Option #4: Purchase an Immediate Fixed Annuity

An *immediate fixed annuity* is a contract you purchase from an insurance company which pays a specific amount to you regularly and starts right away. You could purchase an *immediate fixed annuity* and begin to have regular payments made to you and your spouse for the remainder of your lives. You will no longer need to invest into your retirement account since it will go to the purchase of the annuity. Be sure that there is some type of cost-of-living provision included in the annuity payment schedule so that your standard of living can keep up with inflation.

Be aware that a fixed annuity will be based on a much lower rate of return than you probably would earn on your stock mutual fund portfolio. This translates into lower regular payments to you than you may have anticipated from your original projections. This reduced return could be compensated for if you planned ahead for this scenario. The advantage of an immediate fixed annuity is that you will never outlive your source of income.

Option #5: Ready To Retire Before Age 59 1/2?

Have you thought about retiring before age 59 1/2 but didn't want to pay the 10% early withdrawal penalty? The IRS will actually allow you penalty-free withdrawals if you take them in a series of substantially equal payments (SSEP).

Your qualified plan may allow for this already. You may need to terminate your employment before you can take advantage of this. However, if your plan does not allow for this type of withdrawal, you could arrange to transfer your vested assets from your existing plan to an IRA through a Direct Rollover Option.

What is a Direct Rollover Option? All qualified plans are required to give you the option to have your eligible distribution paid directly to an IRA that you establish. Under this Direct Rollover Option, no tax is withheld from the distribution since it is transferred directly from one retirement account to the trustee of your IRA. Once completed, you could begin your SSEP from the IRA.

Here is an important fact to consider before transferring assets to an IRA. Money in a qualified retirement plan often is protected from creditor's claims. Assets in an IRA often are not protected from creditor's claims. Therefore, moving assets out of a qualified plan into an IRA may subject these assets to judgments against you. If this is a concern to you, you may be better off not disturbing your assets that are currently protected in your qualified plan.

Here's how an early withdrawal program works: A series of substantially equal payments (SSEP) must be made at least annually and must be based on your life expectancy or on the joint life expectancies of you and a designated beneficiary. These payments must not be modified before you reach age 59 1/2, *and* they must be continued for at least five years from the date of the first payment unless you die or become disabled.

If you begin retirement at age 58, for instance, you must continue with your SSEP until age 63 to satisfy the five-year rule. If either of these rules is broken, you will be subject to the 10% penalty on all distributions prior to age 59 1/2 beginning with the first distribution you took. However, once this specified period of time has passed, you can change the amount of the payments you receive and how often you receive them. (Once you reach age 70 1/2, there are minimum required distributions that you must follow. Recent tax law changes have eliminated this requirement for some retirement programs.)

The IRS allows for three different methods to determine a series of substantially equal payments: minimum distribution method, amortization method, annuity method. Only one of the three methods can be used.

Method #1: Minimum Distribution Method. The annual payment can be determined using a method that is acceptable for purposes of calculating the *minimum distribution* required under the rules for IRAs (IRS Publication 590). However, this method to determine a SSEP results in the exact amount required, not the minimum amount. To figure the required distribution for each year, divide the IRA account balance as of the close of business on December 31 of the preceding year by the applicable life expectancy in the year of the distribution. Life expectancy tables are located in the back of IRS Publication 590. Table I is for single life expectancy, and Table II is for joint life expectancy. Your life expectancy can be recalculated each year from Tables I or II, or it can be reduced by "1" for each succeeding year. One or the other method must be chosen and cannot be changed until age 59 1/2 is reached *and* five years have elapsed.

Example: It is 1996, and Dr. Jones is 50 years old with a birthday in April. His IRA account balance on December 31, 1995 was $1.6 million. His life expectancy as of December 31, 1996 is 33.1 years (Table I). He can begin retirement this year with a SSEP of $48,338 ($1.6 million ÷ 33.1). Assume that the account grew to $1.7 million by the end of 1996 after $48,338 had been withdrawn earlier in the year. His life expectancy from Table I as of December 31, 1997 was 32.2 years. Therefore, his required distribution for 1997 would be $52,795 ($1.7 million ÷ 32.2).

Method #2: Amortization Method. The amount to be distributed annually can be determined by amortizing the account balance over a number of years equal to the life expectancy of the account owner (Table I, Publication 590) or the joint life and last survivor expectancy of the account owner and beneficiary (Table II, Publication 590). The interest rate is not to exceed a reasonable interest rate on the date payments begin.

Example: Assuming an interest rate of 8%, Dr. Jones can begin retirement in 1996 with a SSEP of $138,871 by amortizing $1.6 million over 33.1 years at 8%. This amount must be distributed to him each year until he reaches age 59 1/2. Since age 59 1/2 is nine years from the date he started receiving distributions, the five year minimum rule is also satisfied.

Method #3: Annuity Method. The amount to be distributed annually can be determined by dividing the taxpayer's account balance by an annuity factor (the present value of an annuity of $1 per year beginning at the taxpayer's age attained in the first distribution year and continuing for the life of the taxpayer).

The annuity factor must be derived using a reasonable mortality table and an interest rate that is reasonable on the date when payments begin. If substantially equal monthly payments are being determined, the account balance would be divided by an annuity factor equal to the present value of an annuity of $1 per month beginning at the taxpayer's age attained in the first distribution year and continuing for the life of the taxpayer.

Example: Using the annuity factor of 11.109 for a $1 per year annuity (assuming an interest rate of 8% and using the UP-1984 Mortality Table), Dr. Jones can begin retirement in 1996 with a SSEP of $144,027 ($1.6 million ÷ 11.109). As in the previous example, this distribution must continue each year until he reaches age 59 1/2.

The preceding three methods offer you various scenarios to plan for early retirement. Doing *what if* calculations by varying the method, interest rate, and mortality tables used to figure the distribution or by designating different beneficiaries (or using no beneficiary), the distribution can be tailored to meet your needs.

Furthermore, the SSEP exception does not require that all of an individual's IRAs be aggregated when the annual distribution amount is calculated. Individuals

with multiple IRAs can calculate payments from one IRA without considering the balance held in other IRAs. Additionally, similar periodic payments are not required to be made from the other IRAs.

Remember that once you begin your SSEP withdrawal program, it can not be altered until you reach age 59 1/2 *and* five years from the date of the first payment have passed.

As with all retirement and tax planning concerns, you must contact the appropriate professionals who can advise you regarding your specific needs and financial situation. To help you with the IRS guidelines, call the IRS at (800) 829-3676, and request Publication 590 (Individual Retirement Arrangements), Publication 575 (Pension and Annuity Income), and Publication 939 (Pension General Rule).

Don't Get Burned

The IRS can take almost everything you have successfully acquired during your life if you don't take proper steps to prevent it. When you die, there are estate taxes, income taxes, generation skipping taxes, and excess accumulation taxes that can eat up your estate. Here is a worse case scenario:

Dr. and Mrs. Jones have a qualified retirement plan with $2 million accumulated. He dies at age 70 with a taxable estate of over $10 million including the plan benefits. His children are well off so he names his grandchildren as beneficiaries of the retirement benefits. The $2 million distribution to his grandchildren is victim to approximately $1,700,000 in total taxes. That leaves only $300,000 after taxes for his grandchildren—approximately 15% of the original pre-tax balance of the benefits. This is a disaster!

Without proper planning, your estate could fall victim to the same ravaging tax system. Here is a typical scenario about Dr. and Mrs. I. M. Retiring. Consider their objectives and the accompanying course of action they take.

Dr. I. M. Retiring has accumulated a significant amount of money in his retirement account. He and his wife are ready to retire, but they know that their estate could suffer severe taxation if they don't make plans now.

Their objectives are to live on $80,000 a year with annual increases to offset future inflation. They have two adult children and three grandchildren, all of whom they want to share in their estate. Dr. and Mrs. Retiring want to know if there is a simple way they can meet their objectives without their lifestyles being disrupted and without taxes diluting the distributions to their beneficiaries.

I. M. and his wife could consider an immediate annuity for their cash flow needs and an irrevocable insurance trust for the needs of their beneficiaries. Here is how it could work:

Dr. and Mrs. Retiring can roll their retirement account into a Joint Life Annuity with a rider that allows for annual cost-of-living increases. This annuity can be set up to pay I. M. and his wife a monthly income equivalent to their projected needs for the rest of both of their lives. It will start immediately and will offset the ravages that inflation could cause because of the built-in inflation rider.

I. M. and his wife also will set up an irrevocable insurance trust. (This is discussed in chapter 17.) This is a trust whose beneficiaries are their children and grandchildren. The trust will purchase and own a second-to-die life insurance policy on Dr. and Mrs. Retiring's lives. (A second-to-die life insurance policy insures two people and pays the death benefit after the second person dies. This type of policy is less expensive than one for a sole individual.) The death benefit of the insurance policy will be for the amount of money I. M. and his wife have decided they want to leave to their heirs.

The trust will be funded by I. M. and his wife every year. The trust will then purchase the insurance policy and make annual premium payments. The trustee of the insurance trust could be one of their adult children.

After the death of both Dr. and Mrs. Retiring, the proceeds of the second-to-die insurance policy will go to the trust. Since the insurance proceeds are not in the estate of Dr. or Mrs. Retiring, there will be no estate taxes. There also will be no income taxes on the life insurance distribution. Also, with proper planning, there will be no generation skipping taxes to be paid either.

The end result will be that Dr. and Mrs. I. M. Retiring will continue to live their lifestyles as they desire, their children and grandchildren will have the inheritance that I. M. and his wife have planned, and the IRS will not dilute any of the distributed assets.

This scenario is obviously a simplification. But, it should open your eyes to some of the potential tax consequences of not planning properly and how to avoid them. Contact an estate planning professional to see what might work best for you.

Don't Save Too Much ... or Else!

Don't take me wrong. Yes, you must plan for retirement. Yes, you must start early. Yes, you must save enough to maintain the lifestyle you desire for the rest of your life. However, when you are accumulating wealth in a retirement plan, you can get to a point where the IRS steps in to make its presence known.

They do that by imposing taxes. These are excise taxes for taking too much out of your retirement plans or for saving too much within these plans. Here's how these taxes work:

- There maybe an excise tax if your distributions are above a certain amount. If your plan will pay you in 1996 more than $155,000 or a lump sum distribution of more than $775,000 (both are indexed for inflation), you could face a 15% excise tax on the amount you receive above these limits I have just cited. (These taxes have been suspended for qualified retirement plans in 1997, 1998, and 1999.)

- There is also an excise tax if you die with too much money in your retirement plan. If your retirement plan at your death has more money than it would cost to purchase an annuity to pay you $155,000 in 1996 (indexed for inflation) based on your age at the time of your death, then the excess accumulation in your plan would be subject to a 15% excise tax. This tax is in addition to the income tax and estate tax which would be due on the money in your retirement plan. Your estate could actually have a total tax bill as high as 85%!

One way to avoid the excise tax is to take distributions early. Don't wait until you are 70 1/2 to begin your withdrawal program from your retirement nest egg. As I described in Option #5, you could begin a series of payments before age 59 1/2 without penalty.

Also, by naming your spouse as the beneficiary of your retirement plan, he or she could elect to pay the excise tax over a lifetime of distributions. If your spouse is much younger than you, distributions made over a lifetime would be smaller and could escape the excise tax entirely.

On the other side of the story, there are situations where it might be best to continue to defer your withdrawals for as long as possible. If your retirement money were compounding at a high total rate of return, then the growth potential (with taxes being deferred) would be substantial. Any excise taxes to pay at a later date might be offset easily by the greater accumulated wealth within the account.

Contact your tax adviser to review the options that are available to you. Meanwhile, keep investing and accumulating wealth. Enjoy the harvest of your efforts.

You've Arrived!
A Withdrawal Plan

If you follow your financial plan for retirement, you will eventually reach your destination; you will arrive. This chapter assumes that you have arrived and are ready to retire. To assist you with planning once you have arrived, I have developed a Withdrawal Table to help with your projections and actual withdrawals.

A Withdrawal Table projects how much will be left in your nest egg account at the end of each successive future year after (1) you have taken out your annual living needs at the beginning of the year, and (2) the balance of the portfolio has continued to grow from its investments. Each year your annual withdrawal is projected. It is based on your original needs you calculated in chapter 7, and it is increased annually by the projected inflation rate. The annual increase in your withdrawal offsets the decrease in purchasing power as a result of inflation. The bottom line is that your standard of living can be maintained even though inflation continues to increase your cost of living.

I am going to describe the components of the Withdrawal Table first. Next I will return to our young couple, Jodi and Mike, and go through their projected Withdrawal Table.

Beginning Balance: This is the value of your nest egg at the beginning of your retirement. It is the PV button on the financial calculator.

Years to Withdraw: This is the projected number of years before your portfolio is depleted to zero. Most financial planners suggest you use your projected life expectancy and then add another fifteen years or so. It is the N button on the financial calculator. If you prefer not to touch the principal at all, you could enter 100 for N which represents infinity for all intents and purposes. (Life expectancies are in Table 7.10: Life Expectancy.)

Anticipated annually-compounded rate of return: There is no guarantee you will achieve this return. It is based on the historical returns of the funds you choose. It is always wise to underestimate this number. This is the I button on the financial calculator.

Projected inflation rate: This is what you project to be the annual inflation rate. This is also the percent by which you will increase your annual withdrawals in order to keep up with inflation.

Table 16.1: Jodi and Mike's Withdrawal Table

Date_____

Beginning Balance _____$1,480,294_____
Years to withdraw _____40_____
Anticipated annually-compounded rate-of-return ____14%____
Projected inflation rate __4.0%__
Inflation-adjusted rate-of-return _9.6154%_
Annual needs - first year of retirement ___$133,237___

Start Yr	Year	Age	Annual	Target	Actual	Adjust
1	2023		$133,237	$1,535,645		
2	2024		$138,566	$1,592,670		
3	2025		$144,109	$1,651,360		
4	2026		$149,874	$1,711,694		
5	2027		$155,868	$1,773,641		
6	2028		$162,103	$1,837,153		
7	2029		$168,587	$1,902,166		
8	2030		$175,331	$1,968,592		
9	2031		$182,344	$2,036,322		
10	2032		$189,638	$2,105,220		
11	2033		$197,223	$2,175,117		
12	2034		$205,112	$2,245,805		
13	2035		$213,317	$2,317,037		
14	2036		$221,849	$2,388,514		
15	2037		$230,723	$2,459,882		
16	2038		$239,952	$2,530,720		
17	2039		$249,550	$2,600,534		
18	2040		$259,532	$2,668,742		
19	2041		$269,914	$2,734,664		
20	2042		$280,716	$2,797,501		

Table 16.1: Jodi and Mike's Withdrawal Table (continued)

Start Yr	Year	Age	Annual	Target	Actual	Adjust
21	2043		$291,939	$2,856,340		
22	2044		$303,616	$2,910,106		
23	2045		$315,761	$2,957,553		
24	2046		$328,391	$2,997,245		
25	2047		$341,527	$3,027,518		
26	2048		$355,188	$3,046,456		
27	2049		$369,396	$3,051,849		
28	2050		$384,171	$3,041,153		
29	2051		$399,538	$3,011,441		
30	2052		$415,520	$2,959,350		
31	2053		$432,140	$2,881,019		
32	2054		$449,426	$2,772,016		
33	5055		$467,403	$2,627,259		
34	2056		$486,099	$2,440,922		
35	2057		$505,548	$2,206,327		
36	2058		$525,765	$1,915,838		
37	2059		$546,796	$1,560,708		
38	2060		$568,667	$1,130,927		
39	2061		$591,414	$615,044		
40	2063		$615,070	[$26]		
41						
42						
43						
44						
45						
46						
47						
48						

Inflation adjusted rate-of-return: This is the rate after inflation is taken into consideration. It is calculated from the formula in Table 7.12: How Much Does It Take (Step #3). Use four decimal places for accuracy.

Annual needs for first year of retirement: This is what you can withdraw the first year of retirement for your projections to stay on target.

Start Year: Year "1" is the first year that you will withdraw an annual income. In this example, you withdraw an annual income at the beginning of the year, place it in a check-writing money market account, and write yourself a monthly check for your needs.

Year: This is the actual year you begin your withdrawal program.

Age: This is your attained age during that Year.

Annual: This is your projected annual need which increases each year by the projected inflation rate. This is the total that you withdraw at the beginning of the year to meet your needs. (All interest earned in a check-writing, money market account is a bonus and is not considered in these calculations.)

Target: This is the projected balance of your nest egg at the end of each year (1) after you have withdrawn the annual amount at the beginning of the year to be used over the course of the year and (2) after the remainder of the portfolio has grown from its mutual fund investments for that year.

Actual: This is the real time balance of your portfolio at the end of the year. You will record this annually as you monitor your Withdrawal Table.

Adjust: If the *target balance* is less than the *actual balance*, you are in good shape. No adjustment is necessary. If, on the other hand, your *target balance* is more than the *actual balance*, you are running a deficit. Your options at that moment are:
- Shift your mutual funds to better performing funds. (Review the rules for the Lifetime Investing Plan in chapter 13.)
- Withdraw less money in the following year.
- Consider some means of supplementing your income aside from your nest egg account.

Now, let's again interrupt Jodi and Mike to discover how they have put their Withdrawal Table together.

Jodi's Annual Monitor (Table 14.2) will be essentially the same as Mike's. Together, they have projected their combined nest egg to be worth $1,480,294 at the beginning of retirement. They will be 56 years old at that point. From the Table 7.10:

Life Expectancy, they know Mike's life expectancy is approximately 21 more years, and Jodi's life expectancy is approximately 25 more years. To be on the safe side, they add 15 years to this and plan their withdrawals for the next 40 years.

Using their financial calculator and the calculation method in Step #4 of Table 7.12: How Much Does It Take?, Mike and Jodi projected how much they could withdraw at the beginning of their first year of retirement. The calculator entries are: N = 40; I = 9.6154; FV = 0; PV = 1,480,294; PMT = ? = -$133,237. Therefore, the first year of retirement, Mike and Jodi will withdraw $133,237. Each successive year they will withdraw 4.0% more to offset the anticipated inflation rate of 4.0%. This is the only time the inflation-adjusted return is used in this calculation. It compensates for the effects of inflation during the entire withdrawal period.

These, of course, are only educated guesses just as are all of your projections. You will need to reevaluate your calculations and projections annually to be sure amounts are on target. Changes along the way are inevitable.

Continuing with the Withdrawal Table, the annual amounts to withdraw each successive year are increased by the inflation rate.

In the example, Year "2" equals Year "1" plus 4.0%. Year "3" equals Year "2" plus 4.0%, and so on.

To calculate the *target values*, a simple degree of math is required:
1. Begin with the beginning balance ($1,480,294 in Jodi and Mike's case);
2. Subtract out the first year's annual needs ($1,480,294 - $133,237 = $1,347,057);
3. To this balance, add in the expected total return for the year ($1,347,057 + [0.14 times $1,347,057] = $1,535,645).
4. This is the *target value* at the end of that Year.
5. From this *target value*, subtract the second year's annual needs as you did in Step #2. Then proceed to Step #3, and continue to repeat the process until all *target values* have been determined.

Jodi and Mike will fill in this Withdrawal Table through the last year of their projection which is 40 years from the time when they retire. It is not until the year 2062 (15 years beyond their combined life expectancy) that their nest egg is close to being depleted.

As with all of the forms I have described in this book, a blank Withdrawal Table is waiting for you in Appendix I.

Although you have put much thought into creating and realizing your financial goals, have you protected your assets along the way? Bonus chapter 17 addresses this very concern.

Asset Protection

Assure Your Privacy

To protect your assets you first must assure your privacy. The fact that you have a social security number, a personal identification number, a driver's license, and most likely many credit cards places you in harm's way. You are open to scams, hacker attacks, and other invasions of privacy. Let me relate a personal story.

Several months ago, a representative from my long-distance telephone company called me. He introduced himself as an investigator from my phone company. He asked me if I had made any long-distance calls out of the country within the past week; I told him I had not. He asked me if I had lost my phone-card; I told him I had not.

He then informed me that calls had been made using my phone-card to several foreign countries and that my phone history had never shown these types of calls being made. He continued to describe to me how I was a victim of a scam.

He explained how he was going to cancel my old card, credit my account for the fraudulent calls, and issue me a new phone-card. He even told me what my new personal identification number would be. He proceeded to get specific information from me.

I had no reason to question him because he seemed to know a great deal about my telephone habits from the past. He requested final verification of my old personal identification number. I gave it to him without thinking.

After completing our conversation, I hung up. I thought about what had just happened. To be on the safe side, I called the customer relations department immediately to be sure this gentleman was in fact who he said he was.

Guess What! I *was* the victim of a scam, but the scam was perpetrated by the impostor/investigator with whom I just had talked. When I gave the impostor/investigator my personal identification number, he apparently sold that information to other crooks. My phone company traced the impostor's call to a public phone booth at Grand Central Station in New York. Within minutes, phone calls to Ethiopia and China were being charged to my phone-card.

I couldn't believe how vulnerable I was.

It is important for you to be aware of all the information concerning you that is available to anyone. Information about your personal life is on file in over five billion computerized records. Almost 200 federal agencies and departments maintain millions of private records. Mailing lists and private files are manipulated by thousands of magazine companies, catalog companies, retail products companies, etc. Over 450 million records are maintained by the big three credit-reporting companies—TRW, Trans Union, Equifax.

It is estimated that your personal information is moved from one computer to another approximately five times a day! For a fee, you can contact each of the major credit-reporting companies and request a copy of your personal record. You might be amazed at the information they have on you. Here are their toll-free phone numbers: TRW, (800) 392-1122; Trans Union, (800) 916-8800; Equifax, (800) 685-1111.

Here are several ideas about how you can protect your privacy:

Shred Your Trash

You may not believe it, but your trash is a veritable source of private information. The bank statements, charge slips, deposit slips, and other private letters you throw away are just waiting to be exploited.

Be Careful at ATM Machines

People have been videotaped at ATM machines. As they leave and throw away their ATM transaction receipt, scam artists have been able to retrieve these slips. It is only a matter of matching the account numbers on the slip with the personal identification number on the videotape. The thief can then begin withdrawing money from that ATM account.

Withhold Your Social Security and Personal Identification Numbers

Be sure there is a legitimate reason for giving your social security or personal identification numbers to anyone. These numbers allow an individual to gain access to considerable private information about you.

Minimize Recorded Transactions

Every time you purchase something from a catalog, that information is recorded. The catalog company has your name, address, phone number, and credit card number. Although most companies are honest, this information could get into the wrong hands. Request that the company remove your name from their mailing list so it is not sold to mail-list companies.

Consider a Locked Mailbox

Your mailbox is most likely a typical post office approved type. This is easily opened by anyone who wishes to peek at its contents. There are lock boxes that are available. For details, contact: Janzer Corp., 6 Lincoln Center, Hulmeville, PA 19047 or Trail Side Mailbox, Inc., 21000 E. 32nd Parkway, Aurora, CO 80011.

Investigate Electronic Security Devices

Electronic devices exist that can sweep your home and office for "taps and bugs," can scramble your phone calls and faxes, and even can stop your computer from its normal broadcasting of everything you display on the screen. Prices start around $375. You may think this is overkill, but it may not be at all.

You may not feel that your private life is open to anyone who wants admission, but it is. If there is information about you that is written or entered into a computer, it can be tapped by conniving individuals who might have devious intentions. Your best protection is to keep the availability of your private information as limited as possible.

Methods of Asset Protection

After assuring your privacy, you can investigate ways of protecting your assets. Consider the following scenario:

You are financially successful with a level of wealth that may be viewed by some as *more than you need*. There are those who are jealous of individuals who have more than they have. Sometimes, just your visible wealth is enough to foster frivolous lawsuits. Since anxious attorneys perceive you to have "deep financial pockets," you are susceptible to liability suits. Your assets are also vulnerable to the whims and taxes of the government. Presently, you are aware of no potential lawsuits against you, but you have substantial assets with the potential for significant appreciation which could be at risk.

One of your goals is to try to protect these assets from potential lawsuits. Another goal is to protect your assets from government intervention and taxes. Still, another goal is to keep your assets as confidential as is legally possible. What can you do now?

Your first protection for covered risks is *general liability insurance*. Another protection from creditors that also allows for tax-deferred growth of capital is a *qualified retirement plan*. (A word of caution is in order here. An IRA is not qualified retirement plan and may not be exempt from a creditor attack in all of the states. Check with your local counsel to determine if your IRA is an exempt asset.) One vehicle that helps you transfer assets out of your estate thereby making them almost inaccessible to creditors but still lets you have control over these assets is a *family limited partnership*. A vehicle that can protect your assets from creditors as well as take your assets out of the public eye is a *United States based trust*. The following are some examples of U.S. based trusts:

For those who are charitably inclined, *a charitable remainder trust* offers the benefits of removing appreciated assets out of your estate and in addition provides both an income stream and a charitable income-tax deduction to you. For those who want to create and preserve assets for their heirs, an *irrevocable life insurance trust* works well. When you die, there are two testamentary trusts that can reduce estate taxes and give you a say in how assets eventually will be dispersed—a *credit trust* and an *Q-TIP trust*. If you want to preserve assets for generations to come, there is the *dynasty trust*.

Yet, another vehicle that can do most of these things and also may protect your assets from government intervention is a trust outside of the United States. It is called an *offshore asset protection trust*.

Liability Insurance

Liability insurance is the first place to turn for third party help. This is an insurance product that will provide you with a means of transferring the potential financial loss of a judgment from you to an insurance company. Liability coverage is an agreement whereby an insurer, in exchange for a premium, pays those dollars that an insured becomes legally obligated to pay as damages because of bodily injury or property damage. The end results are that the insured avoids the financial loss for covered damages and the insurance company pays the plaintiff.

Various types of policies are available to cover for personal liability, professional liability, and commercial liability. You will need to seek the services of an insurance agent who specializes in liability insurance.

Qualified Retirement Plans

These types of plans are provided by employers and approved by the IRS offer a unique type of asset protection. Your assets that are in qualified retirement plans are usually protected from your creditors. In this way, if there is a judgment brought against you, your creditors can not take your qualified retirement assets to satisfy the judgment.

This protection does not usually apply to the retirement money that you may have in an IRA. It is also important to remember that if you have a qualified retirement plan and then rollover the assets to an IRA, the money that has been transferred to the IRA is usually no longer protected from creditors.

Family Limited Partnership

Your attorney draws up the proper documents for this partnership, and some of your investments (assets) are transferred to it. The partnership units are made up of general units and limited units.

For example, 100 units could be created for your Family Limited Partnership consisting of 90 limited partnership units and 10 general partnership units. Each limited unit carries 1% ownership and 0% control; each general unit carries 1% ownership and 10% control. Total control (100%) is retained in the 10 general units.

Your spouse and you would own all the general partnership units, thereby maintaining 100% control. With respect to the limited partnership units, you may want to gift some of them to family members. As you give away these limited units, they are permanently removed from your estate.

Also, there is usually a *valuation discount* that you can claim with the limited units you give away. A *valuation discount* is a reduction in the fair market value of these limited units because they do not carry any controlling interest. Check with a qualified CPA to discuss the methods of receiving a *valuation discount* for these limited partnership units. Your spouse and you would retain the remaining limited partnership units.

Protection with a Family Limited Partnership only works if it is formed and assets are completely transferred into it, *before* an incident resulting in a creditor judgment. Otherwise, the transfer of assets to the partnership could be considered a fraudulent conveyance and therefore would be disallowed by the courts.

If a large judgment were rendered against you in the future, your Family Limited Partnership would function at least as a major nuisance to your creditors. In most states, a judgment creditor only can obtain a *charging order* against the partnership units. This order gives the creditor only the right to receive income from the partnership if and when it is distributed to you and your spouse. The creditor has no right to take control or gain access to the assets owned by the Family Limited Partnership. Also, the creditor cannot have any effect on you or your spouse who are the general partners. Only you and your spouse will retain total control over the assets.

To further protect these assets, a clause is usually included in the partnership agreement which states that the general partners may retain all of the cash in the partnership for future needs of the partnership.

Interestingly, if the creditor obtains a charging order and is entitled to receive distributed income, the IRS will consider the creditor to be an owner of his share of the partnership income even though it was not distributed. The creditor, therefore, will be required to pay income taxes on the undistributed (phantom) income. This is a real deterrent to the creditor!

Additional protection is available for your assets through an Offshore Asset Protection Trust described later in this chapter. An onshore or offshore specialist in international financial and estate planning would establish this trust in a foreign jurisdiction and have it supervised by an offshore trustee. You and your spouse then would transfer ownership of the limited partnership units to this trust. The limited partnership units must be transferred to the trust before there is a claim made against you or before you are sued, whichever comes first. Once transferred, you and your spouse would continue to own the general partnership units and thereby maintain complete control over the assets. The offshore trustee would only hold the limited partnership units for your benefit.

United States Based Trusts

The use of trusts dates back to premedieval England. Back then, necessity proved to be the mother of invention. The necessity began when kings in days of old would often overtax and over regulate real estate to the chagrin of many land owners. The invention was created by wise attorneys to get around these burdensome laws—so, trusts were born.

Title to land was given by the original owner to persons he could trust. The trustees (the persons who managed the property) administered the land for the original owner. After the original owner's death, the trustee disposed of the property according to the original owner's wishes.

Today, trusts have evolved into highly sophisticated tools for the convenient management of one's assets. Once only the very wealthy knew about and benefited from trusts. However, trusts are available today to anyone who wishes to benefit from them.

Why should you be interested in trusts? Because, you can arrange to educate your children through trusts. You can take care of your elderly parents through trusts. You can avoid probate through trusts. You can protect assets from creditors through trusts. You can even create a retirement income for yourself and your spouse through trusts without including any employees.

Basically, a trust enables you to create a financial plan that meets your needs as well as the needs of your loved ones. It therefore helps to guarantee the future.

By definition, a trust is a legal arrangement which can hold the ownership of assets for the benefit of one or more individuals (beneficiaries). You (the grantor) can establish the trust to fulfill your wishes. You can be the manager of the trust (the trustee) or you can name someone else to be the trustee. The trust files annual tax returns and pays taxes on retained income. This last statement is important for you to realize. The federal income taxes due on taxable retained income above $7,500 is 39.6%!

A trust can be set up that takes effect now (a living trust) or after your death (a testamentary trust). If it takes effect now, it can be either a revocable trust (one whose terms you can change at anytime) or an irrevocable trust (one whose terms you never can change). Most irrevocable trusts can be designed to protect their assets from creditors. All testamentary trusts are irrevocable.

It is important for you to know that if you, the grantor, have any control over the assets in the trust, then the assets in the trust most likely will be included in your estate. On the other hand, if you as the grantor do not have any control over the trust's assets, then usually the assets of the trust will not be included in your estate. Therefore, revocable trusts which you create are generally included in your estate, and irrevocable trusts which you create are generally not included in your estate.

Typical assets which can be placed in a trust include bank accounts, real estate, securities, mutual fund shares, limited partnerships, and personal property such as art, cars, and jewelry. All assets that become part of the trust must have the ownership transferred to the trust. For example, if you placed your car into a trust, the car could no longer be in your name. The title of the car would need to be changed to read, "In trust for. . . the beneficiary's name."

There are many types of trusts for many varied purposes. An attorney who specializes in trusts can advise you regarding how trusts may be able to assist you in reaching and maintaining your financial security. Since trusts are governed by state law, your choice of attorney should be from the state in which you reside.

Living Trusts. Living Trusts have become an integral part of estate planning and are used by many of us as the sole means to protect and pass on our wealth. However, we should be aware that although living trusts are a valuable tool in estate planning, they also have their limitations—especially in their ability to shelter assets from estate taxes and provide asset protection.

Let's first consider what living trusts are able to accomplish.

If properly funded during your lifetime, living trusts are extremely useful in avoiding probate. Probate is a court administered process of transferring assets from a decedent's estate which generally takes nine months, and where the fees are often statutorily based on the gross value of the estate. In some states however, the probate process may be streamlined thereby reducing the time frame necessary to close the proceeding and/or reducing the fees paid to attorneys and executors. In these states it is not uncommon to have testamentary trusts in a will where the decedent's assets are probated as they pass into the trusts. Regardless of what your state's particular laws may be regarding probate, you should be aware you may have a probatable estate even though it may not be subject to estate taxes.

Another popular reason for having a living trust is for tax planning purposes. These types of trusts (ex. Credit Trusts and Q-TIP Trusts discussed later) allow a husband and wife to combine their current $600,000 unified exemption credits so that between them they can pass $1,200,000 free of estate taxes to their beneficiaries. However, non-tax planning types of trusts, where everything is left to the surviving spouse, forfeit the $600,000 exemption of the first spouse to die. This means that although there is no estate tax due at the first spouse's death, now only the survivor's $600,000 may be used.

Also, keep in mind that a limitation of living trusts is that they offer no additional benefit in sheltering estate taxes for individuals. Therefore, don't assume that because you have a living trust your estate will not pay any taxes.

It is a cruel reality that estates which are in excess of $1,200,000 between spouses and those which exceed $600,000 for individuals will ultimately have to pay estate tax. Many people are surprised to learn that our estate tax system is a separate tax system where taxable estates begin to be taxed at a rate of 37.5%, with a current maximum rate of 55%. Further, if a sizable amount of your estate is left to your grandchildren there is also a 55% generation skipping tax in addition to estate taxes. Finally, qualified retirement monies may be especially hard hit with estate, income, and excise taxes which could deplete such monies by over 70% by the time they reach your beneficiaries.

Another limitation of living trusts is that many of us mistakenly believe that they will offer us asset protection from our creditors or from potential lawsuits. The reality is that living trusts afford no such protection since you still retain full control of the assets. Although other types of trusts used in more advanced estate planning can afford such protection in accordance with your state's laws, the revocable nature of living trusts makes asset and creditor protection nonexistent.

Credit Trust and Q-TIP Trust. These two trusts help to minimize estate taxes and provide control over assets. These trusts could be funded while you are alive (living trusts) or they could be funded after your death (testamentary trusts).

The estate and gift tax laws usually tax any transfer of assets unless a specific exemption applies. The three exemptions you are entitled to are the:

- annual $10,000 gift tax exclusion which allows you to give away tax-free up to $10,000 a year to as many individuals as you choose,
- $600,000 unified credit which allows you to exempt a maximum of $600,000 of your assets from estate and gift taxes either while you are alive or after your death, and
- unlimited marital deduction which allows you to give as much as you wish, before or after your death, to your spouse without any gift or estate taxes.

If you were to die and leave everything to your spouse, there would be no estate taxes due at your death. Then, when your spouse died, there would be only $600,000 of the estate which would avoid estate taxes. In addition, after your death, your spouse could dispose of the assets in any way he or she desired regardless of what you had intended. There is a way for you to further reduce estate taxes and to control most of the estate assets.

A Credit Trust will shelter an additional $600,000 from estate taxes, and a Q-TIP Trust will provide control over the assets.

- **Credit Trust**—The $600,000 unified credit allows *each* spouse to avoid taxes on $600,000 of assets owned solely by that spouse. Therefore, each spouse should own up to $600,000 of assets in his or her name only, and a Credit Trust should be established. On the death of the first spouse, $600,000 of that spouse's assets would pass into this Credit Trust and would avoid estate taxes. The trustee would be given the right to pay income from the assets of this trust to the surviving spouse and other beneficiaries. However, income could be retained in this trust if desired, and the value of the trust could grow substantially. After the second spouse dies, the assets of this trust would be distributed as detailed in the trust document and would not be taxed in the second spouse's estate.

- **Q-TIP Trust**—The full name of this trust is Qualified Terminable Interest Property Trust. The surviving spouse would receive all of the income from the trust at least on an annual basis, and no other person would have an interest in the trust during the life of the surviving spouse.

The advantages of this type of trust are that the first spouse to die could specify whether or not the principal of the trust would be available to the surviving spouse and how the trust assets would be distributed following the death of the surviving spouse. In this way, the first spouse to die would have considerable control over the assets in the trust. Also, the assets in the Q-TIP Trust qualify for the marital deduction, and therefore are not taxed in the first-to-die spouse's estate.

Strategy: Create a testamentary Credit Trust; place the balance into testamentary Q-TIP Trust

In this scenario, $600,000 of assets owned by the first spouse to die (the maximum unified credit) would be contributed to the Credit Trust, and the balance would pass to the Q-TIP Trust. This is a complex strategy because two trusts would be created at the death of the first spouse. This technique would eventually save estate taxes for the surviving spouse because $600,000 would be removed from the joint estate by way of the Credit Trust. The remaining assets in the Q-TIP Trust would benefit the surviving spouse until his or her death and then would be taxed in his or her gross estate. The estate of the second spouse to die would receive its own $600,000 exemption. Finally, the assets of the Q-TIP Trust would pass to the beneficiaries as originally determined by the first spouse to die.

There are many more issues to be discussed when considering a Credit Trust and a Q-TIP Trust. Your attorney and accountant need to describe all of the issues to you before you can determine if these vehicles are suitable for your needs. However, the combination of both trusts can help your estate by saving estate taxes and by ensuring you that your assets are handled as you wish.

Charitable Remainder Trust. Here is an estate planning tool to convert investment assets which have a low cost-basis and which generate little if any income into income generating assets for retirement needs. It also takes your assets out of the path of creditors and judgments. It is called a Charitable Remainder Trust. (By the way, this can be set up at any time to provide current cash flow. You do not have to do this as a retirement program.)

The cost-basis is the original cost of the asset and any additional after-tax dollars you put into the asset while you owned it. In the case of stocks or mutual funds, this would include your original purchase price, all of your dollar-cost-averaging, and all reinvested distributions. In the case of real estate, it would include your purchase price and all expenses to improve the property.

Generally, if you wanted to create retirement income out of a low cost-basis asset that generated little income, you would need to sell the asset, pay the capital gains taxes, and invest the balance in an income producing vehicle. A 28% capital gains tax could leave you with an inadequate base from which to obtain your desired income flow. A charitable remainder trust eliminates the 28% tax bite on the sale of the asset and also generates an income tax shelter for the proceeds.

Here is an example:

Steve and Jill are preparing to retire. They have a $1 million portfolio of stock that has a basis of $50,000. The stock generates annual dividends of approximately $30,000 a year. They need more income.

If they sold the stock portfolio, Steve and Jill would have to pay $266,000 in capital gains. This would leave $734,000 to invest. If they invested this into a conservative vehicle yielding 8% annually, they would generate $58,720 a year. This is approximately a 5.9% return on their original $1 million portfolio. They had hoped for more.

If Steve and Jill set up a Charitable Remainder Trust and transferred their $1 million portfolio into it, a different scenario could take place.

The trustee could sell the stock and reinvest the proceeds into the same 8% conservative vehicle. However, the trust would not have to pay a capital gains tax because it is a tax-exempt charity. The entire $1 million therefore could be invested to yield $80,000 a year.

The terms of this irrevocable trust provide that upon the death of both Steve and Jill, whatever is left in the trust would be owned by the charity they had selected. Since the charity owns the remainder of the trust (remainder interest), Steve and Jill receive another benefit.

When Steve and Jill establish the trust, they get an immediate income tax deduction for the charitable gift of this anticipated remainder interest. The IRS publishes a future interest table to establish the present value of the remainder interest. The amount of this income tax deduction is based on the ages of Steve and Jill, the prevailing interest rates, and the percent of the trust to be distributed annually to Steve and Jill.

In this case, the tax deduction for Steve and Jill is approximately $240,000. They will be limited to taking a maximum of 30% of their adjusted gross income as a deduction per year. But, they can take this maximum year after year until the total $240,000 is depleted. However, if all $240,000 is not depleted by the fifth year, the balance is lost.

There are two disadvantages that you must understandf:
- The first disadvantage is that Steve and Jill will not be able to deplete all of the property they have transferred to the trust. Whatever remains in the trust upon their deaths will go to the charity.
- The second disadvantage is that Steve and Jill cannot leave any of this property to their children.

If Steve and Jill want to provide a benefit for their children, they could establish an *irrevocable life insurance trust*. This life insurance trust could purchase a second-to-die policy on Steve and Jill, and could pay the premiums with funds transferred to the trust by Steve and Jill. The money to fund the trust could come from the income tax saving as a result of the charitable deduction from the transfer of assets to the Charitable Remainder Trust.

Here is a summary of the benefits of a Charitable Remainder Trust:
- Increased cash flow from assets
- Immediate charitable deduction against current income

- Greater capital base from which to draw retirement income since no capital gains tax is paid on sale of assets
- Protection of assets from creditors since transferred assets are owned by charitable trust

Irrevocable Life Insurance Trust. Most people believe that life insurance proceeds are tax-free at death. This is only half true. Life insurance proceeds are free from income taxes at death, but they may be subject to federal estate taxes which could be as high as 55%.

Therefore, the challenge is to plan your insurance program so that your life insurance proceeds are not subject to federal estate taxes. If taxed at the estate tax level, the benefits that you thought you had provided for your family to maintain their lifestyle could be diminished greatly. All of your previous efforts to create security for your family might provide only stress and uncertainty for them after your death.

The federal estate tax is not based on who benefits from the insurance proceeds; it is based on who owns and controls the life insurance policy.

For instance, if an insurance policy on your life were owned by your adult child for his or her benefit and you died, the proceeds of the policy would go to your child income-tax-free as well as estate-tax-free. The proceeds would be out of your estate since you were not the owner of the policy.

However, if this same policy were for your child's benefit but were owned by you, and you died, the proceeds would first go to your estate. Only after the estate taxes were paid on these proceeds would your child receive his or her share.

The problem of assigning ownership of your policy to your adult child is that your child may not have the means, the interest, or the maturity to handle the proceeds in the way you intended for them to be used. So, what is the answer?

The solution may be an irrevocable life insurance trust established by you. Here is how it works. Someone other than you would be designated as the trustee. The ownership of the life insurance policy would be transferred to this trust. The trust would be designated as the beneficiary of the policy. You would design the trust document to state how the assets of the trust were to be applied for the benefit of your family members. You would give money to the trust from which the trustee would pay the insurance premiums.

There are several other details to consider when establishing this trust. The trust must have its own bank account so it can pay the life insurance premiums when due and eventually disburse benefits to your family members later on. It will also need to register for its own federal identification number, and it will need to file its own income tax returns.

The major benefit from such a trust is that it will avoid taxation in the estate for both you and your spouse. This can actually double the after-tax value of the life

insurance policy. Another benefit is that you have dictated exactly how the proceeds of the trust will be used. The funds will not be squandered, and they will be out of the reach of creditors.

Technically, the trust must be structured to avoid gift taxes from the transfer of the insurance policy to it. A special provision of the trust called the Crummey Power could allow as much as $5,000 to be given to the trust per beneficiary of the trust without triggering any gift taxes. This would be limited to a maximum of $10,000. (You will need to check with your tax attorney regarding the specifics about this special power.)

For instance, if there were a spouse and two children who would be the ultimate beneficiaries of the trust, the maximum you could give to the trust each year to pay the premiums would be $10,000. On the other hand, if there were only one beneficiary, then the maximum you could give the trust annually to pay the premiums would be $5,000.

Another technical requirement is the *Three Year Rule*. If your policy is transferred to the trust within three years of your death, the proceeds will usually be taxed in your estate. Therefore, early planning is important. To avoid this problem, the trust could be formed first. Then money could be placed into the trust to purchase a new policy on your life.

Remember, this is an irrevocable trust. Once the terms are established, they cannot be changed. If you had a life insurance policy that had a large cash value, transferring this to an irrevocable trust will make the cash value off limits to you forever.

Dynasty Trust. There is a generation-skipping-tax when you try to pass assets on from one generation to another. There is also an exemption from this tax on the first $1,000,000 that is gifted. A Dynasty Trust is designed to maximize the growth of a portfolio as well as minimize the effects of estate and generation-skipping-taxation.

As with all trusts, this is a complex issue that must be discussed with a tax attorney. The important point here is that this trust can avoid multiple generation estate taxes and generation-skipping taxes. Also, there can be potential for significant accumulation of wealth for later generations. Each state regulates how long this type of trust can continue.

Offshore Asset Protection Trust

As with all trusts, the offshore asset protection trust (APT) offers privacy, but because of the extra layers of privacy designed around these trusts, it is very difficult for the prying eye to find out about your offshore wealth.

The APT is a tax-neutral entity and is intended primarily for privacy and asset protection.

Those countries in which an APT is established are chosen because they have different and favorable laws protecting the trust, the trustee, the assets, and hence the beneficiaries. For one thing, they do not entertain frivolous lawsuits. Since they have no income taxes, they do not allow judgments entered in U.S. courts for taxes to be enforced, nor do they allow punitive damages to be collected from you. Your offshore assets are owned by the APT, not you, and the offshore trustee cannot be forced to surrender these assets under a U.S. court order.

Some of the countries that are suited for offshore trusts include Bermuda, the Cook Islands, the Cayman Islands, the British Virgin Islands, the Bahamas, and the Isle of Man.

Bermuda is an example of a typical tax haven, offering excellent political, economic, and social stability. It is also typical of most better tax havens in that it has no income taxes and is easy to reach by plane or cruise ship.

An onshore or offshore service provider specializing in offshore trusts could establish such a trust in one of these countries and appoint an independent trustee in that country. Your spouse and you then would transfer ownership of selected assets to the trust. The offshore trustee could hold cash and tangible assets, or it could only hold title to certain assets. For instance, family limited partnership units could be held by the offshore trustee with total control held by you through your general partnership units.

In August 1996, major U.S. tax law changes were implemented that had sweeping effects upon how pre-existing APTs operated and upon some of the tax advantages (tax deferral, estate reduction, etc.) achieved by using an APT. The full effects of this law have not been digested thoroughly by the pundits at this time. In summary, the IRS reporting requirements of the APT were enlarged. Certain events (loans, gifts, etc.) that were previously tax-free now have become taxable. The death of the settlor (the person creating the trust) triggered new reporting requirements. A U.S. agent for the APT would need to be established to respond to IRS inquiries with respect to the trust. These are but a few of the many changes.

The end result of this new tax law will likely be:

- The APT will continue to be used but not as often and with less privacy.
- Much of the tax deferral and tax avoidance features will be lost.
- U.S. beneficiaries receiving loans or distributions from these trusts will pay income taxes on those funds.
- Costs of alternative structures will likely be more expensive.

Until recently, good, well thought out APTs were expensive but the costs were coming down slowly due to some competition and efficiencies in the so called offshore industry. With the IRS reporting changes mandated by Congress, the pricing should go up again because of new uncertainties, greater reporting requirements and complexities, and the element of the unknown. Two resources to contact for further information are The Global Group Limited at (800) 823-0080 (e-mail: offshore@dnai.com) and Passport Financial, Inc. at (800) 531-5142. A good resource

book is *The Offshore Money Book* by Arnold L. Cornez, J.D., ISBN: 0-942641-72-8. (Arnold Cornez is also the offshore financial and business consultant for The Global Group Limited.)

You have now completed the major text portion of this book. Well, has it helped you?

Before you jump to answer this question, let me emphasize that this book cannot be read only once with complete understanding. It must be reread and digested. It also takes time—actually many years—to realize the true benefits this book can bestow. So, if your answer to my original question is "Yes," read the book again and again. If your answer is "No," read the book again and again.

You see, I know you will get a lot out of this book, but I also know you will need to keep refreshing your memory. Most importantly though, I know I've given you *more than LIP Service!*

Personalized Forms

The following forms are for your use. Make copies of them so that you can maintain your personal data. You should punch three holes in these sheets and store them in a three-ring binder. It is also a good idea to let other members of your family, your accountant, and your attorney know of this binder so that it can be retrieved when necessary in case of an emergency.

Personal Financial Statement
Year:_____

ASSETS   **NOTES**

I. Cash/Cash Equivalents
    A. Checking account _____
    B. Savings account _____
    C. Money market fund _____
    D. Life insurance cash value _____
    E. Cash on hand _____

            Total Cash/Cash Equivalents _____

II. Invested Assets
    A. Portfolio Assets
        1. Money Market Instruments
            a. Certificates of deposit _____
            b. U.S. treasury bills _____
            c. Commercial paper _____
        2. Fixed-Income Securities
            a. U.S. government _____
            b. U.S. agencies _____
            c. Municipal bonds _____
            d. Preferred stock _____
            e. Corporate bonds _____
            f. Notes receivable _____
        3. Common Stocks
            a. Listed _____
            b. Over-the-counter _____
            c. Restricted stock _____
        4. Retirement Benefits
            a. IRA _____
            b. Qualified retirement plans _____
            c. Variable annuities _____
            d. Deferred compensation benefits _____
            e. Other _____
        5. Other Portfolio Assets
            a. Options _____
            b. Mutual funds _____
            c. Collectibles _____
            d. Other _____
    B. Passive Assets
        1. Limited partnerships _____
        2. Real estate _____
    C. Active Assets
        1. Personal business _____
        2. Real estate _____
            Total Invested Assets _____

III. Use Assets
    A. Personal residence _____
    B. Other real estate _____
    C. Automobiles _____
    D. Boat _____
    E. Jewelry _____
    F. Computers _____
    G. Miscellaneous household contents _____
    H. Other _____
            Total Use Assets _____

LIABILITIES   **NOTES**

    I. Short-Term Liabilities (pay-off balances where applicable)
      A. Credit card debt _____
      B. Installment debt _____
      C. Personal notes payable _____
      D. Taxes due _____
      E. Other _____
            Total Short-Term Liabilities _____

   II. Long-Term Liabilities (pay-off balances where applicable)
      A. Loans for investment assets _____
      B. Loans for automobiles _____
      C. Loans for other personal assets_____
      D. Mortgage(s) on personal residence(s) _____
      E. Borrowing on life insurance _____
      F. Notes guaranteed _____
      G. Other _____
            Total Long-Term Liabilities _____

SUMMARY

ASSETS (fair market value)
    Total Cash/Cash Equivalents _____
    Total Invested Assets _____
    Total Use Assets _____
          Total Assets _____

LIABILITIES (pay-off balances)
    Short-Term _____
    Long-Term _____
          Total Liabilities _____

NET WORTH (Total Assets - Total Liabilities) _____

Personal Cash Flow Statement   YEAR: _____

	Jan	Feb	March	April	May	June	July	Aug	Sept	Oct	Nov	Dec
INFLOW:												
Alimony												
Capital gains												
Child support												
Dividend income												
Gross salaries												
Interest income												
Rental income												
Retirement income												
Tax refund												
Other												
TOTAL CASH INFLOW:												
OUTFLOW:												
SAVINGS & INVESTMENT												
Fixed Outflow:												
Alimony payments												
Auto insurance premiums												
Child support												
Debt payments												
Education expenses												
Health insurance premiums												
Income taxes												
Life Insurance premiums												
Mortgage payments/Rent												
Taxes, other												
Telephone												
Utilities												
Other												
TOTAL FIXED OUTFLOW:												
Variable Outflows:												
Attorney / Accountant fees												
Auto: gas, repairs												
Clothing / personal items												
Entertainment / vacations												
Food												
Gifts/contributions												
Home repairs/Maintenance												
Household furnishings												
Medical/Dental care												
Other												
TOTAL VARIABLE OUTFLOW:												
TOTAL CASH OUTFLOW:												

How Much Does It Take?

1. Current need per year = $_____

   (retirement need in TODAY'S dollars)

2. Future Value of TODAY'S retirement need

   PV = $_____

   N = _____ years

   I = _____% inflation rate

   PMT = 0

   FV = -$_____

3. Determine inflation-adjusted return

$$= \left[\frac{1 + \text{rate of return}}{1 + \text{rate of inflation}} - 1 \right] \times 100\%$$

$$= \left[\frac{1 + .\_\_\_\_\_}{1 + .\_\_\_\_\_} - 1 \right] \times 100\%$$

   = (_____ - 1) X 100%

   = _____%

4. Nest egg required at retirement

   N = _____ years to withdraw

   I = _____% (adjusted inflation rate)

   PMT = -$_____ (first year's withdrawal)

   FV = 0

   PV = $_____ (required nest egg at retirement)

College Expense Projection

Cost of college in future?

Cost of 4-year college today (**PV**): _____

Expected average percentage increase in costs until college begins (**I**): _____

Number of years before college begins (**N**): _____

Required cash for 4-year college in N years (**FV**): _____

How much to save yearly?

Set calculator to BEGIN mode.

Current savings for college expenses (**PV**)= _____

Number of years before college begins (**N** from above)= _____

Expected after-tax return, compounded annually from investment (**I**)= _____

Amount needed for 4-year college expenses from above (**FV**)= _____

Annual amount required to invest at the beginning of each year (**PMT**)= _____

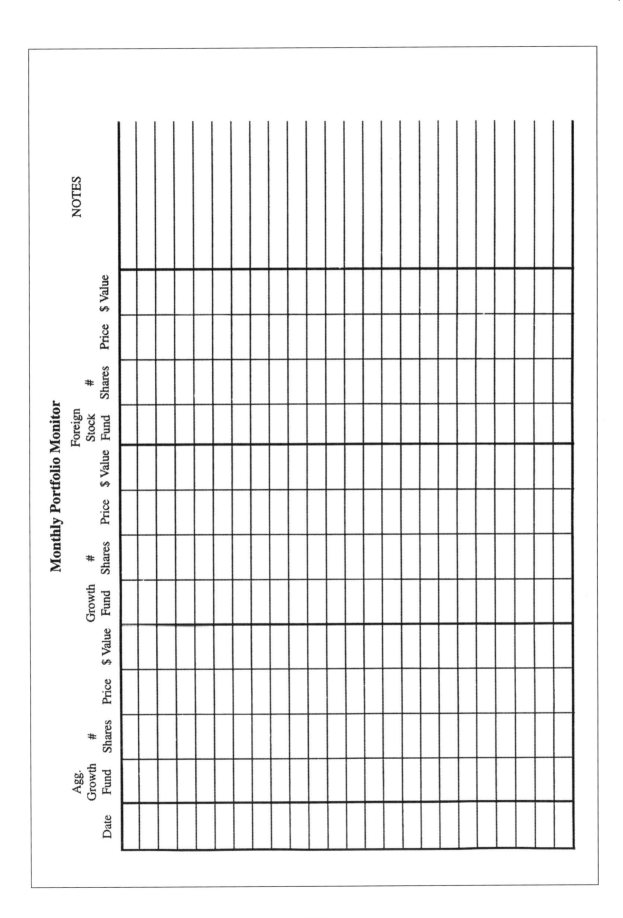

Monthly Portfolio Monitor

Date	Agg. Growth Fund # Shares	Price	$ Value	Growth Fund # Shares	Price	$ Value	Foreign Stock Fund # Shares	Price	$ Value	NOTES

Monthly Portfolio Monitor (contnued)

Date	Emerg. Foreign Stock Fund	# Shares	Price	$ Value	Contrary Style Fund	# Shares	Price	$ Value	Total Portfolio Value	NOTES

FIFO
(First In, First Out)

Fund Name

Purchase/Distrib				Sale				(Fee)	Profit
Date	$ Amt	NAV	# Sh	Date	$ Amt	NAV	# Sh		(Loss)

ANNUAL MONITOR

Date_____

GOAL _____

Years to reach goal _____

Beginning value of portfolio _____

Anticipated annually-compounded rate of return _____

Annual contribution _____

End of Year	End of	Age	Target	Actual	Adjustments
0					
1					
2					
3					
4					
5					
6					
7					
8					
9					
10					
11					
12					
13					
14					
15					
16					
17					
18					
19					

End of Year	End of	Age	Target	Actual	Adjustments
20					
21					
22					
23					
24					
25					
26					
27					
28					
29					
30					
31					
32					
33					
34					
35					
36					
37					
38					
39					
40					
41					
42					
43					
44					
45					
46					

WITHDRAWAL TABLE

Date_____

Beginning Balance ——————————————
Years to withdraw ————————————
Anticipated annually-compounded rate-of-return ——————
Projected inflation rate ————————
Inflation-adjusted rate-of-return ——————
Annual needs - first year of retirement ——————————

Start Yr	Year	Age	Annual	Target	Actual	Adjust
1						
2						
3						
4						
5						
6						
7						
8						
9						
10						
11						
12						
13						
14						
15						
16						
17						
18						
19						
20						

Start Yr	Year	Age	Annual	Target	Actual	Adjust
21						
22						
23						
24						
25						
26						
27						
28						
29						
30						
31						
32						
33						
34						
35						
36						
37						
38						
39						
40						
41						
42						
43						
44						
45						
46						
47						
48						

Danenberg's Lifetime Investing Plan

The following is the most recent issue of the quarterly newsletter you will receive when you purchase this book. The newsletter provides you with the two best performing and riskiest no-load mutual funds for each of the five asset categories that you will be using in the Lifetime Investing Plan.

There are many other features including a "What To Do Now" column, a summary of the LIP Portfolio from Jan. 1, 1985 through the current date of the newsletter, financial planning commentary, and information about the U.S. Business cycle and Relative Value Ratio. There are also descriptions about each of the best performing selected funds.

DANENBERG's Lifetime Investing Plan

a quarterly investment newsletter

September 30, 1996

WHAT TO DO NOW!

**My Recommendation:
Ideally, you should dollar-cost-average <u>monthly</u>. My Lifetime Investing Plan (LIP) requires you to divide your investable dollars equally among the following asset categories and rebalance yearly:**

20% U.S. Aggressive Growth funds: These funds usually invest in small companies and use leverage.

20% U.S. Growth funds: These funds will often invest in more mature companies than those found in the aggressive growth category. Also, these funds will tend not to use leverage.

20% Foreign Stock funds: These funds invest in companies that are located in countries that are considered well-developed such as Germany, Japan, and the United Kingdom.

20% Emerging Foreign Stock funds: These funds are more speculative than the foreign stock category because the companies are located in emerging countries such as China, India, Poland, and Israel.

20% Contrary-Style funds: This is a unique fund category. There are very few funds that fit this style. These funds are basically growth-type funds that also offer the ability to short overvalued sectors. They tend to invest in the stocks of companies that are out of favor with the general investing public.

Danenberg's Lifetime Investing Plan

INVESTING LONG-TERM

Sometimes you don't realize what long-term actually means. For instance, when you invest for a college education, you are investing for a goal that will be realized maybe ten years down the road. This is long-term. When you are planning to purchase a house in seven years, this is long-term. When you need money to live on during the next three years, this is short-term.

Most financial planners suggest that any investment over five year's duration is long-term because it will include various *ups* and *downs* in a normal business cycle. If your investment horizon is less than five years, your investment choices are much more limited because you cannot be sure if you will get caught at the wrong time in the business cycle.

For these shorter-term goals, you should invest in money market funds or perhaps short-term bonds. Another perfect investment for short-term goals is zero-coupon bonds.

At the other extreme, retirement planning is definitely long-term. But, many people believe that when you retire, you should become much more conservative with your investments and move into fixed-income securities. I totally disagree.

When you retire, you still have many years yet to live. This is still long-term. What you should do is liquidate only what you need from your retirement portfolio for the next year, and place those proceeds into some type of fixed-income investments for you to draw from. Repeat this process year after year. ■

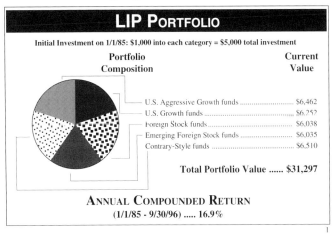

LIP PORTFOLIO

Initial Investment on 1/1/85: $1,000 into each category = $5,000 total investment

Portfolio Composition	Current Value
U.S. Aggressive Growth funds	$6,462
U.S. Growth funds	$6,252
Foreign Stock funds	$6,038
Emerging Foreign Stock funds	$6,035
Contrary-Style funds	$6,510

Total Portfolio Value $31,297

**ANNUAL COMPOUNDED RETURN
(1/1/85 - 9/30/96) 16.9%**

1

BEST OF EACH CATEGORY

Selections below are the two best performing funds with the highest risk levels
for each category over the past 3 and 5 year periods.

Category Fund	Phone #	Risk	annual compounded total return 9/30/96 3 yr.	5 yr.
U.S. Aggressive Growth				
PBHG Growth	800-809-8008	High	24.6%	31.8%
SteinRoe Capital Opportunity	800-338-2550	Above Avg.	28.1%	24.5%
U.S. Growth				
Founders Growth	800-525-2440	Above Avg.	16.9%	19.3%
William Blair Growth	800-742-7272	Average	18.9%	17.7%
Foreign stock				
USAA International	800-531-8181	Average	12.6%	12.7%
Warburg Pincus Int'l Equity	800-257-5614	Above Avg.	11.4%	11.4%
Emerging foreign stock				
Lexington Worldwide Emerging Mkts	800-526-0056	Above Avg.	5.6%	9.4%
Montgomery Emerging Markets	800-572-3863	High	6.5%	NA
Contrary-style				
(This category is relatively new and does not have long-term return data.)				
Robertson Stephens Contrarian	800-766-3863	High	19.8%	NA
Lindner Bulwark (1 Year return: 30.8%)	314-727-5305	High	NA	NA

9/27/96 | **RELATIVE VALUE RATIO**
(3-Mo. T-Bill Yield / S&P 500 Yield)

The **Relative Value Ratio** has moved up slightly from last quarter. It shows that the U.S. stock market is trending into overvalued territory. In the past, this has produced the right environment for a significant correction in the U.S. stock market.

If you are considering moving a large amount of money into the market, perhaps dividing it into equal amounts over the next six to twelve months may prove to be the prudent way to invest it at this time.

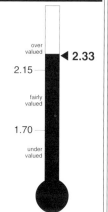

over valued ◄ **2.33**
2.15

fairly valued

1.70

under valued

ISSN XXXX-XXXX
Danenberg's Lifetime Investing Plan is published quarterly by:
Alvin H. Danenberg, DDS, CFP
17 Arabian Dr. • Charleston, SC 29407 • (803) 571-1342

This is an excellent companion update to Dr. Danenberg's book, **More Than LIP Service: *a Lifetime Investing Plan*.**

• Subscription: 1 year (4 issues) ... $13.95 •

Dr. Danenberg may from time to time have positions in the mutual funds mentioned herein. All information is taken from sources believed to be reliable, but accuracy cannot be guaranteed. There is no guarantee that following the investing plan described will be profitable or will equal past results. Individual results will also vary based on which mutual funds are used and when investments are made into them. The investment vehicles described in *Danenberg's Lifetime Investing Plan* are designed to be used for long-term investing (minimum of 5 years). Contact your financial advisor to determine if *Danenberg's Lifetime Investing Plan* fits your individual goals. Dr. Danenberg is a Registered Investment Advisor. A copy of SEC Form ADV Part II is available by writing to the above address.

FOCUS ON FUNDS

U.S. AGGRESSIVE GROWTH

PBHG Growth

This fund invests at least 65% of its assets in stocks issued by companies that have capitalizations or annual revenues of less than $2 billion. Up to 15% of its assets can be in foreign securities. It can also invest up to 5% of its assets in warrants and rights.

It has a close relationship to the Russell 2000 Index of small cap stocks. Its portfolio consists of 91% stocks and 9% cash.

SteinRoe Capital Opportunity

This fund invests in both established companies as well as small companies. Its portfolio consists of 89% stocks and 11% cash. It has a close relationship to the Russell 2000 Index just as the PBHG Growth fund.

U.S. GROWTH

Founders Growth

This fund invests at least 65% of its assets in stocks of well established companies. It may invest up to 30% in foreign companies. Currently, 83% of the fund is in stocks and 17% is in cash. Its style of investing best fits the Wilshire 4500 Index (an index of the 4,500 largest companies without the S&P 500 Index stocks).

William Blair Growth

This fund invests in stocks of companies of all sizes. The portfolio consists of 97% stocks and 3% cash. As with the Founders Growth fund, this fund has a high correlation with the Wilshire 4500 Index.

FOREIGN STOCK

USAA International

This fund invests at least 80% of its assets in countries outside of the U.S. It usually is invested in at least four separate countries. It currently has 91% of its assets in stocks, 3% in cash, and 6% is other securities such as options, futures and warrants. The investment style has a close correlation with the Morgan Stanley Capital International All Country Index. This Index tracks the performance of stock markets in 43 countries, including the U.S. and Japan.

Warburg Pincus International Equity

This fund invests at least 65% in at least three foreign countries. Currently, 95% of the portfolio is in stocks and 5% is in cash. It also has a close correlation to the Morgan Stanley Capital International All Country Index.

EMERGING FOREIGN STOCK

Lexington Worldwide Emerging Markets

This fund invests at least 65% of its assets in emerging countries. It is 97% invested in stocks and 3% in cash. Its correlation is close to the Morgan Stanley Capital International Pacific Index without Japan.

Montgomery Emerging Markets

This fund invests at least 65% of its assets in emerging countries. To select individual securities, the fund uses fundamental analysis so that no more than 35% of its assets are in any one country. It will have at least six emerging countries represented. Its portfolio has 78% in stocks, 5% in cash, and 17% in options, futures, warrants or illiquid securities. Like the Lexington Worldwide Emerging Markets fund, it has a close correlation to the Morgan Stanley Capital International Pacific Index without Japan.

CONTRARY-STYLE

Robertson Stephens Contrarian

This fund invests at least 65% of its assets in stocks from all over the world. No more than 35% of its assets can be in any one country. It currently has 48% in foreign stocks, 22% in U.S. stocks, 26% in cash, and 4% in shorts.

Lindner Bulwark

This fund invests in undervalued equities and precious metals that can maintain value during inflationary periods. It may invest up to 35% in foreign companies. Currently 12% is in foreign stocks, 25% is in U.S. stocks, 56% is in cash, and 7% is in other.

U.S. BUSINESS CYCLE

X = Where We Are Now

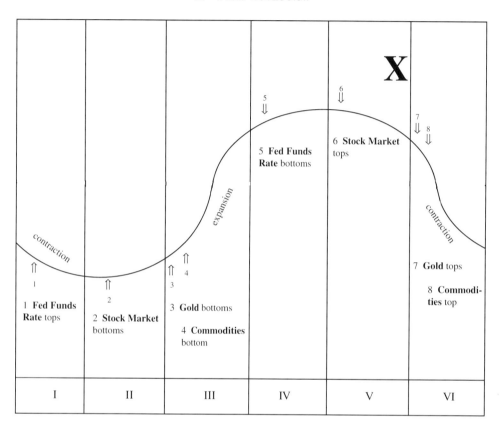

X

5 ⇓

6 ⇓

7 ⇓ 8 ⇓

5 **Fed Funds Rate** bottoms

6 **Stock Market** tops

expansion

contraction

contraction

1 ⇑

2 ⇑

3 ⇑ ⇑ 4

7 **Gold** tops

8 **Commodities** top

1 **Fed Funds Rate** tops

2 **Stock Market** bottoms

3 **Gold** bottoms

4 **Commodities** bottom

I	II	III	IV	V	VI

SUMMARY

The business cycle in the U.S. appears to be nearing a topping phase in which the stock market tends to reach a peak and the commodity markets tend to follow thereafter. If this is the case, the contraction phase of the cycle will begin in the near future. This most likely will take the form of a normal recession. It does not have to be severe. As a matter of fact, many in the country many not even feel it. On the other hand, some recessions have been very severe and have lasted a long time.

The **LIP** invests in such a way that it is not necessary to make any changes in the percentage allocation to the five asset categories. The contrary-style category will help to offset some of the downward bias in a declining stock market.

It is important to remember that all stocks from all over the world will be affected to some extent by a significant market correction in the U.S. There is no way to avoid it completely other than to be out of the market. The problem with that idea is that you can't be sure when the market correction will begin with full force. Even if you could make that determination, you would not know when it was the right time to be back in the market at the end of the correction simply because you would not know it ended until well after the fact.

Another fact to remember is that when the market is very low, there are great bargains to be had. And, dollar-cost-averaging allows that to take place. ■

Danenberg's Lifetime Investing Plan

4

No-Load Mutual Funds by Asset Category

To date there are over 280 no-load mutual funds to investigate from the specific asset categories of: Aggressive Growth, Growth, Foreign Stock, Emerging Foreign Stock, and Contrary-Style. I have also included the gold stock fund asset category which can serve to some extent as a contrary way of investing.

The funds are listed below in alphabetical order under their respective asset categories. You could contact these funds directly by telephone to obtain a prospectus, a statement of additional information, and a recent annual, semiannual, or quarterly report. Rather than contact each fund company, however, you could contact your discount broker to find out if they offer the funds you are evaluating. The discount broker could then send you the reports that you need.

Some funds will close to new investors when they have more cash inflow than they believe they can handle efficiently. These funds may then reopen when their cash levels moderate again. A simple phone call will let you know if the fund you are considering is closed or not. However, once you are an investor with the fund, you will usually be able to continue to add new money even if the fund closes later to new investors.

The list of funds that fits the categories I have described is growing rapidly. Therefore, when you read this, there may be new existing funds that are not included in the following breakdown.

Aggressive Growth Funds

American Heritage 800-828-5050
Baron Asset 800-992-2766
Berger One Hundred 800-333-1001
Berger Small Company Growth 800-333-1001
Bull & Bear Special Equities 800-847-4200
CGM Captial Development 800-345-4048
Caldwell & Orkin Aggressive Growth .800-237-7073
Cappiello-Rushmore Emerging Growth 800-621-7874
Columbia Special 800-547-1707
Crabbe Huson Special 800-541-9732
Dreyfus New Leaders 800-782-6620
Dreyfus Special Growth Investor 800-782-6620

226

Strong Small Cap 800-368-3863
T Rowe Price Capital Opportunity 800-225-5132
T Rowe Price Health Science 800-225-5132
T Rowe Price New Horizons 800-225-5132
T Rowe Price OTC 800-225-5132
T Rowe Price Science & Tech 800-225-5132
Twentieth Century Giftrust 800-345-2021
Twentieth Century Growth 800-345-2021
Twentieth Century Ultra 800-345-2021
Twentieth Century Vista 800-345-2021
USAA Aggressive Growth 800-531-8181
Value Line Leveraged Growth 800-223-0818
Value Line Special Situations 800-223-0818
Vanguard Explorer 800-635-1511
Vanguard Horizon Aggressive Growth 800-635-1511
Vanguard Horizon Capital Opportunity 800-635-1511
Vanguard Index Trust-Small Cap 800-635-1511
WPG Tudor 800-223-3332
Warburg Pincus Emerging Growth 800-257-5614
Wasatch Aggressive Equity 800-551-1770

Growth Funds

AARP Capital Growth 800-322-2282
Acorn 800-922-6769
American Pension Investors-Growth 800-544-6060
Ariel Appreciation 800-292-7435
Babson Enterprise 800-422-2766
Babson Enterprise II 800-422-2766
Babson Growth 800-422-2766
Babson Shadow Stock 800-422-2766
Benham Equity Growth 800-331-8331
Berwyn 800-824-2249
Brandywine 800-656-3017
Brandywine Blue 800-656-3017
Century Shares Trust 800-321-1928
Clipper 800-420-7556
Columbia Growth 800-547-1707
Crabbe Huson Equity 800-541-9732
Dreyfus Appreciation 800-782-6620
Dreyfus Core Value-Investor 800-782-6620
Dreyfus Growth Opportunity 800-782-6620

Dreyfus S&P MidCap Index 800-782-6620
Eclipse Equity 800-872-2710
FAM Value 800-932-3271
Fidelity Discipline D Equity 800-544-6666
Fidelity Dividend Growth 800-544-6666
Fidelity Large Cap 800-544-6666
Fidelity Mid Cap 800-544-6666
Fidelity Retirement Growth 800-544-6666
Fidelity Stock Selector 800-544-6666
Fidelity Trend 800-544-6666
Fidelity Value 800-544-6666
Fiduciary Capital Growth 800-338-1579
First Eagle Fund of America 800-451-3623
Flex Growth 800-325-3539
Flex Muirfield 800-325-3539
Founders Growth 800-525-2440
Fremont Growth 800-548-4539
Gabelli Asset 800-422-3554
Gabelli Growth 800-422-3554
Galaxy II Small Co. Index-Retail 800-628-0414
Gintel 800-243-5808
Gradison McDonald Established Value 800-869-5999
Gradison McDonald Opportunity Value .800-869-5999
Harbor Capital Appreciation 800-422-1050
Harbor Growth 800-422-1050
IAI MidCap Growth 800-945-3863
IAI Regional 800-945-3863
IAI Value 800-945-3863
INVESCO Growth 800-525-8085
INVESCO Strategic Portfolio-Financial 800-525-8085
Janus 800-525-3713
Janus Mercury 800-525-3713
Key Fund 800-422-7273
L. Roy Papp Stock 800-421-4004
Legg Mason Value-Primary Class 800-822-5544
Longleaf Partners 800-445-9469
Longleaf Partners Small Cap 800-445-9469
Loomis Sayles Growth 800-633-3330
M S B Fund 212-797-2730
Mairs & Powers Growth 612-222-8478
Marshall Stock 800-236-8560
Marshall Value Equity 800-236-8560

Mathers 800-962-3863
Maxus Equity 800-446-2987
Meridian 800-446-6662
Monetta 800-666-3882
Montgomery Growth 800-572-3863
National Industries 800-367-7814
Neuberger & Berman Focus 800-877-9700
Neuberger & Berman Genesis .800-877-9700
Neuberger & Berman Manhattan 800-877-9700
Neuberger & Berman Partners .800-877-9700
New Century Capital Portfolio .617-239-0445
Nicholas 414-272-6133
Nicholas II 414-272-6133
Nicholas Limited Edition 414-272-6133
Northeast Investors Growth 800-225-6704
Northern Growth Equity 800-595-9111
Oakmark 800-625-6275
Pennsylvania Mutual 800-221-4268
Preferred Growth 800-662-4769
Reich & Tang Equity 800-221-3079
Rightime 800-242-1421
Royce Premier 800-221-4268
S B S F 800-422-7273
Safeco Northwest 800-624-5711
Salomon Brothers Opportunity 800-725-6666
Schroder US Equity 800-953-6786
Schwartz Value 810-644-2701
Scout Regional 800-422-2766
Scudder Capital Growth 800-225-2470
Scudder Value 800-225-2470
Scudder Quality Growth 800-225-2470
Selected Special Shares 800-243-1575
Sentry 800-533-7827
Skyline Special Equities II 800-458-5222
Sound Shore 800-953-6786
SteinRoe Growth Stock 800-338-2550
SteinRoe Young Investors 800-338-2550
Stonebridge Growth 800-367-7814
Strong Discovery 800-368-3863
Strong Growth 800-368-3863
Strong Opportunity 800-368-3863
Strong Schafer Value 800-368-3863

T Rowe Price Capital Appreciation 800-225-5132
T Rowe Price Growth Stock 800-225-5132
T Rowe Price MidCap Growth 800-225-5132
T Rowe Price New America Growth 800-225-5132
T Rowe Price New Era 800-225-5132
T Rowe Price Small Cap Value 800-225-5132
T Rowe Price Value 800-225-5132
Turner Growth Equity 800-932-7781
Tweedy Browne American Value 800-432-4789
Twentieth Century Heritage 800-345-2021
Twentieth Century Select 800-345-2021
UAM DSI Disciplined Value 800-638-7983
UAM ICM Small Company Portfolio 800-638-7983
USAA Growth 800-531-8181
Value Line 800-223-0818
Vanguard Index Trust-Extended Market 800-635-1511
Vanguard Index Trust-Growth Portfolio 800-635-1511
Vanguard Morgan Growth 800-635-1511
Vanguard Primecap 800-635-1511
Vanguard Specialized Portfolio-Energy 800-635-1511
Vanguard Specialized Portfolio-Health Care 800-635-1511
Vanguard Tax Managed Capital Appreciation 800-635-1511
Vanguard US Growth 800-635-1511
Vista Large Cap Equity 800-648-4782
Vontobel US Value 800-527-9500
Warburg Pincus Capital Appreciation 800-257-5614
Wayne Hummer Growth 800-621-4477
Weitz Value Portfolio 800-232-4161
Weston Century Capital 617-239-0445
William Blair Growth 800-742-7272
Yacktman 800-525-8258

Foreign Stock Funds

Acorn International 800-922-6769
BB&K International Equity 800-882-8383
Babson-Stewart Ivory International 800-422-2766
Bartlett Value International 800-800-4612
Dreyfus International Equity 800-782-6620
Fidelity Diversified International 800-544-6666
Fidelity International Value 800-544-6666
Fidelity Overseas 800-544-6666

Founders Passport 800-525-2440
Harbor International 800-422-1050
Harbor International Growth 800-422-1050
Hotchkis and Wiley International 800-346-7301
IAI International 800-945-3863
INVESCO International-European 800-525-8085
INVESCO International-International Growth 800-525-8085
INVESCO International-Pacific Basin 800-525-8085
INVESCO Specialty European Small Comany 800-525-8085
INVESCO Specialty Latin America 800-525-8085
Japan 800-225-2470
Loomis Sayles International Equity 800-633-3330
Montgomery International Small Cap 800-572-3863
Nomura Pacific Basin 800-833-0018
Northern International Select Equity 800-595-9111
Northern International Growth Equity .800-595-9111
Oakmark International 800-625-6275
Preferred International 800-662-4769
Schroder International Equity 800-953-6786
SIT International Growth 800-332-5580
Schwab International Index 800-266-5623
Scudder Greater Europe Growth 800-225-2470
Scudder International 800-225-2470
Scudder Latin America 800-225-2470
Scudder Pacific Opportunities 800-225-2470
SteinRoe International 800-338-2550
Strong Asioa Pacific 800-368-3863
Strong International Stock 800-368-3863
T Rowe Price European Stock 800-638-5660
T Rowe Price International Discovery .800-638-5660
T Rowe Price International Stock 800-638-5660
T Rowe Price Japan 800-638-5660
T Rowe Price Latin America 800-638-5660
T Rowe Price New Asia 800-638-5660
Twentieth Century International Equity 800-345-2021
UAM TS & W International Equity 800-800-6387
USAA International 800-531-8181
Vanguard International Equity Index-Europe 800-635-1511
Vanguard International Equity Index-Pacific 800-635-1511
Vanguard International Growth 800-635-1511
Vanguard Trustees' Equity-International 800-635-1511
Vontobel EuroPacific 800-527-9500

Warburg Pincus International Equity 800-257-5614
William Blair International Growth 800-742-7272

Foreign Emerging Countries Stock Funds

Lexington Worldwide Emerging Markets 800-526-0057
Montgomery Emerging Markets 800-572-3863
Robertson Stephens Developing Countries 800-766-3863
T Rowe Price International Emerging Markets Stock 800-638-5660
Twentieth Century International Emerging Markets 800-345-2021
USAA International Emerging Markets 800-531-8181
Vanguard International Equity Index Emerging Markets 800-635-1511

Gold Funds

Benham Global Gold 800-331-8331
Blanchard Precious Metals 800-245-0242
Bull & Bear Gold Investors Limited 800-847-4200
INVESCO Strategic Portfolio-Gold 800-525-8085
Lexington GoldFund 800-526-0057
Midas 800-400-6432
Scudder Gold 800-225-2470
US Gold Shares 800-873-8637
US World Gold 800-873-8637
USAA Gold 800-531-8181
Vanguard Specialized Portfolio-Gold and Precious Metals 800-635-1511

Contrary-Style Funds

Lindner Bulwark 314-727-5305
Robertson Stephens Contrarian 800-766-3863

APPENDIX IV

Getting the most from Prospectus, Statement of Additional Information, and Current Reports

Let's look at those documents you requested for the funds you are considering: a Prospectus, a Statement of Additional Information, and Current Reports (annual, and semiannual and/or quarterly). Some are written in small print on thin paper with no creative graphics or color making reading a boring and dreadful task. Others are written on glossy, 8 1/2" X 11" paper with large print and plenty of color and graphics, giving at least a more appealing look. Despite their appearance, they will tell you everything you need to know about the funds you are going to entrust with your hard earned money. To help you get the most out of them, I'll briefly describe some of their highlights.

Before I even begin, let me mention that the Securities and Exchange Commission is currently revising their requirements for the Prospectus. When they are finished, the new Prospectus will be easier to read and understand. Also, risk will be much more clearly described for the average investor.

The Prospectus

This is a detailed document that has specific sections which are required by the Securities and Exchange Commission. With this also comes an application to become an investor. I'll go through each section and summarize the important facts you should know.

There is a brief description at the beginning of the prospectus that summarizes the fund's objective and some of its investing concepts. If this information is contrary to what you thought the fund was all about, then stop right here and move on to the next Prospectus.

Expense Summary. Here you will find a table that summarizes an investor's maximum transaction costs from purchasing shares. These include sales loads, redemption fees, and exchange fees. Then management fees, 12b-1 fees, and other expenses are listed as a percentage of the fund's average net assets. Following these numbers, there

is a hypothetical example that depicts how many dollars each of these expenses would cost over a one-, three-, five-, and 10-year period if you invested an initial $1,000, the fund experienced a 5% total return, and you sold the shares at the end of each period.

The most important point to this section in my opinion is to know if there are any additional expenses that are added to the NAV of the shares when you purchase them or when you sell them (i.e., load, redemption, and exchange fees).

Financial Highlights. Here is another table that is an audited financial summary showing the NAV at the beginning of a year, income from investments per share, distributions per share, and the NAV at the end of a year. Ten years of data are included or the number of years the fund has been in existence if less than10.

In addition, financial ratios such as (1) net operating expenses to average net assets and (2) net investment income (loss) to average net assets are stated. Finally, the portfolio turnover rate and the net assets at the end of each year are listed.

The most important information in this section is the total return the fund experienced for each year.

Investment Objective and Policies. This is the place where you can find the details of what the fund is all about. The specific investment goals are discussed as well as some of the methods of investing used to reach these goals. This is a very important section.

Other Investment Practices and Risk Considerations. This is another very important section. This is the place where the specific methods of investing and their associated risks are discussed. Such methods as investing in small companies; taking short positions; investing in foreign securities; investing in debt securities; methods of borrowing, and using leverage, options, and futures are all identified. There is a discussion of defensive strategies that may be employed and a discussion of the portfolio turnover rate (i.e., how long securities are held before they are sold).

The following sections are informative. Usually, however, they are not factors that will help you make your decision to invest or not invest:

- Management and managers of the fund.
- Administrative services.
- How to purchase shares.
- How to redeem shares.
- Dividends, distributions, and taxes.
- How NAV is determined.
- How performance is determined.
- Names and addresses of various professionals involved with the fund's activities.

Statement of Additional Information

This is a much more detailed document than the Prospectus. All of the sections of the Prospectus are discussed in more depth. In addition, there is an audited financial statement for the fund. You don't need to read this document to understand your fund, but you can use this document as an additional reference regarding the risks and investing methods the fund manager takes to reach the fund's objective.

Current Reports

These are easy reading. The fund manager has more leeway in what he or she can say. There will be a general highlight section describing the fund's investments. There is also a letter to the shareholders from the portfolio manager.

The portfolio manager can sometimes get too optimistic in his or her comments. Read it for what it is worth—commentary about the way the portfolio manager sees things. This may or may not be the way events will occur.

There is usually a chart that depicts the fund's total return over the last 10 years or since its inception along with a comparison to that of the S&P 500 Index.

Next is a breakdown of the largest sector holdings. Following is a complete list of all the securities in the portfolio as of the date of the report. The number of shares and dollar value of each security is specified. All other assets are also noted.

At the end of the report is a Statement of Net Assets, a Statement of Operations, a Statement of Changes in Net Assets, and Other Financial Highlights. These are followed by Notes to Financial Statements.

To me, the most important sections of the current reports are what the manager has to say in his or her letter to shareholders and the Notes to Financial Statements at the very end of the report. These Notes often identify any pertinent information you need to know as an investor.

Now what do you do with all of this paper? Consider keeping a file for each fund in which you invest. Place the most recent Prospectus, Statement of Additional Information, and Current Report in it. These files will serve as important resources to any questions you may have about your funds in the future.

LIP Gloss
(Lifetime Investing
Plan Glossary)

$10,000 annual gift-tax exclusion. This allows you and your spouse to give away up to $10,000 individually to as many individuals as you wish every year without gift tax consequences. For example, if you and your spouse gave $10,000 to each of your two children this year, the two of you would have given away $40,000 free of gift taxes. This is an excellent way to reduce your estate worth.

$125,000 capital gain exemption. When you reach 55 years of age, you can sell your home, and you will not have to pay capital gains taxes on the first $125,000 of profit.

$600,000 unified credit. This allows you to exempt a maximum of $600,000 of your assets from your estate and gift taxes either while you are alive or after your death

12b-1 fees. These are expenses for some of a fund's distribution and marketing costs. However, 12b-1 fees do not come out of each investment when you purchase or sell shares as do load fees. The 12b-1 fees, like other fund expenses, are subtracted from profits each day before the Net Asset Value (NAV) is calculated at the day's close.

401(k) plan. A very popular qualified retirement plan with employees since they can determine how much of their own pay is to be contributed to the plan on their behalf. Sometimes the employer adds an additional amount of money that matches the amount of the employee's contribution. This is a valuable incentive to the employee to make a contribution.

2503(c) trust. The primary feature of this trust is that assets transferred into it will qualify for the $10,000 annual gift-tax exclusion. Just as with the Uniform Gifts to Minors Act (UGMA) or the Uniform Transfers to Minors Act (UTMA), you and your spouse can jointly give as much as $20,000 a year for each of your children if you desire into the 2503(c) Trust without gift taxes. The specific pay-out date of the trust is when your child reaches age 21. However, you can arrange the trust in such a way to retain the assets beyond age 21.

Accrued interest. Interest that has accumulated in a fixed income security but has not been received by the owner of the security.

Active assets. Assets which produce income or loss for the taxpayer. The taxpayer actually participates in their activities. Examples are individually owned businesses.

Actuary. Person who calculates retirement plan and annuity rates (among other things) using life expectancy tables and other statistical data.

ADV. A document that a financial planner has filed with the Securities and Exchange Commission (SEC). It discloses information about the financial planner and any conflicts of interest. It consists of two parts, Part I and Part II. The planner is required to give you ADV Part II (or another document of disclosure that has been approved by the SEC) for your information.

Age-Weighted Profit Sharing Plan. This qualified retirement plan offers the benefits of a Profit Sharing Plan but permits a larger portion of the contributions to be allocated to the accounts of older employees.

Aggressive growth funds. An asset category of mutual funds. The investment objective of this category is maximum capital gains. These funds invest primarily in stocks with significant growth potential as well as high risk and may use leverage by borrowing money to purchase securities and by trading in options and futures.

Alpha. A measure of the difference between how a fund actually performs and how it is expected to perform based on its benchmark index. When Alpha is positive, it indicates that the fund performed better than expected; when it is negative, it indicates that the fund performed worse than expected.

Annual Monitor. The Annual Monitor (see Appendix I) projects what the values of your portfolio account should be for a specific financial goal at the end of each year. It succinctly monitors where you are and where you should be. If you are off track, you will be made aware of it quickly.

Annual reports. At least once a year, a mutual fund must send an annual report to its shareholders describing the fund's activities over the past year. The report provides a listing of all investments and their market values as of the end of the reporting period. The fund also can distribute more current accounts of its investments and views by way of semiannual and quarterly reports.

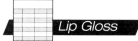

Annualized rate of return. See *Compounded annual rate of return*.

Annuity. A contract sold by a life insurance company that guarantees a fixed or variable payment to the annuitant (beneficiary of the annuity) beginning some time in the future and usually continuing for a lifetime.

Asset allocation. The apportioning of investment dollars among various asset categories. The types of asset categories are usually chosen to offset one another's volatility. This helps to smooth out the overall volatility of one's portfolio and therefore reduces the overall risk of the portfolio.

Asset categories. Types of assets can be organized into various entities or categories. They can be organized by major classifications (such as stocks, bonds, cash, etc.) or along specific industry lines (such as natural resources, communication, health, etc.) or investment styles (such as U.S. aggressive, U.S. growth, foreign, etc.). Each category tends to respond differently when compared to the overall markets. All of the asset categories put together make up the entire world markets.

Asset. Anything that has commercial or exchange value and is owned by a business, institution, or an individual is an asset.

Attorney-in-fact. See *Power of attorney*.

Average annual interest rate. The total interest earned over a period of time divided by the number of years the interest was earned. This is not the same as the *compounded annual rate of return*.

Average cost basis. For mutual funds, you can use this method to determine the average price of all of the shares you purchased and all of the shares that were reinvested from distributions. You can then use this average price to determine profit or loss when you sell shares.

Baby Boomers. Individuals born between 1946 and 1964.

Balanced funds. An asset category of mutual funds. Within these funds, a large portion of the portfolio is devoted to stocks and bonds. Some funds may have a fixed allocation percentage (ex. 40% bonds, 60% stocks), or some funds may allow the fund manager to switch between stocks and bonds based on the conditions in the marketplace. There is significant overlap between this category and that of *growth & income*.

Bear market. Prolonged period of falling stock, bond, or commodity prices.

BEGIN mode. When using a financial calculator, this is a calculator setting that means periodic investments are added at the beginning of an interest period and will earn interest for that entire period.

Benchmark. An Index designed to describe a particular market sector.
- **Dow Jones Industrial Average:** This is a price-weighted average of 30 actively traded blue chip stocks. It is the oldest and most widely quoted of all the market indicators.
- **Dow Jones Transportation Average:** This is a price-weighted average of 20 actively traded transportation stocks.
- **Dow Jones Utility Average:** This is a price-weighted average of 15 actively traded utility stocks.
- **LBAB Index:** The Lehman Brothers Aggregate Bond Index is an overall bond benchmark.
- **MSCI EAFE Index:** This is the Morgan Stanley Capital International Europe, Australia, and Far East Index. It is an aggregate of 15 individual country indices that collectively represent many of the major markets of the world, excluding Canada and the United States.
- **MSCI Emerging:** This is Morgan Stanley's international index for emerging countries. It includes Argentina, Brazil, Chile, Greece, Indonesia, Jordan, Korea, Malaysia, Mexico, the Philippines, Portugal, Taiwan, Thailand, and Turkey.
- **NASDAQ Composite Index:** National Association of Securities Dealers Automated Quotations Composite Index represents all domestic over-the-counter stocks.
- **NYSE Composite Index:** The New York Stock Exchange Composite Index represents all NYSE stocks.
- **Russell 800 Index:** This represents the smaller 800 stocks of the Russell 1000 Index and is considered a benchmark for medium-sized companies.
- **Russell 1000 Growth Index:** This index is composed of those 1000 stocks with the highest price-to-book and earnings ratios and the lowest dividend yields.
- **Russell 1000 Index:** This represents the 1,000 largest companies in the U.S. market as well as the most actively traded. It is closely correlated with the S&P 500 Index.
- **Russell 1000 Value Index:** This index is composed of those 1000 stocks with the lowest price-to-book and earnings ratios and the highest dividend yields.
- **Russell 2000 Index:** This is the smaller 2000 stocks of the Russell 3000 and is considered a benchmark for small-capitalized companies.
- **Russell 3000 Index:** This represents the 3,000 largest companies in terms of market capitalization.

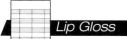

- **S&P 500 Index:** The Standard and Poors 500 Index is a market value-weighted index that contains 500 stocks of which most are on the NYSE.
- **S&P MidCap 400 Index:** This index does not contain any of the stocks of the S&P 500 Index. It consists of 400 stocks that are considered medium-sized companies.
- **Value Line Composite Index:** This is an equally-weighted average of approximately 1700 stocks on the New York Stock Exchange, the American Stock Exchange, and the over-the-counter market. It is designed to reflect price changes of typical industrial stocks, and it is not distorted by the price of more expensive stocks or the size of large company stocks.
- **Wilshire 4500 Equity Index:** This is the Wilshire 5000 Equity Index minus the stocks that make up the S&P 500 Index.
- **Wilshire 5000 Equity Index:** This is the broadest of all the averages and indices. It is market value-weighted and represents the value in billions of dollars of all NYSE, AMEX, and over-the-counter issues for which quotes are available. There are actually over 6,000 stocks in this index.
- **Wilshire REIT Index:** This is an index of real estate investment trusts.

Beneficiaries. See *Trust*.

Beta. A measure of a fund's relationship to the benchmark index for the market as a whole. The benchmark for stock funds is usually the S&P 500 Index. The benchmark for fixed income (bond) funds is usually the LBAB Index. Beta measures the relative volatility inherent in a mutual fund against the volatility of the marketplace. It is therefore a measure of the overall market risk that a particular fund exhibits. It does not measure any volatility that is the result of other factors outside of market risk.

Bond funds. An asset category of mutual funds. These funds usually invest in fixed-income securities (bonds). This category is further subdivided into corporate, government, mortgage-backed, general, and tax-exempt bond funds.

Bonds. Bonds are certificates of debt (fixed-income securities). The corporation borrows money from an investor, pays interest on the borrowed money, and then returns the principal at a specified date in the future.

Building Stage. During this first stage of wealth accumulation using dollar-cost-averaging, the dollar amount of the annual contributions to your program are more than the total return on your portfolio that year.

Bull market. Prolonged period of rising stock, bond, or commodity prices.

Business Risk. A company's success is influenced by many factors that you cannot control which are considered that individual company's business risk. These include inexperienced management, poor products, and weak marketing to name a few. Also, the company may not be well established or properly capitalized. Its operating costs may be extremely high. In addition, its stock may be illiquid. These risks can be off-set by diversifying among other company's stocks.

Buy low / Sell high. An investor buys an investment at a low price and then sells it in the future at a higher price for a profit.

Call Options. Options to buy a security.

Capital accumulation. The saving and investing of money in specifically identified accounts to be used in the future for defined purposes.

Capital gain. The difference between an asset's selling price minus the purchase price when it is positive. Long-term gains come from securities that are held for more than one year. Short-term gains come from securities that are held for one year or less.

Capital loss. The difference between an asset's selling price minus the purchase price when it is negative. Long-term losses come from securities that are held for more than one year. Short-term losses come from securities that are held for one year or less.

Capital. Money that is invested; also the value of an asset rather than the income from that property.

Cash equivalents. Highly liquid securities which means they can be turned into cash immediately with no loss of principal.

Cash Flow Statement. A Cash Flow Statement (see Appendix I) will outline where all of your money comes from and where all of your money goes usually during the course of one year.

Cash value. The amount of cash that accumulates in an insurance policy that the insurer will return to the policyholder on cancellation of the policy.

Certificates of deposit. A debt instrument issued by a bank that usually pays interest. Maturities vary from a few weeks to several years.

Certified Financial Planner (CFP). An individual who successfully completes a pro-gram of financial planning, investment planning, estate planning, income tax plan-

ning, insurance planning, and retirement planning and who passes a ten-hour comprehensive exam. There is also a work requirement of three years in a financial related field before the designation is bestowed.

Certified Public Accountant (CPA). An accounting professional who has passed a state administered examination that is based on accounting, auditing, and tax issues. This individual is not required to have a financial planning background.

Charging order. If there is a judgment against you, and you have a family limited partnership, this order gives your creditor only the right to receive income from this partnership if and when it is distributed to you and your spouse. The creditor has no right to take control or gain access to the assets owned by the family limited partnership. Also, the creditor cannot have any effect on you or your spouse who are the general partners.

Charitable remainder trust. This trust can be used for retirement funding or to create current cash flow. You donate assets to this trust, and the trust is owned by a charity. You, the donor, receive an income tax charitable deduction for a portion of the value of the assets donated. You and your spouse will also receive an annuity for life based on the total value of the assets in this trust. Also, when the assets in this trust are sold by the trustee, there are no capital gains taxes to be paid because the charity is exempt from taxation.

Chartered Financial Analyst (CFA). An individual who has successfully completed a study program in financial accounting, portfolio management, securities analysis, and economics.

Chartered Financial Consultant (ChFC). An individual who has successfully completed a program consisting of insurance, taxation, estate planning, and economics. There is also a work requirement of three years in a financial related field before the designation is bestowed.

Collateral. An asset that is pledged to a lender until a loan is repaid.

Commodities. Bulk goods such as grains, metals, and foods that are traded on a commodities exchange.

Common stocks. Units of ownership of a public corporation. Owners have the right to vote as well as to receive dividends. If the company is liquidated, the claims of common stock holders may be the last to get paid after other creditors and preferred stock and bond holders. Because of the added risk, common stock has more potential for appreciation over bonds or preferred stock.

Compounded annual rate of return. The yearly rate at which an investment grows along with interest, dividends, and capital gains being reinvested as they are earned.

Compounding. Interest being earned on principal plus interest that was earned earlier and reinvested.

Consumer Price Index. Reported monthly by the U.S. Department of Labor and is considered a relatively good reflection of the inflationary rate in the United States.

Contrary-style funds. A relatively new asset category for mutual funds. It is not recognized by all investors and is difficult for many research firms to categorize. These funds invest in asset categories that are out of favor with the majority of investors. This style of fund also takes short positions in overvalued stocks or industries. Generally, these funds have a negative correlation to the rest of the market.

Convertible bonds. Bonds that can be converted into common stocks at a later date.

Correction. A downward movement in the price of a stock, bond, commodity, or market as a whole which otherwise was rising.

Correlation. A statistical term that refers to the degree to which the movements of one asset category or stock are related to another or to the market as a whole. For example, a strong positive correlation between two asset categories means that both usually move up at the same time or move down at the same time. A strong negative correlation between two asset categories means that both usually move in opposite directions to one another.

Cost basis. The purchase price of an asset plus any transaction costs or commissions paid at the time of purchase. When you go to sell the asset, you subtract the cost basis and any additional selling costs or commissions from the selling price to determine your profit or loss.

Cost-of-living increases. Annual increases due to the rate of inflation.

Coupon yield. The annualized interest rate you earn on the purchase price of a Treasury Bill.

CRB (Commodity Research Board) Index. An index of commodity prices.

Credit trust. A trust that shelters $600,000 from an individual's estate taxes.

Creditor judgment. A court order that allows your creditor to come after specific assets you own to satisfy a debt that you owe.

Crummey Power. The right given to a beneficiary to withdraw up to $10,000 per year from a trust when gifts of such amount are made to the trust. This enables the person making the gift to qualify the trust for the $10,000 annual gift-tax exclusion and avoid any gift tax.

Currency devaluations. The lowering of the value of a country's currency relative to gold or to the currencies of other nations.

Current income. Income that is received today.

Custodial accounts. Accounts that parents establish for a minor, usually at a bank, brokerage house, or mutual fund company.

Death benefit. The dollar amount a beneficiary receives upon the death of the insured.

Defined Benefit Plan. A qualified retirement plan that requires mandatory contributions that are higher for older employees. The main advantage of this plan is that the annual contributions are not limited to a specific percentage of salary or to a specific dollar amount. The actual benefit at retirement is determined (or defined) based on a formula that incorporates the employee's current salary.

Deflation. The actual decline in the prices of goods and services. During deflation, borrowing capacity is reduced because personal income drops further and faster than interest rates. Deflation is financially painful.

Depression. A long-term debt liquidation process which occurs when cash flow is insufficient to handle debt payments. Debt liquidation can occur either in an orderly process (slow growth) or a disorderly process (deflation).

Derivatives. Financial instrument whose value is based on another security. Example: an option is a derivative because its value is based on the stock it represents.

Direct Rollover Option. The option to have your eligible distribution paid directly to an IRA that you establish. Under this Direct Rollover Option, no tax is withheld from the distribution since it is transferred directly from one retirement account to the trustee of your IRA.

Discount brokers. Brokerage houses that execute orders to buy and sell securities at commission rates sharply lower than those charged by full service brokers.

Discount Rate. The cost banks must pay to borrow money from the Federal Reserve.

Discounted. The manner of selling securities such as Treasury Bills. For example, you don't pay the face value of the Treasury Bill which you receive at a specified time in the future. You pay the discounted price today which represents the face value you get in the future minus the interest rate you will earn between now and when the bill comes due in the future.

Discretionary income. Current income that an individual can spend after essentials like food, housing, utilities, clothing, medical costs, and debts have been covered.

Disinflation. A slowdown in the rate at which prices are rising. During this time, borrowing capacity can increase because interest rates decline relative to personal income. Disinflation is the end result of a recession.

Distributions. Dividends, interest, and capital gains that are paid to shareholders.

Diversified fund. At least 75% of the assets of the fund is invested in cash, bonds, government securities, and stocks. No more than 5% of the assets of the fund can be invested in one security, and no more than 10% of the outstanding shares of a security can be owned by the fund.

Diversify. Spread risk by investing into several asset categories that do not correlate well.

Dividend reinvestment program. Automatic reinvestment of shareholder dividends in more shares of the company's stock.

Dividend. Distribution of earnings to shareholders.

Dollar-cost-averaging. A disciplined form of regular investing. By dollar-cost-averaging, you invest the same amount of money at specific intervals (ex. monthly) into a financial vehicle such as a no-load mutual fund. Most importantly, dollar-cost-averaging helps the investor develop a discipline to stay committed to a financial goal.

Due diligence. Research to determine if a particular security fits an investor's investment criteria.

Durable health care power of attorney. A legal document that gives an individual you designate broader powers than a living will to make health care decisions for you that are not only life and death decisions.

Durable Power of Attorney. A legal document that will immediately allow an individual or individuals to act on your behalf legally when you are not physically or mentally able to do so.

Dynasty trust. A trust that takes advantage of the $1 million exemption for giving assets to grandchildren, great grandchildren, and others at least two generations below the donor.

Earned income. Income generated by providing goods and services (usually wages and salaries).

Education Account. A savings or investment plan to accumulate a specific amount of money for your child's education. It could also be for you or your spouse to obtain additional education.

Emergency Account. An account to handle unforeseen financial emergencies. The experts suggest that this account should consist of three to six months of living expenses. Ideally it should be a separate account, properly named, and invested in a safe, liquid vehicle.

Emerging Markets. Countries that are beginning their economic development and possess at least one of the three following characteristics: a low or middle per capita income; an economy that has not been industrialized; an underdeveloped financial infrastructure. Most of the emerging countries are located in Asia, Latin America, and Eastern Europe. Other emerging countries are located in Africa and the Middle East.

END mode. When using a financial calculator, this is a calculator setting that means periodic investments are added at the end of an interest period. The first periodic payment made will come at the end of its first periodic interest and therefore will not earn interest for that period.

Equities: *See Stocks.*

Estate tax. A transfer tax that the federal government assesses on your right to transfer assets on your death. The tax generally applies only to estates worth more than $600,000 (because of the $600,000 unified credit).

Eurodollars. U.S. currency held in banks outside of the United States and usually used for settling international transactions.

Exchange rate risk. The potential loss resulting from changing values of foreign currencies.

Excise tax. A tax imposed by the federal government. If you withdraw more than a specified amount during retirement from your retirement account, or if you don't take out enough from your retirement account past the age of 70 1/2, or if you die leaving more than a specified amount in your retirement plan, then you may be subject to an excise tax.

Executor. A person designated to manage your estate upon your death. See *Probate*.

Factory operating rate. A measure of how overworked our factories are.

Factory utilization rate. See *Factory operating rate*

Fair market value. The price at which buyers and sellers trade similar items in an open marketplace. If there is no specific market price, it is the estimated highest price a buyer would be willing to pay to a seller for the item.

Family limited partnership. A partnership owned within a family consisting of general partnership units (which contain all of the control and a proportionate amount of ownership) and limited partnership units (which contain no control and a proportionate amount of ownership).

Federal Funds Rate. Interest rate charged by banks with excess reserves at a Federal Reserve district bank to banks needing overnight loans to meet reserve requirement.

Federal Open Market Committee (FOMC). Sets short-term monetary policy for the Federal Reserve. It consists of seven Federal Reserve governors and the presidents of six Federal Reserve Banks.

Federal Reserve Board of Governors. Consists of seven members appointed by the President of the United States and confirmed by the Senate. The board establishes Federal Reserve System policies such as reserve requirements, discount rate, availability of credit in the economy, and margin requirements.

Federal Reserve System. Made up of the Federal Reserve Board of Governors, a network of Federal Reserve Banks located throughout the country, and the Federal

Open Market Committee (FOMC). Its main functions are to regulate the national money supply, set reserve requirements, supervise the printing of currency, act as a clearinghouse for the transfer of funds throughout the banking system, and examine member banks to make sure they meet various Federal Reserve regulations.

Fee-only Certified Financial Planner. A Certified Financial Planner who only receives a fee for services rendered and does not sell financial products for a commission such as insurance products, mutual funds, etc.

Fiat money. Has no value itself. It only has the value people are willing to accept. It is money that is created by the government without the backing of gold or any other commodity. It is considered the legal tender of the land.

Fidelity bond. Insurance coverage against losses due to employee dishonesty. Your investment club may want to buy a fidelity bond which will protect the club against fraud. Unfortunately, it is possible for a club treasurer to embezzle.

Fiduciary. A person in a position of trust and responsibility, such as the trustee of a trust.

Financial calculator. A calculator that does, among other functions, time value of money calculations.

Financial independence. A time when you can live the lifestyle you have chosen solely from the cash flow generated by your investment vehicles.

Financial risk. Debt creates financial risk. Excessive debt can make it difficult for a company to repay its obligations especially if sales decline in an economic downturn for the company. If sales declined significantly, leaving insufficient profits to pay its creditors, a company could be faced with bankruptcy if debt holders had to foreclose on the firm's assets.

Financial vehicles. Investments that are purchased to appreciate in value and/or produce a stream of income. Such vehicles include: stocks, bonds, mutual funds, real estate, collectibles, gold, etc.

First In / First Out (FIFO). The generally accepted method to determine profit or loss. The first shares purchased are the first shares sold.

Fixed cash outflows. Part of a cash flow statement. These are expenses over which you have no (or little) control. Such things as rent, utilities, telephone, and mortgage payments (to name a few) are costs of living that you must meet to maintain your lifestyle.

Fixed income securities. These pay a fixed rate of return. They usually refer to government, corporate, or municipal bonds which pay a fixed rate of interest until they mature. Also included are preferred stocks which pay a fixed dividend.

Fixed rate. The interest rate does not vary.

Foreign Country Risk. Risk associated with individual foreign countries. These countries may have unstable governments, economies based on only a few commodities or industries, or runaway inflation. Their stock markets might be illiquid, or their political systems could be subject to scandals and upheavals. Even the healthiest companies within an adverse environment like this could suffer.

Foreign stock funds of emerging countries. An asset category of mutual funds. It consists of stocks of companies located in the emerging countries of the world. These funds tend to be very volatile. They also do not correlate well with other mutual fund asset categories.

Foreign stock funds. An asset category of mutual funds. These funds invest in stocks of foreign companies. There is added risk beyond U.S. stock funds because of government instability as well as currency fluctuations to a lesser degree. Foreign stock funds can be further subdivided into foreign stock funds of developed countries and foreign stock funds of emerging countries.

Fraudulent conveyance. Something transferred with the intention to deceive.

Fundamental indicators. Past records of assets, earnings, sales, products, management, and markets help to predict future trends in a company's success or failure. Factors such as interest rates, U.S. growth rate of goods and services, inflation, unemployment, and inventories help to predict the future direction of the economy.

Future Value (FV): This is a keystroke on the financial calculator. It is the amount of money you are calculating in the future. A specific sum of money today known as the present value (PV) is worth a different amount in the future (FV) based on the time period between now and then (N), the compounded interest rate that it experiences (I), and the amount of money that is added or subtracted at different time intervals between now and then (PMT).

Futures. An agreement to buy or sell a specific amount of a commodity or financial instrument at a particular price on a stipulated date in the future. Because it only takes a small amount of money to control a large futures position, there is tremendous leverage. Serious money can be made, but serious money can also be lost in trading futures. The risk is extremely high.

General Investment Account. This capital accumulation account can be used for large purchases such as a down payment on a home, a boat, a vacation, etc.

Government obligations. U.S. government debt instruments such as Treasury bonds, bills, notes, and savings bonds that the government has pledged to repay and which is backed by the full faith and credit of the U.S. government.

Government securities. U.S. government obligations and other securities issued by U.S. government agencies. These other securities have high credit ratings, but they are not government obligations and are not directly backed by the full faith and credit of the government as Treasuries are.

Grantor. See *Trust.*

Gross Domestic Product (GDP). Total value of goods and services produced in the country being described (ex. U.S. Gross Domestic Product).

Growth & income funds. An asset category of mutual funds. These funds will invest in securities of well established companies that usually pay high cash dividends. Income is an important objective along with long-term growth.

Growth funds. An asset category of mutual funds. These funds are similar to aggressive funds except they usually do not engage in leveraging. They generally invest in growth oriented companies that are more mature and that may pay some cash dividends.

Hedging. The practice of offsetting the potential of future loss. For example, if a stockholder thought that the U.S. market was going to drop sharply, he could purchase a *Put Option* on the S&P 500 Index. This will *hedge* some of that individual's U.S. stock portfolio for a specific period of time.

Household Account. A capital accumulation account. This is most likely where you keep your money in order to pay your daily, weekly, and monthly expenses. It will usually be a checking account through a local bank that may or may not also be an interest bearing account.

Illiquid. Difficult to sell or difficult to obtain original cost without loss.

Immediate fixed annuity. A contract you purchase from an insurance company which pays a specific amount to you regularly and which starts right away. Regular payments are made to you and your spouse for the remainder of your lives. The advantage of an immediate fixed annuity is that you will never outlive your source of income.

Incompetent. Not able to engage in legal transactions due to mental or physical incapacity.

Index: *See Benchmark.*

Index funds. Funds which invest in the stocks that make up specific market indices such as the S&P 500 Index, the Over-the-Counter Index, etc. Their purpose is to mimic the up and down trends of the indices they represent. They usually have much lower management fees than all of the other categories already described because there is little change in their portfolios.

Individual retirement account (IRA). An individual retirement savings arrangement. It is not considered a qualified plan, but it is a tax-deferred vehicle. It can be used by anyone who has earned income.

Inflation adjusted rate-of-return. A rate of return that is reduced to offset the loss of purchasing power as the result of a specific inflation rate.

Inflation. A rise in the prices of goods and services when spending increases relative to the supply of goods and services.

Initial public offering. When a new stock or bond comes into the market. The proceeds of the offering go directly to the company. This is known as the primary market. Thereafter, these securities trade in the secondary markets, and the companies represented by the securities do not receive any more proceeds from the purchase and sale of their securities.

Interest. Cost of using money.

Interest (I). This is a keystroke on the financial calculator. It is the average compounded rate of return your investment will experience (or is expected to experience) at regular intervals over the course of a specific period of time. A specific sum of money today known as the present value (PV) is worth a different amount in the future (FV) based on the time period between now and then (N), the compounded interest rate that it experiences (I), and the amount of money that is added or subtracted at different time intervals between now and then (PMT).

Interest Rate Risk. Interest rate trends often drive the market. When interest rates are trending down, the equity markets become more attractive and rise in price. Inversely, when interest rates are trending up, the equity markets become less attractive and fall in price. All stocks in all sectors can be affected by interest rates.

International bond funds. An asset category of mutual funds. These fixed-income securities are from foreign companies and governments. There is more risk involved than with U.S. bond funds because of currency rate fluctuations and foreign government instability.

Invested assets. Assets that have a commercial or exchange value and are used to create more money.

Investing. Using capital to create more money. It connotes the idea that the safety of your investment dollars is most important.

Investment banker. A firm that acts as an intermediary between a company that is issuing a new stock or bond and the investing public.

Investment clubs. A group of people getting together to pool their talents and cash in order to invest as a group. This is a good way to share your knowledge and also to learn from others.

Investment vehicles. See *Financial ehicles*.

Irrevocable life insurance trust. A trust intended primarily to hold life insurance and formed to keep insurance proceeds out of the taxable estate of the insured.

Irrevocable trust. A trust whose terms you can never change.

Joint Life Annuity. An annuity that will last all of your life and the life of your spouse.

Joint life and last survivor expectancy. The life expectancy of you and either your spouse or another beneficiary.

Kiddie tax. A tax levied at your top tax rate on your child's unearned income if the child is under age 14. The amount subject to this kiddie tax is anything above $1,300 in 1996. This amount is adjusted each year for inflation.

Leverage. Buying a security with borrowed money; controlling more of an asset with little extra investment (examples: options, futures).

Liabilities. Debts or other financial obligations for money, goods, or services received.

Liability insurance. An insurance product that will protect you against injury, damage, or loss to others.

Life expectancy. The average number of years you have left to live at your current age based on statistical data.

Lifetime Investing Plan. My program of investing for a lifetime. It is basically a plan that incorporates risky no-load mutual funds in five different asset categories that offset one another's volatility. The result is a relatively conservative overall portfolio with the expectation of high total returns. The plan becomes a withdrawal program during one's retirement years.

Limited power of attorney. A document in which you grant certain people the authority to handle specific financial matters on your behalf.

Living trust. A trust that takes effect now while you are alive. The assets in a living trust avoid probate.

Living Will. A written declaration instructing a physician to withhold or withdraw life-sustaining medical procedures in the event of a terminal condition.

Line of credit. A bank's commitment to make a loan up to a certain amount usually over a specified period of time that can be renewed.

Load funds. Funds that have a sales commission added to the NAV of the fund which is a fee paid to brokers and agents who sell the funds.

Long-term capital gains. See *Capital gains*.

Long-term care insurance. An insurance policy that pays a specific daily amount for certain types of care in nursing homes or in your own home for a specified period of time.

Long-term goal planning. Planning for future goals whose time horizon is more than five years away.

Long-term liabilities. Debts that are to be paid off in more than 12 months.

Lump-Sum Investing. The initial investment into an investment vehicle.

M1. A measure of the U.S. money supply that includes all currency, traveler's checks, and checkable deposits.

M2. A measure of the U.S. money supply that includes M1 plus passbook savings deposits, small denomination certificates of deposit (CDs), money market funds, money market deposit accounts, overnight repurchase agreements issued by commercial banks, and overnight Eurodollars.

M3. A measure of the U.S. money supply that includes M2 plus large denomination CDs and term repurchase agreements.

Margin. The collateral someone puts up to back a loan for an investment in securities. Borrowing on margin produces leverage because the customer deposits an amount of money with a broker as collateral and then borrows more than that to purchase various securities.

Marginal tax rate. Amount of tax on the next dollar of income.

Market risk. The up and down movement of prices that affects all securities.

Market timing. A means of deciding when to buy or sell mutual funds or other investments based on technical or fundamental indicators which try to identify the current trend (or direction) of the market and the future direction it will take.

Maturity date. The date when a fixed income security becomes due and payable; the date when a minor child reaches legal age (example: 18 years old in most states).

Medicare. A federal program which provides health insurance at minimal or no cost. To be eligible, you must generally be 65 years old and meet other Social Security requirements. Or, you must have been receiving Social Security disability benefits for at least 24 months, regardless of age.

Medicare taxes. Taxes taken out of earned income to pay for Medicare insurance benefits. Currently, this is 1.45% of earned income.

Medigap insurance. Insurance that covers some of the gaps in the Medicare program. Medigap covers the deductibles and the coinsurance portions not covered by Medicare. However, many gaps still remain.

Minimum distribution method. The annual payment for a **Series of substantially equal payments (SSEP)** can be determined by using a method that is acceptable for purposes of calculating the *minimum distribution* required under the rules for IRAs (IRS Publication 590).

Momentum stage. During this second stage of wealth accumulation using dollar-cost-averaging, the momentum stage begins when your total annual contributions to your investment plan equal the total return of your portfolio annually. This stage lasts until your total return is twice your annual contributions.

Momentum. Rate of acceleration in the price of a stock or the growth of the economy.

Money market funds. Money market funds invest in money market instruments and earn the current money market rates.

Money market instruments. Money market instruments are short-term debt instruments such as repurchase agreements, government obligations and securities, certificates of deposit, and other highly liquid and safe securities that have maturities of less than three months.

Money Purchase Pension Plan. A qualified retirement plan in which annual contributions by the employer are mandatory. As much as 25% of salary is allowed as a contribution.

Monthly Portfolio Monitor. This tool (see Appendix I) summarizes all of your portfolio activity at the end of each month. It provides a convenient place to keep score of your funds in each asset category.

Mortality table. Life expectancy table.

Moving average. An average of a certain body of data, for instance the weekly closing prices of a stock fund over the last 10 months. As each week goes by, the new week's closing price is added and the oldest week's closing price is dropped from the calculation.

Municipal bonds. Debt obligations of a state or local government. Public purpose bonds are tax-exempt from federal income taxes and may or may not be exempt from state income taxes. Private purpose bonds are usually taxable for both federal and state income taxes.

NASDAQ (National Association of Securities Dealers Automated Quotations). See *Over-the-counter*.

Net asset value. The price of each share of a fund. It is equal to the value of the assets in the portfolio after all expenses have been paid divided by the number of shares outstanding.

Net worth. The total value of all possessions minus all outstanding debts. Possessions are at fair market value and debts are determined as pay-off balances.

No-load funds. Funds that are sold directly by the fund company and have no sales commissions added onto the NAV. I include mutual funds that fit this criteria even if they charge 12b-1 fees as part of their overall expenses.

No-transaction-fee funds. Funds that are offered by discount brokers with no commission or transactions fees charged to the investor. The fund companies compensate the discount broker out of the fund's operating expenses for the broker's services.

Non-Deductible IRAs. Investors who are covered by other qualified retirement plans may not be able to deduct their contributions to an IRA from their income taxes. However, these non-deductible IRAs still continue to offer tax-deferred growth within the IRA.

Number (N): This is a keystroke on the financial calculator. It is the number of intervals before you reach your goal (i.e., future value). It may be calculated in years, quarters, months, etc. A specific sum of money today known as the present value (PV) is worth a different amount in the future (FV) based on the time period between now and then (N), the compounded interest rate that it experiences (I), and the amount of money that is added or subtracted at different time intervals between now and then (PMT).

Offshore asset protection trust. As with all trusts, the offshore asset protection trust offers privacy. Because of the extra layers of privacy designed around these trusts, it is very difficult for the prying eye to find out about your wealth held in this trust.

Old Age, Survivors and Disability Insurance trust fund. The source of dollars to provide the Social Security benefits as mandated by the U.S. Congress.

Options are the right to buy or sell an underlying security such as a stock, a commodity, or a stock index at a specific price at a specific time in the future. Since the option buyer must put up only a small amount of money to control a large amount of the security, options trading provides a great deal of leverage.

Ordinary income. This includes earned income, interest, and dividends.

Over-the-counter (OTC). Market in which securities are traded that are not listed or traded on an organized exchange. The NASDAQ (National Association of Securities Dealers Automated Quotations) is a computerized system that provides brokers and dealers with price quotations for OTC securities.

Overvalued. The price of a stock or the overall price level of the market that is above what would be determined to be the normal value at a specific time.

Passive assets. Passive assets produce income or loss for the taxpayer who does not materially participate in these activities. Examples are limited partnerships.

Pay-off balance. If you owe money to a lending institution that you are paying off over a period of time, the pay-off balance is the dollar amount it would cost you to pay off the entire debt immediately. The pay-off balance does not include the additional interest that would accrue if you had continued to make payments.

Payment (PMT). This is a keystroke on the financial calculator. This is how much you will put into your investment at regular intervals. It is the dollar-cost-averaging part of investing. The PMT function key is also used to figure how much you will take out of your investment at regular intervals in a withdrawal program. [A specific sum of money today known as the present value (PV) is worth a different amount in the future (FV) based on the time period between now and then (N), the compounded interest rate that it experiences (I), and the amount of money that is added or subtracted at different time intervals between now and then (PMT)].

Personal Financial Statement. Defines your net worth (see Appendix I). It summarizes everything you own and everything you owe.

Personal residence trust. Through this vehicle, you can gift your home to your children. Your children will receive the home after a specified period of time, and your estate will save on estate taxes because your home will be removed from your estate.

Portfolio. Combined investment holdings.

Power of attorney. A legal document which allows you, the principal, to grant another individual, an attorney-in-fact, the power to act legally on your behalf. This power can either be granted for very limited use or for very broad use. However, if you should die or become incompetent, the power given to the attorney-in-fact terminates immediately.

Precious metals funds. An asset category of mutual funds. By definition, these are actually sector funds. However, precious metals funds are the most volatile and therefore the most risky of all mutual funds. They deserve a separate category. These funds invest in mining stocks as well as precious metal bullion. Some precious metals funds also invest in other natural resources companies.

Preferred stocks. Units of ownership that pay dividends at a specified rate and have preference over common stocks in the payment of dividends and the liquidation of assets. Preferred stock holders usually do not have voting rights.

Present value (PV). This is a keystroke on the financial calculator. This is today's starting amount of money. If you are starting with nothing, then the present value is zero. This present value (PV) is worth a different amount in the future (FV) based on the time period between now and then (N), the compounded interest rate that it experiences (I), and the amount of money that is added or subtracted at different time intervals between now and then (PMT).

Primary market. When a company initially issues new securities to the investing public and the company receives capital from this initial public offering.

Principal. Basic amount invested.

Probate. The process where a will is presented to a court, and an executor is appointed to carry out the will's instructions.

Profit Sharing Plan. This is one of the most common qualified retirement plans. Contributions are made as a percentage of salary. The same percentage must be used for all employees.

Prospectus. Formal written document describing a mutual fund's financial objectives and policies, risk factors, distribution and performance information, method of purchasing and selling shares, and other pertinent information.

Purchasing Power Risk. Rising inflation makes the purchasing power of the dollar decrease over time. The risk of losing purchasing power occurs when inflation exceeds the after-tax total return from your investments.

Put Options. Options to sell a security.

Q-TIP trust (Qualified Terminable Interest Property Trust). A trust that qualifies for the unlimited marital deduction. The surviving spouse would receive all of the income from the trust at least on an annual basis, and no other person would have an interest in the trust during the life of the surviving spouse. The advantages of this type of trust are that the first spouse to die could specify whether or not the principal of the trust would be available to the surviving spouse and how the trust assets would be distributed following the death of the surviving spouse. The assets in the Q-TIP Trust are not taxed in the first-to-die spouse's estate. The assets are taxed in the second-to-die spouse's estate.

Qualified retirement plans. Retirement plans that are approved by the IRS. They are for the exclusive benefit of employees or their beneficiaries; must be communicated to the participants in a written document; and cannot discriminate in favor of officers, stockholders, or highly paid employees. These plans must also comply with minimum eligibility, vesting, and funding requirements.

R-squared. A mathematically derived statistic (known as the coefficient of determination) which defines the percentage of a fund's movements that can be related to its benchmark index. This statistic can also relate one asset category to another.

Rate of return. The relationship of the growth of an investment plus all of the dividends, interest, and capital gains paid on an investment usually over the course of one year divided by the original cost. This is expressed as a percentage.

Real money. The medium of exchange that represents a store-of-value.

Recession. An actual downturn in economic activity which generally begins when the Federal Reserve tightens the money supply. A recession is the contraction phase of a normal business cycle.

Recourse. The right to demand compensation from someone.

Registered Investment Advisor (RIA). An individual who has filed a form (ADV) with the Securities and Exchange Commission (SEC) and has paid a registration fee. There are no education requirements, but some states require examination. However, the SEC does require full disclosure of education, experience, and investment strategy. A registered investment advisor can give financial advice to clients for a fee.

Registered Representative. This individual is more commonly known as a stockbroker or an account executive.

Reinvestment Rate Risk. This refers to the dilemma faced by an investor with cash to invest after interest rates or stock prices have declined. This is particularly important to bondholders with periodic interest payments to reinvest, but it also can affect stockholders who wish to reinvest dividends or capital gains.

Reinvestment. Putting the money received from dividends, interest, and capital gains back into the investment so that it may continue to compound.

Relative Value Ratio (RVR). An indicator that helps to determine when the overall U.S. stock market is overvalued or undervalued based on the S&P 500 Index and the 13-week U.S. Treasury Bill.

Replacement value. The cost to replace personal property.

Repurchase agreement. Agreement between a seller and a buyer, where the seller agrees to repurchase specific securities (usually U.S. Government securities) at an agreed upon price and at a stated time.

Reserve Requirements. Federal Reserve System rule mandating the financial assets that member banks must keep in their own vaults in the form of cash as a percentage of all of its demand deposits (checking accounts) and time deposits (savings accounts and certificates of deposit).

Retirement Account. This account forms the nest egg from which a steady cash flow will maintain one's retirement. This should be started early in life and planned appropriately so that enough wealth can accumulate to meet retirement needs. This account could be established within one of several tax-deferred retirement accounts so that your money will grow without current taxes being taken out.

Retirement benefits. The assets that have accrued for an individual within various types of plans. Examples of plans include qualified retirement plans, individual retirement accounts, annuities, etc. They are usually available to an individual at retirement or to an employee upon termination of employment.

Return. Profit on an investment. See *Rate of return*.

Reverse mortgage. Mortgage instrument that allows an elderly person to live off the equity in a fully paid-for house. Usually a bank will guarantee a lifelong fixed monthly income in return for gradually giving up ownership of the house. At the owner's death, the bank gains title to the real estate.

Revocable trust. A trust whose terms you can change at anytime.

Rider. Added stipulations that are attached to an insurance policy.

Risk avoidance. One way to eliminate risk is to avoid it. For example, if you don't snow ski, then you will avoid the risk of being disabled from a skiing accident.

Risk reduction. In order to reduce risk, you can take measures to prevent mishaps. If you do snow ski, you can take lessons from qualified instructors and use the proper equipment to try to prevent serious accidents from occurring.

Risk retention. A method of managing risk is to assume part of the risk. This can be done through the use of deductibles with your insurance. If you snow ski and break your leg, and if you have a $300 deductible with your health insurance, then you know that you will have to pay the first $300 before the insurance kicks in. By assuming a higher deductible or cost of the risk, you can lower your insurance premium and still maintain the proper coverage to prevent financial ruin.

Risk transfer. With this method of managing risk, your risk is actually transferred to another. Insurance is a means of transferring financial risk to an insurance company in return for a premium payment. If you snow ski and are involved in an accident, then your health insurance and possibly your disability insurance would cover most of your medical expenses and financial loss.

Risk. A measure of the chance of losing something. In investing, it is the chance of losing principal. In insurance, it is the chance of losing property or one's life or one's health.

Savings Account. Money that is put into a bank that earns interest as determined by the bank. Money can be withdrawn usually at the discretion of the owner of the account.

Savings Incentive Match Plan for Employees (SIMPLE). New retirement program that goes into effect in 1997. Basically, self-employed individuals and small-business owners can elect to contribute up to $6,000 a year with certain restrictions into a SIMPLE IRA or a SIMPLE 401(k).

Secondary market. After securities have been issued by a company, this is where these shares are traded back and forth by investors.

Second-to-die life insurance. This insurance policy insures two people and pays the death benefit after the second person dies. This type of policy is less expensive than one for a sole individual.

Sector funds. These funds are industry specific. For example, there are funds investing only in health related companies, or utilities, or financial institutions, or communications, etc. When one sector may be strong, another may be weak. These funds are much more risky than diversified funds.

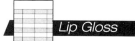

Securities and Exchange Commission (SEC). Federal agency created to administer the securities markets.

Securities. Stocks, bonds, convertible bonds, options to purchase or sell, and stock warrants.

Self-Propelled Stage. During this third stage of wealth accumulation using dollar-cost-averaging, the self-propelled stage begins when the total annual return on your portfolio is more than twice your annual contribution. This is when the power of compounding and exponential growth becomes obvious.

Series of substantially equal payments (SSEP). To avoid the 10% IRS penalty on early withdrawals from a tax-deferred retirement program, a series of substantially equal payments must be made at least annually and must be based on your life expectancy or on the joint life expectancies of you and a designated beneficiary. Several methods are allowed by the IRS to determine the SSEP.

Short selling. Refers to the sale of a security that is not owned by the seller. The investor borrows the security certificate at the market price from a broker. This borrowed security must be returned to the broker at a later date. If the short seller can purchase the actual stock at a lower price later, he can return the borrowed certificate to the broker and will make a profit. If he must purchase the security later at a higher price, he will return the borrowed certificate to the broker and will have a loss.

Short-term liabilities. Short-term liabilities are debts that are to be paid off within 12 months.

Simplified Employee Pension (SEP). The SEP works like a Profit Sharing Plan when it comes to contributions. These contributions are made by the employer to each of the employee's IRAs. SEPs are also available to self-employed individuals. It is the easiest and least expensive defined contribution plan to establish.

Social Security taxes. These taxes are based on earned income. Currently, this tax is 6.2% for employed individuals and 12.4% for self-employed individuals. For 1996, the maximum earned income to be taxed is $62,700.

Speculation. Investing that implies far more risk.

Standard Deviation (SD). A statistic which quantifies past volatility. It identifies the variation of a fund's total return above and below its average return.

Statement of additional information. This document elaborates on the prospectus. You usually will not get this publication with a prospectus unless you specifically request it.

Step-up in basis. When the owner of an asset dies, the cost basis of that asset rises to the current market price for that asset. This step-up in basis becomes the new cost basis for the beneficiary of the asset.

Stock exchange. A market place where actual transactions of securities occur.

Stock index. Benchmark indicators used to measure and report value changes in various stock groupings.

Stock market. A general term that refers to the organized trading of securities.

Stock warrants. See *Warrants*.

Stocks. Certificates of ownership. They represent a piece of the total corporation. In the initial offering of stock, the company exchanges stock certificates for a sum of money. Money is transferred into the corporation from the investor, and the investor now owns a portion of the company along with certain rights. The company does not have to pay any principal back to the shareholder. The company often pays dividends to shareholders, but it does so as a result of profits.

Store-of-value. An asset that maintains its purchasing power over time after inflation is taken into consideration. Gold usually is considered a store-of-value.

Systematic risk. This cannot be eliminated by diversifying. It can be thought of as a risk that is part of the *system* of investing. It tends to affect all securities to some extent, rather than being unique to a particular company. These types of risk include market risk, purchasing power risk, interest rate risk, reinvestment rate risk, foreign country risk, and exchange rate risk.

Target Benefit Plan. This qualified retirement plan functions like the Age Weighted Profit Sharing Plan, but the annual contributions are mandatory.

Tax-deferral. Taxes are not due until money is withdrawn. This allows more money to compound over time.

Technical indicators. Trading volume and prices create signals for investors to time the purchase and sale of various securities.

Telephone switching privileges. Most mutual funds and discount brokers allow you to call by telephone to place buy and sell orders.

Term life insurance. Pure life insurance. Premiums are based on the chance of you dying at your age and with your health record. Future premiums increase as your age increases. No cash value is included in this policy.

Testamentary trust. A trust that takes effect after you die.

Three Year Rule. If a life insurance policy that you own on your life is transferred to an irrevocable insurance trust within three years of your death, the proceeds will usually be taxed in your estate.

Time value of money. The change of the value of money from the present to the future. The present value of money grows over time as a result of it earning some stated rate of return over a specific period of time. A financial calculator makes these calculations easy and quick.

Titling of Property. There are nine legal methods by which property can be owned and titled:
- **Separate Ownership** - When you own property solely, you have total control.
- **Tenancy in Common** - Joint ownership with at least one other person or entity such as a corporation, trust, or partnership. You have the right to sell, transfer, gift, or bequeath your interest to anyone you wish without the expressed permission of the other joint owners. However, in order to dispose of the entire asset, all joint owners must agree to sign.
- **Joint Tenancy with Rights of Survivorship (JTWROS)** - Most common form of joint ownership. It carries the same advantages and disadvantages of tenancy in common with one major exception. When one of the owners dies, the decedent's share automatically passes on to the surviving tenants. And, this transfer takes precedence over any will or trust document.
- **Community Property** - There are nine states that have a form of co-ownership of property known as community property, and they are Arizona, California, Idaho, Louisiana, Nevada, New Mexico, Texas, Washington, and Wisconsin. Community property is owned by both husband and wife and is subject to liens from creditors just as with the previous forms of ownership discussed. One major tax advantage of community property over other types of ownership occurs when one spouse dies. When either spouse dies, the cost basis of the entire property is stepped-up to the market value at the time of death. In JTWROS and tenancy in common, the cost basis of the deceased's portion of the property is the only portion that is stepped-up.

- **Tenancy by the Entirety** - This is joint ownership between a husband and wife and is allowed in many non-community property states. It functions much like JTWROS, but it can only be terminated by joint agreement of both spouses.
- **Custodial** - Minor children and incapacitated persons are not considered to have legal capacity and therefore cannot enter into a binding contract. Therefore, accounts set up for these people must have a custodian named who can trade, buy, and sell assets in this account. A custodian does not personally own the asset for himself; he oversees the asset for the benefit of another.
- **Partnership** - Two or more adults can form a partnership and own property. The partners can be either general partners or limited partners. General partners are personally liable for any claims against the partnership. Not only are the assets subject to judgments, but each general partner is 100% liable for any legal actions against the partnership. On the other hand, limited partners are not personally liable for any claims.
- **Corporation** - A corporation can be formed by one or more individuals and can own property. The major benefit is that judgments against the corporation usually cannot also be placed against the individuals.
- **Trust** - Property can be placed in a trust and administered by a trustee. The trustee holds title to this property for the benefit of another and thereby has a fiduciary responsibility.

Total return. Annual return on an investment including appreciation, dividends, interest, and capital gains.

Trading-range breaks. This is where a price for a stock is able to move above a previous high or to move below a previous low.

Treasury Bills. Short-term securities with maturities of one year or less issued at a discount from face value. These are U.S. Government obligations and are considered risk-free investments. They are free of state income tax.

Trust. A trust is a legal arrangement which can hold the ownership of assets for the benefit of one or more individuals (beneficiaries). You (the grantor) can establish the trust to fulfill your wishes. You can be the manager of the trust (the trustee) or you can name someone else to be the trustee. The trust files annual tax returns and pays taxes on retained income.

Trustee. See *Trust*.

U.S. Business Cycle. An economic cycle. It develops as a wave which falls during its contraction phase, reaches a bottom, rises through its expansion phase, reaches a top, and then repeats itself.

U.S. Government Savings Bonds (Series EE). The purchase price of a bond is 50% of its face amount. The denominations are $50, $75, $500, $1,000, $5,000, and $10,000. There is a $15,000 purchase price limit per person per calendar year. Unfortunately, the interest rates are low and they vary every six months. Taxes can be deferred on the accrued interest until the bond is cashed in. Interest accrues for a maximum of 30 years.

U.S. Government Savings Bonds (Series HH). EE Bonds can be exchanged for HH Bonds, and the accrued interest in the EE Bonds would continue to be deferred. The HH Bonds pay a fixed rate of return every six months which is taxable on your federal income tax. HH Bonds can be held for up to twenty years. When the HH Bonds are redeemed, the tax-deferred interest from the EE Bonds becomes taxable on your federal income tax. The interest continues to be excluded from state tax.

Umbrella insurance. A liability insurance policy that covers an insured above the limits of regular liability coverage.

Undervalued. The price of a stock or the overall price level of the market that is below what would be determined to be the normal value at a specific time.

Underwriting. When an investment banker offers the company (who is issuing a new stock or bond) a guarantee to sell their newly issued securities. The banker also agrees to retain any of the securities which are not sold.

Unearned income. Interest, dividends, capital gains, rents, royalties, and pension and annuity income.

Uniform Gifts to Minors Act (UGMA). Cash and securities can be placed into this account for the benefit of your minor child. Either the parents or an independent trustee can be the custodian. Usually, the assets become the child's property at age 18.

Uniform Transfers to Minors Act (UTMA). This is like the UGMA but also allows the transfer of real estate, personal property, and intangible property into the account.

Unlimited marital deduction. This allows you to give as much as you wish, before or after your death, to your spouse without any gift or estate taxes. These assets will become part of your spouse's estate.

Unsystematic risk. This risk is unique to a particular company or sector and includes business risk and financial risk. This can be minimized by diversifying among various unrelated stocks or asset classes.

Use assets. Use assets are physical items that an individual uses in his or her life. They have a value, but they are not usually held as an investment with the intention of being sold in the future for a profit. Examples are household furnishings, automobiles, and a primary residence.

Valuation discount. This is a reduction in the fair market value of the limited partnership units from a family limited partnership because they do not carry any controlling interest.

Variable annuities. Variable annuities are basically mutual funds wrapped inside an insurance product. The life insurance component may insure that your beneficiary will receive at least the amount of all your contributions even if the equity value in the annuity falls below the total of all your contributions. Payout options range from withdrawals at your discretion to guaranteed lifetime annuities for you and your spouse. Assets within a variable annuity grow tax-deferred. This makes variable annuities an excellent retirement planning tool.

Variable cash outflows. This is part of a cash flow statement (see Appendix I). These expenses are at your discretion most of the time.

Variable interest rate. Interest rates that move up and down based on the current rates of money market instruments.

Vesting. The right an employee gradually acquires over the length of employment at a company to receive benefits from employer sponsored qualified retirement plans.

Volatility. The daily up and down fluctuations in the stock market.

Warrants. A security that entitles the holder to purchase a proportionate amount of common stock at a specified price for usually a period of years before it expires. (Options are similar to warrants, except options usually expire in less than one year.)

Whole life insurance. Form of life insurance policy that provides a death benefit on the death of the insured and also builds up cash value. Usually the insured pays a set annual premium for life which does not rise as the person grows older. The earnings on the cash value are tax-deferred and can be borrowed against. The death benefit is reduced by whatever loan amount was not repaid.

Will. A legally enforceable declaration of what a person wants done at death with his or her property and other matters.

Withdrawal Table. A Withdrawal Table (see Appendix I) projects how much will be left in your nest egg account at the end of each successive year into the future after (1) you have taken out your annual living needs (adjusted for inflation) at the beginning of the year, and (2) the balance of the portfolio has continued to grow because of its investments.

Yield to maturity. The total return an investor earns on a bond that takes into account the purchase price, the redemption value, the time to maturity, and the total interest paid while holding the bond.

Zero Coupon Bonds. Zero coupon bonds are purchased from a broker at a deep discount from their face value of $1,000. No interest is received until the bond reaches maturity. However, taxes are due each year on the accrued interest. This is a good way to provide a specific sum of money at a specific time in the future.

Index